GLOBAL POLITICS AND STRATEGY

Volume 50 Number 4 | August–September 2008

The International Institute for Strategic Studies

Arundel House | 13–15 Arundel Street | Temple Place | London | WC2R 3DX | UK

Tel +44 (0)20 7379 7676 Fax +44 (0)20 7836 3108 E-mail survival@iiss.org Web www.iiss.org

Survival Online www.informaworld.com/survival

Aims and Scope *Survival* is one of the world's leading forums for analysis and debate of international and strategic affairs. Shaped by its editors to be both timely and forward thinking, the journal encourages writers to challenge conventional wisdom and bring fresh, often controversial, perspectives to bear on the strategic issues of the moment. With a diverse range of authors, *Survival* aims to be scholarly in depth while vivid, well written and policy relevant in approach. Through commentary, analytical articles, case studies, forums, review essays, reviews and letters to the editor, the journal promotes lively, critical debate on issues of international politics and strategy.

Published for the IISS by
Routledge Journals, Taylor & Francis, 4 Park Square,
Milton Park, Abingdon, Oxfordshire OX14 4RN, UK.

GLOBAL POLITICS AND STRATEGY
Volume 50 Number 4 | August–September 2008

Contents

Cover: Getty Images

www.iiss.org
Visit the IISS website for up-to-date information on *Survival* and other IISS publications and events.

On the web
Interviews with the editor and authors in the current and previous issues.

React to articles
Send Letters to the Editor to survival@iiss.org. Look for *Survival*'s new online forum later in 2008.

Plus

Review Essays

From the Archives

Closing Argument

About the IISS The IISS, a registered charity with offices in London, Washington and Singapore, is the world's leading authority on political–military conflict. It is the primary independent source of accurate, objective information on international strategic issues. Publications include *The Military Balance*, an annual reference work on each nation's defence capabilities; *Strategic Survey*, an annual review of world affairs; *Survival*, a bi-monthly journal on international affairs; *Strategic Comments*, a monthly analysis of topical issues in international affairs; and the *Adelphi Paper* monograph series on policy-relevant strategic issues.

SUBMISSIONS

To submit an article, authors are advised to follow these guidelines:

- *Survival* articles are around 8,000 words long including endnotes. A word count should be included with a draft.
- All text, including endnotes, should be double-spaced with wide margins.
- Any tables or artwork should be supplied in separate files, ideally not embedded in the document or linked to text around it.
- All *Survival* articles are expected to include endnote references. These should be complete and include first and last names of authors, titles of articles (even from newspapers), place of publication, publisher, exact publication dates, volume and issue number (if from a journal) and page numbers. Web sources should include complete URLs and DOIs if available.
- A summary of up to 150 words should be included with the article. The summary should state the main argument clearly and concisely, not simply say what the article is about.
- A short author's biography of one or two lines should also be included. This information will appear at the foot of the first page of the article.

Submissions should be made by email, in Microsoft Word format, to the Managing Editor, Jeffrey Mazo, survival@iiss.org. Alternatively, hard copies may be sent to *Survival*, IISS, Arundel House, 13–15 Arundel Street, Temple Place, London WC2R 3DX, UK. Please direct any queries to Jeffrey Mazo.

The editorial review process can take up to three months. *Survival*'s acceptance rate for unsolicited manuscripts is less than 20%. *Survival* does not normally provide referees' comments in the event of rejection. Authors are permitted to submit simultaneously elsewhere so long as this is consistent with the policy of the other publication and the Editors of *Survival* are informed of the dual submission.

Readers are encouraged to comment on articles from the previous issue. Letters should be concise, no longer than 750 words and relate directly to the argument or points made in the original article. A response from the author of the article will normally be solicited.

ADVERTISING AND PERMISSIONS

For advertising rates and schedules

USA/Canada: The Advertising Manager, Taylor & Francis Inc., 325 Chestnut Street, 8th Floor, Philadelphia, PA 19106, USA Tel +1 (800) 354 1420 Fax +1 (215) 625 2940

UK/Europe/Rest of World: The Advertising Manager, Routledge Journals, Taylor & Francis, 4 Park Square, Milton Park, Abingdon, Oxfordshire OX14 4RN, UK
Tel +44 (0) 207 017 6000 Fax +44 (0) 207 017 6336.

SUBSCRIPTIONS

Survival is published bi-monthly in February, April, June, August, October and December by Routledge Journals, an imprint of Taylor & Francis, an Informa Business.

Annual Subscription 2008

Institution	$502	£279	€418
Individual	$132	£80	€106
Online only	$477	£265	€397

A subscription to the institution print edition, ISSN 0039-6338, includes free access for any number of concurrent users across a local area network to the online edition, ISSN 1468-2699.

Dollar rates apply to subscribers in all countries except the UK and the Republic of Ireland where the pound sterling price applies. All subscriptions are payable in advance and all rates include postage. Journals are sent by air to the USA, Canada, Mexico, India, Japan and Australasia. Subscriptions are entered on an annual basis, i.e. January to December. Payment may be made by sterling cheque, dollar cheque, international money order, National Giro, or credit card (Amex, Visa, Mastercard).

Periodicals postage paid at Jamaica, NY by US Mailing Agent Air Business Ltd, c/o Priority Airfreight NY Ltd, 147–29 182nd Street, Jamaica, NY 11413.

US Postmaster: Please send address changes to Air Business Ltd, c/o Priority Airfreight NY Ltd, 147–29 182nd Street, Jamaica, NY 11413.

ORDERING INFORMATION

USA/Canada: Taylor & Francis Inc., Journals Department, 325 Chestnut Street, 8th Floor, Philadelphia, PA 19106, USA.

UK/Europe/Rest of World: Routledge Journals, T&F Customer Services, T&F Informa UK Ltd, Sheepen Place, Colchester, Essex CO3 3LP, UK.

Back issues: Taylor & Francis retains a three-year back issue stock of journals. Older volumes are held by our official stockists: Periodicals Service Company, 11 Main Street, Germantown, NY 12526, USA to whom all orders and enquiries should be addressed. *Tel* +1 518 537 4700 *Fax* +1 518 537 5899 *e-mail* psc@periodicals.com *web* http://www.periodicals.com/tandf.html

The issue date is August–September 2008.

The print edition of this journal is printed on ANSI conforming acid free paper by Bell & Bain, Glasgow, UK.

Carrying China's Torch

Robert Ayson and Brendan Taylor

China's government has gained international recognition for what appeared to be a swift, coordinated and in many ways sensitive response to the Sichuan earthquake. In contrast to the refusal of Myanmar's ruling junta to acknowledge the scale of the devastation caused by recent floods and to make the most of sincere offers of international assistance, Beijing's leaders came across as much more transparent, accountable and responsible managers of a serious natural disaster. In the lead-up to the August Olympics, China's international reputation has received an unplanned boost.

The earthquake and its aftermath diverted attention from China's very long and laboured Olympic torch relay. Beijing's leaders expected the relay to be a triumphant prelude to the 29th Olympiad, an event intended to confirm China's status as a genuine great power. But the 2008 procession quickly descended into farce. The torch's passage was disrupted by demonstrations, particularly in early portions of the relay through London and Paris. As the relay went on, local governments, most notably in China's Asian neighbourhood, contrived to make the torch's journey as benign as possible by, for instance, curtailing routes and directing runners along safer and more predictable pathways. At the surreal extreme was the Mount Everest leg, which had been years in the planning, employing 80 space scientists and costing millions. Well before a special high-altitude torch was taken to the summit, Everest was effectively shut down. Chinese authorities banned climbers

Robert Ayson and **Brendan Taylor** are scholars with the Australian National University's Strategic and Defence Studies Centre.

Survival | vol. 50 no. 4 | August–September 2008 | pp. 5–10 DOI 10.1080/00396330802328776

from the northern side of the mountain and restricted media coverage of the event from Tibet. Following Beijing's lead, Nepalese authorities deployed two dozen armed security personnel, enforced a no-climb rule above Camp 2 (at an altitude of 6,500 metres), and banned laptops and satellite and Internet communications from Base Camp on the southern side of the mountain. Through the fog of censorship a report from one alpinist suggested that China had also sent security personnel to Everest's Nepalese flank.

The relay has been a test of how various communities around the world see China. In contrast with the near universal sympathy the country received after the earthquake, the mixed experiences of the relay have been a more accurate measure of the international reception China can expect as its power grows.

The torch relay left little doubt about China's very considerable aspirations and reveals much about Chinese power today. Most impressive and yet largely unanticipated was the mobilisation of the Chinese diaspora, particularly on the South Korean and Australian legs. In Australia, thousands of Chinese students arrived early and en masse to secure pre-determined vantage points along the relay's route. Enthusiastically waving embassy-supplied flags and patriotically screaming 'One China', these loyal young cadres outnumbered and strategically out-positioned their 'splittist' counterparts. In so doing, they reminded the world that quantity has a quality all of its own.

The relay has also underlined the potency of China's growing economic power. Corporate sponsors contributed an estimated $15 million to the relay, and refused to be cornered into criticising Beijing or withdrawing their support, even as hopes for the torch's 'harmonious journey' vanished. The reasons for their reluctance became obvious when rumours surfaced that the French retailer Carrefour was bankrolling the Dalai Lama. Many Chinese citizens responded by boycotting the supermarket chain, and nationwide protests erupted outside Carrefour stores. Somewhat unsurprisingly, Carrefour rapidly doused these allegations and pledged its unswerving allegiance to the Beijing Olympics.

These protests, while short-lived, further highlighted some of the sources and limits of Chinese power. That they were organised using mobile phones and the Internet is somewhat ironic. Traditionally, such technologies have been considered the 'Achilles' heel' of the Chinese government. They have been portrayed as a threat to Beijing's longstanding stranglehold on information and a conduit for the dissemination of new political ideas throughout China.

During the torch relay, however, mobile phones and the Internet were used not to undermine, but to rally support for the Chinese leadership. They have also served as a catalyst for Chinese nationalism more generally. Yet the manner in which Beijing has sought to regulate the resultant outpourings of patriotic sentiment also suggests an ongoing sense of vulnerability. Having allowed the anti-Carrefour protests to run for several days, Beijing abruptly ordered a cessation of such activities. Mobile phone messages and Internet chat rooms referring to the French retailer were also reportedly blocked. This pattern is consistent with Beijing's response to the mass anti-Japanese protests of April 2005. The Chinese Communist Party is not entirely sure whether popular nationalism is a useful force that can be utilised and even encouraged to provide legitimacy in a post-socialist era, or a dangerous beast that can easily run out of control.

Beijing was not the only Asian capital seeking to regulate popular sentiment during the torch relay. On the Indian leg, for instance, the centre of New Delhi went into complete lockdown. Fifteen thousand security personnel were deployed and almost 300 protestors (mostly Tibetan) were arrested. Manmohan Singh's government, eager to preserve and build on improvements in its vital relationship with China, also publicly advised the Dalai Lama to take a low-key role. In Indonesia, the relay was held within the confines of the Bung Karno sports stadium, with only 2,500 'guests', and the same number of security personnel, in attendance.

The centre of New Delhi went into complete lockdown

Security was also tight in the Japanese city of Nagano, with authorities deploying 3,000 police and shutting the public out at torch stopping points. Still, a major Japanese temple refused to host the torch as planned, and scuffles between Chinese students and Japanese nationalists broke out on the fringes of the relay. But given the proven potential of the underlying tension in Sino-Japanese relations to produce large-scale protests in both countries, the relatively smooth Nagano leg was no small achievement. Overall, while security measures in Asian countries were partly a reflection of concerns about domestic order, they also indicated a sense of deference to China's Olympic sensibilities. This in itself is testament to China's growing power and influence in the region.

South Korea proved the unexpected exception to this Asian rule. In Seoul, 8,300 police were unable to prevent Chinese students from assaulting a small number of local protesters, prompting threats of deportation from the South Korean government and official complaints to Beijing's ambassador. Yet these diplomatic gymnastics paled in comparison with the defiance that greeted the torch on its 'disharmonious' journey through Europe. A Paris-based media-rights group disrupted the torch-lighting ceremony in Olympia, unfurling a banner criticising Chinese human-rights practices; members of China's 'Sacred Torch Protection Unit' were labelled 'thugs' by the head of London's Olympic organising committee, Sebastian Coe, even as anti-China protesters tried to extinguish the torch during its journey through the city; and the cover of the prominent German magazine *Der Spiegel* depicted China's leaders beneath Olympic rings made of barbed wire.

Perhaps most controversially, China's 'angel in a wheelchair' – the paraplegic fencer Jin Jing – was jostled by pro-Tibetan protesters while carrying the torch through Paris. Despite issuing an apology and inviting Jin to return to France, President Nicolas Sarkozy continued to lead calls for a boycott of the Olympic opening ceremony. British Prime Minister Gordon Brown and German Chancellor Angela Merkel were quick to take up the baton, publicly confirming their non-attendance. These developments have given rise to a worrying spike in anti-Western sentiment within China. This feeling has been further fuelled by a widely held perception of Western media bias, epitomised by CNN commentator Jack Cafferty's characterisation of China's leaders as a 'bunch of thugs and goons'.

Princeton professor John Ikenberry recently argued that a rare opportunity exists to integrate an increasingly powerful China into the current

Western-led international order. To the extent that this window exists, it may close quickly if growing numbers of Chinese citizens do not feel that their country is respected or wanted as a member of that order, and especially if they imagine a Western conspiracy designed to keep their nation shackled.

'The West' is a heterogeneous amalgam and the varying reactions of some Western leaders to the torch relay have been significantly more nuanced than the popular Chinese view suggests. Most intriguing has been the approach taken by Australian Prime Minister Kevin Rudd. Since his election late last year, Rudd has been caricatured as a 'Manchurian candidate' because of his fluency in Mandarin and strong interest in China. Yet he surprised many with the fairly robust approach he took during Australia's turn with the torch. In the days prior to the Canberra leg of the relay, Rudd and his spokespeople repeatedly corrected Chinese officials over the role of the 'Sacred Torch Protection Unit'. He publicly threatened to arrest any members of this paramilitary squad who sought to play a direct security role. And when two members of the infamous blue-track-suited brigade tried to get close to the flame during the relay, they were forcibly removed by Australian Federal Police officers.

What distinguishes Rudd from his European counterparts is his sophisticated understanding of Beijing's 'red lines' in relation to the Olympic games and the Tibet issue. Speaking to a group of Peking University students in March of this year, Rudd openly acknowledged Tibet's 'significant human-rights problems'. But at the same time, he described himself as a *zhenghou* (true friend) of China and delivered his criticisms in that capacity. He also reaffirmed Australia's recognition of China's sovereignty over Tibet. Most importantly, he stated his opposition to boycotting the Olympics. In so doing, Rudd demonstrated his understanding of the symbolic importance of the upcoming Olympics to China. He is a student of Chinese history and knows well that this is the platform from which China will announce its arrival as a great power and shed its 'victim mentality' resulting from a 'century of shame' under Western domination.

Similarities are evident in Washington's response to the torch relay, although some aspects of the US tour echoed the European experience. The San Francisco leg, for instance, was marred by violent clashes which evoked memories of Paris and London. Pro-Tibetan congressional supporters, led by House Speaker Nancy Pelosi, have urged President Bush to boycott the games, as have presidential hopefuls John McCain and Barack Obama. Yet Bush's response to this mounting pressure has been most revealing. He has declined to openly politicise the Olympics, indicating that US pressure regarding Beijing's approach to Tibet has been and will continue to be exerted in private. Like Rudd, Bush appears to be pursuing a more sophisticated 'third way' between indulging and directly confronting China's Olympic sensibilities.

By contrast, China's heavy-handed approach during the torch relay is at odds with its own sophisticated diplomacy in recent years. Yet despite the public-relations disaster which parts of the torch relay have become for China's foreign relations – Pew polling data collected in March and April, for instance, shows a sudden spike in global anxieties over China's growing power – the domestic advantages for Beijing have made it a game worth the candle. It is no coincidence that six weeks of the relay have been dedicated to running the Olympic torch through 46 major Chinese cities, where it has been largely greeted by further displays of patriotism.

The Sichuan earthquake has also helped reinforce a sense of national unity and took much heat out of the criticism China attracted from some quarters over the torch relay. But the relay's broader strategic significance should not be lost amidst the rubble of this terrible natural tragedy. The torch's travels reveal much about the sources and limits of Chinese power, demonstrating just how intense the fires of Chinese nationalism can be when fanned. They provide important insights into the potentially combustible nature of ties between China and the West. Most importantly, the relay sheds new light on approaches for dealing with a China increasingly fearful that its Olympic dream, and the international re-emergence it symbolises, might still backfire.

When Nazi Germany invented the Olympic torch relay in 1936, sending it eastward, the *New York Times* presciently dubbed its route a 'strategic highway'. China's 2008 relay – and the controversies it sparked – are no less revealing about a quite different regime whose growing power promises to define a new era in world affairs.

An Agenda for Human Dignity

Marc Perrin de Brichambaut

The debate about promoting democracy continues to beat strong, and for good reason. If in the early 1990s democracy seemed triumphant across the globe as the single most legitimate and effective form of governance, this may no longer be the case. International relations feature today a handful of countries with rising international influence and growing capitalist economic systems, but whose form of government is not democratic. In some, the trappings of democratic form are maintained, while the substance of politics is quite different. More countries today pay allegiance to democracy, but its spirit is not spreading inexorably through the world.

These circumstances raise a difficult question: how to continue to support democracy in countries and regions where the notion is challenged and resistance is growing?

The Organisation for Security and Co-operation in Europe (OSCE) has something unique to contribute to this debate. This is, first, because the OSCE played a key role underpinning democratic transformation in Eastern Europe in the 1990s and remains active today across wider Europe. The OSCE has supported societies undergoing difficult transitions and it has helped build legitimate institutions in war-torn regions. As importantly, the OSCE has even longer experience in promoting the essential value that democracy is designed to promote: the inherent dignity of the individual, as embodied in his or her fundamental freedoms and human rights. The

Marc Perrin de Brichambaut is Secretary General of the Organisation for Security and Co-operation in Europe.

 DOI 10.1080/00396330802328792

OSCE has pursued what might be called a 'human dignity' agenda since its creation in 1975 as the Conference on Security and Co-operation in Europe (CSCE). At a time when democracy itself faces challenges, it is worth remembering the essentials.

The legacy of Helsinki

Since 1975, the OSCE has developed a solid foundation of commitments regarding the protection of the inherent dignity of the individual. It has also developed a useful toolbox for helping the 56 OSCE states implement these commitments.

The Helsinki Final Act was signed in Helsinki in 1975 by a group of 35 countries, ranging from Austria to Yugoslavia and including the United States and the Soviet Union. In the Final Act, these states pledged to 'promote and encourage the effective exercise of the civil, political, economic, social, cultural and other rights and freedoms, all of which derive from the *inherent dignity of the human person* and are essential for his free and full development'.[1]

The Final Act was a complex package of compromises struck between the antagonistic blocs. Nonetheless, the Final Act's commitment to the dignity of the individual became a powerful platform for advocating change in the Soviet bloc. The United States and its European allies pressed the Soviet Union to ensure human rights and fundamental freedoms, including religious freedoms and the right to freedom of movement. The tone was set at the first CSCE Follow-up Meeting in Belgrade in 1977–78, when individual cases of violations were raised. Dissident groups sprung up all across the Soviet bloc inspired by the principles developed in the Final Act.

According to one of its drafters, US diplomat John Maresca, the content of the Final Act created a 'vast political and historical dimension of opportunity'.[2] The space became filled with content once the context had changed sufficiently inside states and across Europe. The CSCE did not change the USSR; the USSR itself changed. Still, the unremitting focus on the inherent dignity of the human person helped till the ground for that change.

'Democracy' itself made it onto the agenda of the OSCE when change in wider Europe was gathering speed. This happened at a meeting in

Copenhagen in June 1989, when states agreed that 'pluralistic democracy and the rule of law are essential for ensuring respect for all human rights and fundamental freedoms'.[3] During that meeting, states also spelled out the institutional components of democratic governance – underlining the role of free and fair elections, an independent judiciary and representative government to ensure that individual fundamental freedoms were respected.

The November 1990 summit in Paris was a crowning moment when the changes that were occurring and the values that had accompanied them were enshrined at the highest level.[4] The Paris Charter placed democracy itself at the heart of the OSCE process: 'We undertake to build, consolidate and strengthen democracy as the only system of government of our nations'.

On these foundations, the OSCE has developed a varied toolbox to assist states in protecting fundamental freedoms and human rights and strengthening democratic institutions. Today, the OSCE has 19 field operations deployed across the OSCE area with mandates to support states and their societies. The organisation also has a central Secretariat and specialised institutions that provide targeted assistance – the Office for Democratic Institutions and Human Rights, the Representative on Freedom of the Media, and the High Commissioner on National Minorities.[5] In practice, the OSCE works across the spectrum – for instance, by helping states strengthen independent judiciaries, monitor media freedoms, build democratic police forces, and ensure the protection of human rights in the struggle against terrorism. The OSCE is also pushing to settle unresolved conflicts in the former Soviet Union, is active across all of Kosovo, and provides a key forum for building trust in military affairs across wider Europe. At the heart of all these activities, there remains the principle that security and democracy starts with the 'inherent dignity of the human person'.

Difficult times

In Central and Eastern Europe, the vision embodied in the Paris Charter was a remarkable success. The decade that followed the end of the Cold War saw the region's transformation. With the EU and NATO, the OSCE was vital in underpinning this historic change. In other parts of wider Europe, however, progress has been more uncertain.

Major reforms have occurred in Southeastern Europe and the former Soviet Union to consolidate state institutions and build new political systems. But the conditions have been difficult, featuring devastating wars in the western Balkans and conflicts further east. Events in Georgia since November 2007 and Armenia after the presidential elections of February 2008 highlight the challenges still facing democratic consolidation, even when major advances have been made.

The challenges to fundamental freedoms and human rights have mutated with time. For instance, the jailing of journalists for political reasons was a key threat to freedom of the media in the OSCE area. Today, problems arise more from the abuse by the authorities of the very legislation that was put in place to protect the media. Also, the business of media has changed dramatically; stubborn independent media voices have great difficulty today finding employment in some countries.

Challenges to human rights have mutated with time

In some countries, the experience of the 1990s, often associated with severe domestic economic hardship and the undermining of traditional social structures, has soured perceptions of 'democracy' as a practice of government. In Russia, former President Vladimir Putin often presented the 1990s as period of chaos and weakness, not to be repeated. In some countries, authoritarian forms of rule have arisen.

Some actors within the OSCE have started revisiting the practice in the field of election observation that was built on the 1990 Copenhagen commitments. The challenge from Russia and some of its partners in the Commonwealth of Independent States (CIS) has focused on the legitimacy of existing practices in the field of election observation, a flagship OSCE activity. These tensions led the OSCE to decide not to send an observation mission to the Russian parliamentary elections (2007) and presidential elections (2008) because of restrictions placed on the size, duration and freedom of movement of the planned team.

Insecurity remains deep in parts of the OSCE area. The break-up of the former Yugoslavia is still running its course, and conflicts remain unsettled in the former Soviet Union. As long as first-order questions of statehood remain, providing for fundamental freedoms will remain a fraught process in these regions, and democratic consolidation will be difficult.

In addition, all OSCE states face the challenge of integrating diversity into increasingly complex societies. Intolerance, hate crimes and terrorism are creating fear in our multicultural cities and societies. Stereotyping, marginalisation and a lack of integration may rip the fibres of interwoven communities, leading to anger and resentment that breeds hate, even violence.

UK Foreign Secretary David Milliband recently said that, 'since the millennium, there has been a pause in the democratic advance'.[7] Wider trends have an impact on the OSCE area. While the vast majority of states around the world are now rooted in a nominal sovereignty of 'the people' and most retain the external trappings of democratic governance, the onward march of liberal values that seemed self-evident a decade ago is no more. The combination of apparently sustainable economic growth with various shades of authoritarianism may be, to some leaders, an increasingly attractive alternative.

All of this means that issues of individual dignity and democracy remain high on the agenda of wider Europe.

Patience and perseverance

The human dignity agenda is tried and tested. It may not be the fastest or the most radical path, but it is one where the basics are not forgotten and where patience is married with perseverance. Since 1975, through the Cold War and after its end, the OSCE has proven its ability to foster change peacefully and resiliently.

Reaffirming an insistence on the 'inherent dignity of the human person' offers an inclusive platform upon which to build deeper cooperation between states and within them, with the long-term objective of supporting and strengthening democracy. The perspective provided by the human dignity agenda, based on the rich body of commitments shared by the OSCE participating states, is already central for the OSCE in tackling new challenges, such as promoting human rights in counter-terrorism and strengthening tolerance and non-discrimination. This agenda also guides OSCE rehabilitation activities in the conflict zones of Transdniestr and South Ossetia. It is the same insistence on protecting the dignity of the individual that inspires OSCE action in the fight against the trafficking of persons. The point is that the OSCE promotes the inherent dignity of the human person in specific, not abstract, terms. In practice, this has meant, for instance, addressing the circumstances of journalists in Azerbaijan, clarifying the fate of prisoners in Belarus, and advocating the rights of Europe's marginalised Roma and Sinti population. Working in parallel with structural support to democratic institution-building, the combination is powerful.

Since 1975, during the Cold War and after its end, the OSCE has developed useful operating principles for promoting human dignity and supporting democracy in a fully complementary way. A first principle reflects the need to create consensus. In the field operations and across the OSCE area, the OSCE seeks to work with the grain of local conditions to craft with elites and societies greater political space for protecting human dignity and consolidating democracy. This is not easy, and it takes time.

A second principle is patience married with perseverance. The transformation of Eastern Europe in the 1990s saw all good things coming together at the same time. The speed of this success should not detract, however, from the historical patience that may be required in other parts of wider Europe. The Helsinki Final Act and the process that followed were visionary in framing the protection of human rights and fundamental freedoms, but also patient in their expectation for success.

Finally, the OSCE has a comprehensive approach. Promoting the dignity of the human person and democratic institutions are *part* of a package, not the package itself, designed to build security in wider Europe through work also on political-military transparency and economic and environmental good governance. The focus is not exclusively state orientated; civil society in the widest sense, including non-governmental organisations and professional groups, has a vital place. The starting point of the OSCE remains as radical as it was in 1975: that genuine and comprehensive security begins at the level of individuals and their fundamental freedoms and human rights. It is on this foundation that a lastingly secure wider Europe may be built

In the heated political debate about the pitfalls of promoting democracy, the human dignity agenda ensures that fundamentals are not left aside. Protecting human dignity is the objective; democratic institutions are the means.

Notes

1 On the negotiations of the Final Act, see Jacques Andréani, *Le Piège, Helsinki et la chute du communisme* (Paris: Odile Jacob, 2005); Andrei Zagorski, *The Helsinki Process* (Moscow: Human Rights Editions, 2005); and John J. Maresca, *To Helsinki, the Conference on Security and Co-operation in Europe, 1973–1975* (Durham, NC: Duke University Press, 1985).

2 John J. Maresca, 'The CSCE at its Inception: 1975 in Myth and Reality', in *OSCE Yearbook 2005* (Baden-Baden: Nomos Verlagsgesellschaft, 2006), pp. 29–38.

3 *Document of the Copenhagen Meeting of the Conference on the Human Dimension of the CSCE*, 29 June 1990.

4 *Charter of Paris for a New Europe*, Paris, 19–21 November 1990.

5 For information on OSCE activities, including those related to the fight against terrorism, police support and the fight against human trafficking, see http://www.osce.org.

6 See *Document of the Copenhagen Meeting of the Conference on the Human Dimension of the CSCE*. For more information on OSCE methodology, see *Election Observation Handbook*, 5th ed. (Warsaw: OSCE, 2005) and *Handbook for Long Term Election Observers* (Warsaw: OSCE, 2007).

7 David Milliband, 'The Democratic Imperative', St Hugh's College, Oxford University, 12 February 2008.

Noteworthy

Seventh IISS Shangri-La Dialogue in Singapore

'Any speculation in the region about the United States losing interest in Asia strikes me as either preposterous, or disingenuous, or both.'

US Secretary of Defense Robert Gates speaks on US commitment to security in Asia-Pacific at the 7th IISS Shangri-La Dialogue, 31 May 2008[1]

'We need a system of sanctions to stop the scandal of having hundreds of thousands of people dying, with help waiting outside, and having a lecture about non-interference in domestic affairs. I am sorry to change the tone of this very polite international gathering, but I think it is my duty to do so.'

Pierre Lellouche criticises Myanmar's response to international offers of assistance following Cyclone Nargis[2]

'We warmly welcome any assistance and aid, which are provided with genuine goodwill, from any country or any organisation, provided that there are no strings attached.'

Major-General Aye Myint, Deputy Minister of Myanmar's Ministry of Defence, speaks on his country's willingness to accept foreign assistance in the wake of Cyclone Nargis[3]

'It is essential that the Japanese people living in this century accurately understand the grief and bitterness which Japan left to the people of Asia and win [their] trust … We feel that we have done something for which we have no excuse, for which we feel very sorry.'

Shigeru Ishiba, Japan's Minister of Defence, acknowledges Japanese wrongdoing during the Second World War during his speech at the 7th Shangri-La Dialgoue[4]

'We will not enter the arms race and we will not be a military threat to any country. We will never seek hegemony or expansion.'

Lieutenant-General Ma Xiaotian, Deputy Chief of Staff of the People's Liberation Army, China, speaks on Chinese intentions within the East Asian region[5]

Closing window

'I do think the parties, both the Israelis and the Palestinians, realise that the opportunity for a two-state solution is not always going to be there.'

US Secretary of State Condoleezza Rice speaks with Mamoun Fandy, IISS Senior Fellow for Gulf Security, in Washington on 8 May 2008[6]

Plain speaking

'In the case of what Iran is doing in Iraq, it is so damn obvious to anybody who wants to look into it I think we ought to just drop the word "alleged".'

Colonel H.R. McMaster, IISS Consulting Fellow, insists that there is no reason to doubt Iran's role in encouraging violence in Iraq[7]

DOI 10.1080/00396330802328917

History lesson

'Some seem to believe that we should negotiate with the terrorists and radicals, as if some ingenious argument will persuade them they have been wrong all along … We have an obligation to call this what it is – the false comfort of appeasement, which has been repeatedly discredited by history.'

President George W. Bush addresses the Knesset in Jerusalem in honour of the 60th anniversary of the founding of Israel, 15 May 2008[8]

'Election' in Zimbabwe

'We in the MDC have resolved that we will no longer participate in this violent, illegitimate sham of an election process.'

Opposition leader Morgan Tsvangirai pulls out of Zimbabwe's presidential run-off, 22 June 2008[11]

'The outcome did not reflect the true and genuine will of the Zimbabwean people or produce a legitimate result.'

UN Secretary-General Ban Ki Moon criticises Zimbabwe's presidential election, which went ahead in spite of international protests[12]

'He was elected, he took an oath, and he is here with us, so he is President and we cannot ask him more. He conducted elections and I think he won.'

President Omar Bongo of Gabon defends Robert Mugabe at a summit of African leaders[13]

'I, Robert Gabriel Mugabe, do swear that I will well and truly serve Zimbabwe in the office of president, so help me God.'

Robert Mugabe is sworn in as President of Zimbabwe on 29 June 2008[14]

23%

Percentage of time on US TV news broadcasts devoted to Iraq, first 10 weeks of 2007

3%

Percentage in first 10 weeks of 2008[9]

Massaging the intel

'He took occasion to let drop some Africa figs before the senate. And on their admiring the size and beauty of them, he presently added, that the place that bore them was but three days' sail from Rome.'

Cato hypes the threat from Carthage before the third Punic War, ca 151 BCE[15]

Rule of law

'We hold that Art. I, §9, cl. 2, of the Constitution has full effect at Guantanamo Bay.'

The Supreme Court of the United States restores habeas corpus for Guantanamo detainees[10]

Sources: **1–5** http://www.iiss.org/conferences/the-shangri-la-dialogue/plenary-session-speeches-2008/ **6** http://www.iiss.org/whats-new/iiss-in-the-press/may-2008/mamoun-fandy-speaks-with-condoleezza-rice/ **7** 'After the Iraqi Offensive: An Address by Colonel H.R. McMaster', American, Enterprise Institute, Washington DC, 13 May 2008,http://app2.capitalreach.com/esp1204/servlet/tc?cn=aei&c=10162&s=20271&e=9461&&espmt=2 **8** http://www.whitehouse.gov/news/releases/2008/05/20080515-1.html **9** Project for Excellence in Journalism, 26 March 2008, http://journalism.org/node/10365 **10** Boumediene et al. v. Bush, President of the United States, et al., No. 06-1195, 12 June 2008, http://caselaw.lp.findlaw.com/scripts/getcase.pl?court=US&vol=000&invol=06-1195 **11** 'Opposition Leader Pulls Out of Zimbabwe Election', video by AP, http://www.washingtonpost.com/wp-dyn/content/video/2008/06/23/VI2008062300518.html?sid=ST2008062300046 **12** 'Outcome of Zimbabwe Polls Illegitimate, says Ban', UN News Centre, http://www.un.org/apps/news/story.asp?NewsID=27208&Cr=Zimbabwe&Cr1= **13** David Blair, 'Zimbabwe's Robert Mugabe "a Hero", say African Leaders', *Telegraph*, 1 July 2008 **14** 'Mugabe is Sworn In for Sixth Term', BBC video, http://news.bbc.co.uk/1/hi/world/africa/7479853.stm. **15** Plutarch, *Life of Cato*, p. 27, discussed in Robin Lane Fox, *The Classical World: An Epic History of Greece and Rome* (London: Penguin, 2005), p. 338.

Early Days in Iraq: Decisions of the CPA

L. Paul Bremer, James Dobbins and David Gompert

With the fall of Baghdad in April 2003 and in the immediate aftermath of Saddam Hussein's immensely destructive three-decade reign, the US-led coalition faced three fundamental challenges: (1) to provide security for the Iraqi people; (2) to set Iraq on the path to a more open, humane and democratic society; and (3) to reform Iraq's closed and moribund economy. The coalition military had primary responsibility for the first task, the Coalition Provisional Authority (CPA) for the latter two.

As security deteriorated, coalition forces came to be seen as occupiers, not liberators. Sunni–Shi'ite tensions, in Iraq and in the surrounding region, proved to be greater than anticipated. Iraq's neighbours did not look kindly on the US occupation or on Iraqi democracy. Iraqi oil revenue was insufficient to fund the normal functions of government, let alone major investments in the nation's dilapidated infrastructure. Despite these and other handicaps, the CPA was able to leave behind a durable democratic political framework and a more open economy, providing Iraq's elected

L. Paul Bremer's diplomatic career spanned eight administrations, during which he served on the personal staff of six Secretaries of State. He was American Ambassador to the Netherlands, Ambassador at Large for Counter Terrorism, and Presidential Envoy to Iraq and Administrator of the Coalition Provisional Authority. He served as Chairman of the bipartisan National Commission on Terrorism and on the President's Homeland Security Advisory Commission. During his time in the private sector, Bremer served as Managing Director of Kissinger Associates and as Chairman and CEO of March Crisis Consulting. **James Dobbins** is a former Assistant Secretary of State for Europe, Ambassador to the European Community, and American Special Envoy for Somalia, Haiti, Bosnia, Kosovo and Afghanistan. He is currently Director of the International Security and Defense Policy Center at the RAND Corporation. **David C. Gompert** is a Senior Fellow at the RAND Corporation and on the faculty of the US Naval Academy. He is former Senior Adviser for National Security and Defense, Iraq, and has served in senior positions in several US administrations, in private industry and at RAND.

Survival | vol. 50 no. 4 | August–September 2008 | pp. 21–56 DOI 10.1080/00396330802328925

leaders with an opportunity to create a legitimate state, a free society and a better life for their people.

The authority's tasks were made more difficult when many of the assumptions that American authorities had made prior to the invasion concerning post-war conditions proved unrealistic. The Iraqi state that the US-led coalition inherited was much more dysfunctional than anticipated. The economy had collapsed. For 30 years political life had been dominated by a small, brutal clique. Under the shock of the invasion, the Iraqi army had ceased to exist as a coherent organisation. The Iraqi police were a force in name only, at half strength, with a deserved reputation for corruption and brutality and unable to provide day-to-day security.

Despite the urging of CPA leaders, during the CPA period the coalition did not field sufficient armed forces, nor did the existing forces implement an effective counter-insurgency strategy to secure the Iraqi population. This failure seriously complicated all the CPA's efforts in the political and economic areas. As of July 2008, violence in Iraq has dropped dramatically due in large part to the decision in 2007 to adopt an effective counter-insurgency strategy, supplemented by additional US forces – the so-called 'surge'. Now, despite the significant problems Iraq has experienced since the overthrow of Saddam Hussein, there is a real opportunity to build on the political and economic foundation laid during the CPA period to realise the goal of a more stable and democratic Iraq at peace with its neighbours.

Here we examine several of the most controversial decisions of the CPA between April 2003 and June 2004 concerning both governing Iraq and the transition to Iraqi self-rule. We do so with the benefit of hindsight, but also in recognition of the information, resources and options available to the CPA at the time the decisions were made. Two of us served with the CPA, and the other helped lead several earlier American efforts at post-war reconstruction.

'Disbanding' the army

Security was the first major problem the coalition faced. Saddam's security forces were essentially gone. By the time Baghdad fell on 9 April 2003, the Iraqi army had simply dissolved. In a 17 April secure video conference with

Deputy Secretary of Defense Paul Wolfowitz, General John Abizaid, then deputy and soon to be the top commander of all US forces in the Middle East, reported that 'there are no organized Iraqi military units left'.[1] As General David Petraeus later confirmed to Congress, the pre-war assumption that Saddam's army would be available 'did not transpire'.[2] The Iraqi police had also deserted their posts in all major cities. Looting was widespread and caused billions of dollars in damage. All major government ministries, police stations and government buildings were effectively destroyed. The Iraqi people and remnants of the Saddam regime were left with the question whether the coalition would provide security. After having suffered three decades of vicious rule, many Iraqis feared (and a small minority of Sunni loyalists hoped) that Saddam would return to power, as he had done once before.

Because the Iraqi army had 'self demobilised', as the Pentagon put it,[3] pre-war plans to use the Iraqi military for post-war stability operations were rendered irrelevant. The question facing the coalition was whether to try to reconstitute Saddam's army. There were compelling practical and political arguments against such a course.

The majority of Saddam's soldiers had been young Shia draftees. These soldiers were frequently abused, often brutally, by their primarily Sunni officers. Grateful to be alive, hundreds of thousands of draftees simply deserted the army and went back to their farms and families. They did not go home empty-handed; soldiers and other looters stripped military bases and barracks clean. They took everything that was not nailed down, and much that was: sinks, faucets, toilets and even the tile and piping in the bathrooms. In many military bases, not a single building was left standing. The coalition recognised that many Shia draftees would not willingly return to an army they hated to serve under officers who had treated them brutally. As a practical matter, if they were to be recalled to service, coalition forces would have to use force to bring some, perhaps most, of them back to destroyed bases.

In many bases not a single building was left standing

The political arguments against recalling Saddam's army were even stronger. The army had conducted a decade-long war against Iraq's Kurds, killing hundreds of thousands of them and forcing tens of thousands from their homes. Saddam had used Iraq's security forces to crush a Shia uprising after the First Gulf War, killing hundreds of thousands of innocent men, women and children. The Kurds had fought alongside the coalition to liberate Iraq. Following guidance from Grand Ayatollah Ali al-Sistani, the Shi'ites were cooperating with the coalition. Together the Kurds and Shi'ites constitute over 80% of Iraq's population. Both groups made clear to the CPA that any attempt to recall the army would give lie to the coalition's stated goal of ridding Iraq of Saddam's regime. Kurdish leaders told the coalition that if Saddam's army were recalled, they would secede from Iraq, causing the country's breakup and likely precipitating both a civil war and a wider regional war.[4]

The political consequences which would have resulted from recalling even parts of Saddam's army were dramatically illustrated in April 2004. The US Marines, without coordination with the CPA, took it upon themselves to recall a single brigade of Saddam's army, purportedly to help control the city of Falluja. The recall caused a public political explosion which almost blew apart the Iraqi government. And the 'Falluja Brigade', instead of helping the Marines, wound up supporting the very insurgents it was supposed to suppress and itself had to be disbanded.[5]

Nevertheless, the security situation demanded a solution. The US government examined the question of whether it should try to recall the army or to build a new volunteer army open to both vetted members of the old army and new recruits. In the 17 April video conference General Abizaid favoured the second approach. In the weeks after Abizaid's recommendation, the CPA's designated national security adviser, former Undersecretary of Defense (in the Clinton administration) Walter Slocombe, discussed options with top officials in the Pentagon, including Deputy Secretary of Defense Wolfowitz. These officials believed that an early recall of the former army and would be a practical and political mistake.[6]

On 9 May 2003, Secretary of Defense Donald Rumsfeld circulated to members of the National Security Council a memo entitled 'Principles for Iraq–Policy Guidelines' that specified that the coalition 'will actively oppose Saddam Hussein's old enforcers — the Baath Party, Fedayeen Saddam, etc.'

and that 'we will make clear that the coalition will eliminate the remnants of Saddam's regime'.[7] This approach was consistent with pre-war thinking reflected in the State Department's 'Future of Iraq' study, which in May 2002 had concluded that 'the Iraqi Army of the future cannot be an extension of the present army, which has been made into a tool of dictatorship', and called for the coalition to 'rebuild the Iraqi army in a manner that will ensure its professional and military conduct ... distancing itself from any political role'.[8]

Slocombe's consultations with Americans officials in Washington and Baghdad convinced him that most agreed that the only viable course was to build a new, all-volunteer, professional force open to screened members of the former army. Slocombe drafted an order to accomplish these objectives. In early May, drafts of this order were forwarded for comments to Rumsfeld; Wolfowitz; Under Secretary of Defense for Policy Douglas Feith; the Defense Department's general counsel; General Tommy Franks (head of Central Command); and Jay Garner (the coalition's top civil administrator at the time).

On 12 May, Garner and the CPA administrator sent Stephen Hadley, deputy national security adviser, a memo noting their intention to pay all former Iraqi government employees except uniformed military and members of the intelligence services. On 13 May, en route to Baghdad, Slocombe briefed senior British officials in London on this proposal. They told him they recognised that 'the demobilisation of the Iraqi military is a fait accompli'. His report to Washington following that visit added that 'if some U.K. officers or officials think that we should try to rebuild or reassemble the old R.A. [Republican Army], they did not give any hint of it in our meetings, and in fact agreed with the need for vigorous de-Baathification, especially in the security sector'.[9]

Over the following week, Slocombe continued discussions about the planned order with top Pentagon officials, including Feith. During that same period, Lieutenant-General David McKiernan, the field commander of the coalition forces in Iraq, received and cleared the draft order. Rumsfeld was kept regularly informed about these discussions and on 19 May received a final draft of the proposed order for his approval.[10] Apart from minor edits to the order, none of these military or civilian officials raised objections to the proposal to create a new Iraqi army or to formally dissolve Saddam Hussein's security apparatus. On 22 May the full National Security Council, with the president in the chair, was briefed on the plan. No one raised objections.[11]

While some American officers in the field have stated that they believe a number of Iraqi soldiers would have been willing to return to service, the practical and political arguments against their recall at the time were decisive. Iraqis consulted by the US government before the war said that 'the Iraqi armed forces are often cited as a national institution that has an organizational and command structure and can therefore replace the regime of Saddam Hussein. This argument it without merit ... the military establishment itself requires thorough reform and depoliticization.'[12] And at the time, this decision was not regarded as controversial. General Richard Myers, former chairman of the Joint Chiefs of Staff, confirmed that there had been 'no robust debate' about the decision at the time.[13] When Slocombe held a press conference in Baghdad on 23 May to explain the decision, only two reporters showed up — neither of them Americans.

In retrospect it was a mistake to label the decision as 'disbanding' an army which, in point of fact, no longer existed. More importantly, and more harmfully, the formal dissolution of the army was not immediately accompanied by a clear-cut commitment to pay career officers and non-commissioned officers pensions for some period based upon their time in service. It took another month for such a step to be announced and somewhat longer for it to be implemented, for two reasons. First, there were American political concerns about the impact of paying soldiers who, just weeks before, had been killing Americans. Secondly, it was not until the middle of June that the coalition was able to obtain the personnel roster of the pre-war Iraqi army, which was necessary to make payments. Until then, and having access to only limited Iraqi government funds, the CPA could not estimate the costs of paying soldiers of the former army. Once that list was obtained, the CPA announced stipends for former officers at levels equal to or greater than they would have received under pre-war arrangements and higher than salaries being paid to Iraqi civil servants. Payments were begun in early July 2003 and continued for the entire 14 months of the CPA's existence, and under successive sovereign Iraqi governments.

As soon as the coalition announced its intention to pay Saddam's army soldiers these stipends, organised demonstrations by former officers stopped, leading coalition military intelligence to drop 'former officers' as a threat category. Moreover, the CPA policy encouraged former army soldiers to apply for service in the new all-volunteer Iraqi army. They did so by the thousands. By the time the CPA left Iraq, almost all enlisted men and over 80% of officers were from the former army.[14] Nonetheless, during this period, financial uncertainty among this class of individuals, most of whom were Sunni, may have contributed to support for the emerging insurgency. Some members of the former army did join the insurgency, not because they had no income after self-demobilisation (they did), but because they wanted to reinstate by force either Saddam or, at least, a Sunni-dominated government. Still, a better prepared and resourced programme for disarmament, demobilisation and reintegration would almost certainly have both attenuated the reaction to the army's 'disbandment' and made reconstitution of a new force somewhat easier. Such programmes have become routine components of most post-conflict reconstruction missions over the past 20 years, and the failure to develop, fund and staff such a programme prior to the invasion proved a costly mistake. Under no circumstances would the coalition have wished to keep the entire Iraqi army under arms. Thus the need for a disarmament, demobilisation and reintegration programme was foreseeable, even if the scale of the eventual demobilisation could not have been predicted.

The CPA was unable to integrate former soldiers into the civilian economy

The CPA proved unable to implement plans to reintegrate those former soldiers who did not volunteer for service in the new army into the civilian economy. Given the state of that economy at the time (the Iraqi Ministry of Planning told the CPA administrator that his ministry estimated post-war unemployment at over 60%, and virtually all Iraq's state-owned enterprises were closed down), this would under any circumstances have been very difficult. The CPA contracted with the International Organisation for Migration, a UN agency, to undertake a comprehensive programme of reintegration of former army soldiers. But when, on 19 August 2003, the UN office in Baghdad was bombed, the organisation, like all UN-connected organisations, had to withdraw from Iraq in accordance with UN security procedures and was unable to fulfil the contract.

Some have criticised the decision to rely on civilian contractors to train the new Iraqi army. In fact, in June 2003, General Ricardo Sanchez, commander of Coalition forces in Iraq, proposed to CPA leaders that the US Army take on this task. The CPA agreed. Sanchez forwarded the proposal through military channels but it was not approved.

On a final note, today two of the most effective and respected institutions in Iraq are the new Iraqi army and the central bank, both recreated by the CPA. In contrast, the police, an institution that was not 'disbanded', remains ineffective, corrupt and abusive. Starting from scratch with the army has certainly had its costs, but also its benefits.

Reforming Iraqi political structures

The nature of Saddam's regime affected all CPA efforts at political reform. Saddam modelled his political system on Hitler's Germany and Stalin's Soviet Union. He admired Hitler's use of the Nazi Party and its security services to control the German population. In Iraq membership in Saddam's Ba'ath Party was required for all senior government jobs. Teachers had to be party members and to use school books full of Ba'athist ideology and Saddam worship.

Under Saddam, all political life was tightly controlled and scripted. The press was a tool of the government. Citizens were denied access to independent sources of information and communication, such as satellite TV, the Internet and mobile phones. Like Hitler's and Stalin's secret services, Saddam's much-feared Mukhabarrat (intelligence service) recruited children to inform on their parents. Dissent and criticism, even if only suspected, were answered with summary brutality. Men and women were regularly abducted, tortured, raped and killed. Saddam's regime, dominated by the minority Sunnis, systematically punished both the Kurds and the Shi'ites.

By the time the coalition liberated Iraq in 2003, Saddam had been in power three times longer than Hitler had led Germany. His brutality had had a major impact on Iraqi society.

De-Ba'athification

Had Saddam been forced from power before the American-led invasion, another military or political figure might have taken his place without otherwise changing the regime. But having intervened to force Saddam's ouster, the coalition had no real option but to also break the Ba'ath Party's hold on power. Iraqi participants in the State Department's 'Future of Iraq' study before the war concluded that 'the Baath party merely serves propaganda purposes and no member in it has any stature in the country'. The Iraqis urged that steps be taken after Saddam's overthrow to 'ensure that Baathist ideology in whatever guise does not seep into the public realm' and to 'block the appointment or promotion of any figure who has Baathist sympathies or loyalties or who expresses Baathist "thought"'.[15] Consistent with these views, on 16 April 2003, General Tommy Franks, commander of Coalition forces, issued his 'Freedom Message' in which he outlawed the Ba'ath Party.[16]

No one in Washington, any other capital, or Iraq itself seriously suggested any other possibility, nor did prominent American foreign and defence policy experts, including critics of the invasion. In March 2003 the International Crisis Group, later a critic of the CPA on this issue, recommended excluding 'core' members of Saddam's regime. It was clear that there would be some level of de-Ba'athification, but a key question remained: what was to become of the Ba'athists?

The CPA's policy was intentionally designed to avoid the excesses of the early phases of de-Nazification in Germany, which comprehensively barred Nazi party members not just from government jobs but from a much wider range of commercial professional and managerial positions. In contrast, the CPA order prohibited only the top 1% of party members from working for the Iraqi government. They were free to find work in the private sector, admittedly no easy task given the state of the economy. According to the carefully drawn terms of the CPA's policy, therefore, the vast majority of former

Ba'athists (99%) could keep their government jobs, while all the rest would retain their property except those accused and convicted of specific crimes. Moreover, the CPA authorised scores of exceptions to this lenient policy, permitting ranking former party members to stay in government jobs. The de-Ba'athification decree was, not surprisingly, welcomed by the majority of Iraqis. Shia leaders described themselves as 'jubilant' because the decree had quashed growing speculation that, after the overthrow of Saddam, the United States intended to restore 'Saddamism without Saddam'.[17]

Some civilians in Baghdad, including Jay Garner, expressed concerns about the scope of the intended decree. But within two days after it was issued, the CPA senior adviser overseeing Iraqi ministries reported her surprise at how welcomed the decree was among Iraqis in government. Contrary to some reports, the de-Ba'athification policy did not lead to a collapse of the Iraqi government. Most senior Ba'athist officials in ministries had already fled by the time the decree was issued and many of the career civil servants remaining in those ministries proved to be competent and responsible individuals. After 1 September 2003, all Iraqi ministries were led by Iraqis appointed by the interim Iraqi government.

From the outset, the CPA stated that Iraqi political leaders would have responsibility for implementing a policy which required fine distinctions only Iraqis could make between those who were irreconcilable Ba'athists and those who had joined the party just to get along and had committed no crimes.[18] But Iraqi politicians pressed the CPA for a much more extensive house-cleaning, one also encompassing party members in the business community and in civil society, as Iraqis involved in the Future of Iraq study had urged. They also complained that the CPA was not implementing its own policy ruthlessly enough. Responding to Iraqi demands for more authority over the process, in November 2003, the CPA empowered Iraqi politicians to implement the de-Ba'athification policy. This proved a mistake. The Iraqi political leaders greatly expanded the definition of individuals subject to de-Ba'athification, exacerbating tensions with the Sunni community and provoking plausible claims that the politicians were more interested in creating job openings for their cronies than in weeding out lower-level Ba'athists who had truly misused their positions. Iraqi politician Ali Allawi, a prominent Shia politician who served as minister of trade and minister of finance, has underscored that the de-Ba'athification process became divisive in Iraq at precisely the point it was transferred from CPA to Iraqi control.[19] A better path would have been for the CPA to retain its authority in this area, or to empower a non-politicised Iraqi judicial body to oversee implementation of the order, assuming one could have been formed.

Apart from its flawed implementation, was the aim of de-Ba'athification correct? Loosely speaking, the model was de-Nazification in post-Second World War Germany, though with a much narrower intended effect. Might an altogether different approach have been better, such as the one taken in post-communist Eastern Europe? There, high-level communists were driven from power but not, in most cases, systematically excluded from public office purely on the basis of their former rank, or even, in most cases, held legally accountable for past abuses. Successors to the East European Communist Parties have continued to compete in free elections, generally under new names, and occasionally returned to power, which in the main they have exercised with due deference to the new democratic norms. Might the Ba'ath Party have made such a transition?

Neither the German nor East European analogies are entirely apt. The German Nazis and the East European Communists were national, not narrowly sectarian phenomena. Their overthrow did not result in the displacement of one ethnic or religious group by another. In Iraq, by contrast, the Ba'ath Party had long been dominated by one sect, the Sunnis, so the Shi'ites and Kurds regarded de-Ba'athification as essential to creating a political system in which they could play a role commensurate with their share of the population. In contrast, many Sunnis regarded de-Ba'athification less as a punishment for past abuses than as a prelude to permanent Shia domination. In this respect Iraq in 2003 looked less like Germany or Eastern Europe and more like several other Second and Third World societies that had been rebuilt by the international community throughout the 1990s in the aftermath of sectarian conflicts. In places like Haiti, Bosnia, Kosovo, Namibia,

The Shi'ites and Kurds regarded de-Ba'athification as essential

Mozambique, Cambodia and the Democratic Republic of the Congo, intervening powers sought to avoid large-scale purges, although a small number of individuals were sometimes brought before international tribunals. Rather, the international community has generally sought to co-opt elements of the former regime and bring them into the new, more democratic political process as rapidly and thoroughly as possible. Even the Khmer Rouge, whose genocidal record in Cambodia rivalled that of Hitler on only a slightly smaller scale, was invited by the UN to participate in democratic politics in the early 1990s, when that country was emerging from civil war.

In retrospect, these post-Cold War models may have been more relevant to the situation the United States found in Iraq in spring 2003 than the earlier, post-Second World War paradigm. Some level of de-Ba'athification was justified, and in any case inevitable, given the pent-up grievances of the Shia and Kurdish majority of the population. Perhaps a smaller initial number of party members could have been disqualified, though such a step would certainly have exacerbated the already-strong criticism by most Iraqi Shi'ites of what they considered to be the coalition's already weak de-Ba'athification policy.

The CPA did eventually seek to reverse the broader implementation of its decree carried out by Iraqi politicians, for example in the case of several thousand teachers. But by this point the CPA's authority was waning, and the dominant Shia and Kurdish political factions in Baghdad had little or no interest in allowing even innocent Ba'athists back into public office. The difficulties three successive Iraqi governments have since encountered making even modest changes to the coalition's policy demonstrate the continuing sensitivity of the role of former Ba'athists in Iraqi society.

Democratisation

With the fall of Saddam, American authorities faced two basic decisions about the political future of Iraq, one strategic and the other tactical. Strategically, the choice was between building democracy in Iraq or replacing Saddam with another authoritarian government of more moderate cast. This issue was considered by the US government before the war. By the time the CPA was established, President George W. Bush had decided squarely in favour of building a democratic Iraq. This should not be seen as a radical choice: since the end of the Cold War the United States, NATO and the UN have repeatedly employed military force to underpin the formation of democratically elected governments in places such as Haiti, Bosnia, Kosovo, Albania, Macedonia, Afghanistan, Namibia, Mozambique, El Salvador, East Timor, Sierra Leone, Liberia and the Democratic Republic of the Congo. None of these have become model societies, but most are still at peace and all are currently ruled by freely elected governments. Having ousted Saddam, it was never likely that the United States would seek to do less in Iraq. Nor, given the record elsewhere, was the US effort in Iraq foredoomed to fail. The State Department's Future of Iraq Study had concluded that the 'United States should make a commitment to Iraq like Japan and Germany'.

Washington's decision to promote representative government in Iraq was thus fully consistent with US and international practice and with the views of Iraqis consulted beforehand. The rhetoric that accompanied this effort may have been counterproductive, however. It was at a minimum impolitic to suggest that success in Iraq would lead to comparable changes throughout the surrounding region, given the need to secure the cooperation of Iraq's neighbours. The prospect of democracy sweeping through the greater Middle East was clearly not designed to appeal to those in power in most neighbouring states, and the prominence of this theme in American rhetoric only increased the hostility with which many of these governments viewed Washington's project for Iraq.

With the strategic decision made to move Iraq toward representative government, the tactical question remained of how best to effect a transition from collapsed dictatorship to infant democracy. The two alternatives were handing over authority to an unelected Iraqi government immediately or retaining authority while following a slower, more deliberate political process toward restoration of sovereignty. Before the war, Bush favoured the first option. But even before the CPA was set up, the president had switched to the second.

In May 2003, the president's instructions to the CPA leadership were clear: the coalition was not to rush to appoint an interim Iraqi government, but rather to create lasting conditions for a representative and legitimate one. Democratisation was an overriding objective of the United States. The president's senior advisers understood that this was to be American policy. At an 8 May 2003 meeting of America's top national-security officials, Secretary of State Colin Powell said that 'the President says we should take our time before setting up an Iraqi Interim Administration'.[20] Instead, the United States should plan and implement orderly political progress. At a full National Security Council meeting the next day, the president reiterated that the political transformation of Iraq 'will take a long time'.[21]

This decision to take the time needed to establish a representative government in Iraq also reflected Rumsfeld's thinking; he noted in a memo on 'Policy Guidelines', circulated to the National Security Council on 8 May 2003, that 'the transition from despotism to a democracy will not happen fast or easily. It cannot be rushed. It will evolve over years.'[22] Two weeks later, Rumsfeld underscored the president's guidance in a 21 May memo to Feith and the CPA administrator in Baghdad: 'we need to lay a foundation for self-government. The way to get a non-theocratic system is to go slowly … We should not rush to elections.'[23]

The administration had concluded that a rapid turnover would endanger the strategic goal of a democratic Iraq. At the time of the invasion there were no Iraqi political leaders inside the country with any appreciable following to whom power could have been transferred, other than in the Kurdish region. No one Iraqi figure was acceptable to the entire country. The only avenue open for an early transfer of power would have been to establish an Iraqi government made up largely of exiles who had led the pre-war Iraqi opposition abroad. However, these were far less known to the people of Iraq than to Washington officials. The thinking, speech and dress of many were of men who had been living in another world – the West. Others had been resident in neighbouring Iran or Syria.

The émigré leadership did not reflect Iraq's population

Moreover, the émigré leadership did not reflect a balance of Iraq's population. Sunnis were hardly represented; Kurds were overrepresented. Women and members of important Iraqi minorities, such as Christians and Turkomans, were not represented at all. Nor did this small group prove ready to broaden itself to remedy these shortcomings, despite repeated requests by the coalition that it do so, both before and after the invasion.

There were also practical problems associated with an early transfer of authority to Iraqi hands. The immediate establishment of a provisional government might well have accelerated, rather than avoided, the inter-communal conflict which eventually emerged. Shia exile leaders were constantly urging the CPA to incorporate their sectarian militia forces intact into the police and military, to then be used against the Sunni resistance. The CPA's position was that the members of these militias could come into national forces as individuals, but not as organised units; that the central government should have a monopoly on the sanctioned use of force; and that Iraq's security should depend on reconstituted state security (that is, police) forces. If a representative (that is, a Shia-dominated) provisional government had been installed quickly, it would likely have sanctioned the use of party militias, further alienating the Sunnis, deepening sectarian tensions and precipitating civil war. Two years later, after sovereignty had been returned to an Iraqi government, many of these feared developments occurred. Making such a transfer earlier would likely have exacerbated the sectarian conflict earlier, when Iraqi political institutions and security forces would have been even less capable of coping.

Moreover, such a government would have operated in a legal and political vacuum, answering to no one – least of all to the people of Iraq. It would have assumed power with no constitution and no accepted procedures for structuring or choosing a government or for making decisions or passing and enforcing laws. There would have been no restraining framework to encourage compromise and power sharing, no assurance that Iraqi leaders would even move in the direction of representative government. Lacking the accountability and checks and balances a constitution can provide, a provisional government would have exacerbated tensions among Shi'ites, Sunnis and Kurds. Political life would have been characterised by power grabs, not power sharing, with decisions forced upon the disempowered Sunnis. To deal with this obvious vacuum, leading Iraqis urged the CPA to help Iraqis write a new constitution. From May 2003 onward, it was US policy that Iraq needed such a constitution before sovereignty could safely and responsibly be returned by the coalition.[24]

Turning Iraq over to an unelected government shortly after the invasion would also have provoked a confrontation with Grand Ayatollah Ali al-Sistani, the most widely respected religious authority in the country. The acknowledged spiritual leader of Iraq's majority Shia sect, al-Sistani had encouraged the Shi'ites, who comprise about 60% of the population, to cooperate with the coalition, so a large part of the country and population was initially quite peaceful. Yet, throughout the entire existence of the CPA, al-Sistani repeatedly insisted that Iraq's new leaders be chosen by election. While his demand initially extended only to Iraq's constitution-drafting body, in November 2003 he broadened his demand, insisting that any post-CPA government also be elected. From the scores of communications the CPA had with the ayatollah over 14 months, it is certain he would have seen coalition efforts to set up a provisional government absent an agreed roadmap leading to elections as an illegitimate effort to abort Iraqi democracy, which he considered a core principle and a vital Shia interest. A move to install an unelected government of former émigrés in spring 2003 would thus certainly have provoked the ayatollah's opposition, and likely open opposition, at a fateful time, putting at risk the continued cooperation of millions of Iraqi Shi'ites. As the CPA learned, once al-Sistani opposed a political course, his enormous influence in Iraq made it effectively impossible to proceed.

When the group of exiles with which the US government had been in contact proved unable or unwilling to increase its representation, the CPA itself sought out Iraqi leaders who could broaden the group. A team of American, British and other coalition experts worked under the leadership of two of America's ablest diplomats, Ambassadors Hume Horan and Ryan Crocker, both fluent Arabic speakers with extensive prior diplomatic service in the region and in Iraq. Horan had been the US ambassador to Saudi Arabia, Crocker ambassador to Lebanon. In addition, the CPA drew on the regional expertise of many other coalition diplomats, including Ambassador John Sawers, a British Arabist then serving concurrently as British ambassador to Egypt and as the senior British representative in the

CPA. Travelling throughout Iraq, this team identified Iraqis from all walks of life, all sectors of society, and all parts of the country who could represent the broad streams of Iraqi society. On 13 July 2003, 60 days after the CPA was set up, a 25-member, broadly representative Iraqi Governing Council was announced by UN Special Envoy Sergio de Mello, who had assisted in its recruitment.

It was an imperfect process with an imperfect result. After weeks of wrangling, this council adopted a cumbersome nine-man rotating presidency, greatly complicating its subsequent deliberations. Despite urging by the CPA, the council was unable to make decisions or even to give useful advice on the many urgent issues confronting Iraq. Its leaders had no experience working together, and little mutual trust. The group was understandably concerned about the deteriorating security situation and its members struggled to make the transition from opposition, whose sole mission was to criticise Saddam's government, to a government body with responsibility to act.

Some have suggested that the Governing Council would have acted more responsibly had it been given more responsibility, though the argument overlooks the comprehensive authorities granted the council.[25] Nonetheless, the criticism cannot be definitively disproved, though the inability of this group to agree upon even the most basic questions of its own internal functioning suggests that it was not ready to govern Iraq, or even to share substantially in such responsibilities. In fact the CPA gave the council full authority to appoint Iraqi ministers to run the government and encouraged the council to hold those ministers responsible for their performance. While the council did appoint the ministers, who in effect ran Iraq's government, it never managed to install a system of accountability. It resisted repeated advice to staff the council with assistants who could help it exercise its authorities.

The CPA gave the council full authority to appoint Iraqi ministers

The political challenge facing the CPA and the Governing Council was to establish a process leading to democratic government. Iraqi political leaders told the CPA that Iraq needed a new constitution to guide the way forward and to provide a democratic framework for Iraq's political life. The CPA and the council agreed that the first step was for the latter to convene a conference to draft a new constitution. This would then be ratified by the Iraqi people, leading to elections, a sovereign Iraqi government, and the end of the occupation. This political sequence was outlined to top coalition leaders within weeks of the CPA's establishment.[26]

The plan was greeted by a fatwa from al-Sistani insisting that members of the constitutional conference be chosen by the people of Iraq in an election. But election experts from the UN and independent experts consulted by the CPA were unanimous in their assessment that it would take up to two years to organise free, fair and orderly elections. There had been no reliable census for a half-century. Iraq had no laws concerning political parties or elections, no constituency boundaries, and no system or plans to create them or to conduct a census. These circumstances left the CPA and the Governing Council in a bind.

The ayatollah's stance also underscored why the Afghan model of an immediate transfer of authority would have been difficult to apply to Iraq. At the Bonn Conference in late 2001, Afghans from inside and outside the country had agreed over a period of ten days on an interim constitution and a provisional government, and did so even before the Taliban had been fully ejected from power. Al-Sistani was insisting that no unelected Iraqi leaders could assume such responsibility.

The CPA hoped that the Governing Council would find a way around al-Sistani's order, which threatened a prolonged delay in returning sovereignty to Iraq. But it became clear that several Shia members of the council would not buck al-Sistani and the other council members would not overrule them.[27] So on 15 November 2003, with the approval of the US government, the CPA and the Governing Council laid out a new plan. Working with Iraqi legal experts, the council was to draft an interim constitution which would establish the framework for Iraq's politics and lead to elections. The agreement provided for an indirectly elected Iraqi government to assume sovereignty from the coalition. When al-Sistani objected to this aspect of the agreement, the CPA and the UN worked to answer his concerns and were able to gain a broad consensus on the transition process. All parties agreed that the interim constitution would be drafted by the Governing Council and Iraqi legal experts in spring 2004, and that the CPA would then hand sovereignty to a non-elected but representative interim government by 1 July 2004.

This interim constitution, or Transitional Administrative Law, was the CPA's most important contribution to Iraq's political future, as even some of the CPA's strongest critics have conceded. The law established the principles of democracy, individual rights and federalism on which Iraq's permanent constitution came to be based, and thus laid a foundation for open, representative and legitimate government. It established basic rights for all Iraqis, irrespective of gender, sect, religion or ethnicity. It committed Iraq to the rule of law and established such principles as the right of the accused to be assumed innocent until proven guilty, to confront his accusers and to have legal counsel. Freedom of religion was confirmed, though the document recognised that Islam is the religion of the majority of Iraqis. It also established the architecture of Iraq's government, based on the separation of powers, including an independent judiciary and civilian control of the military. The Iraqis would later import the law's provisions for the protection of human rights into Iraq's permanent constitution approved by referendum in 2005.

This agreement gave Iraq the opportunity to remain a united country while becoming a democratic one. It took the landmark step of establishing a framework for Iraqi federalism, key to balancing national unity with local self-government. The federal structure reversed the millennia-long domination of Mesopotamia by Baghdad. It recognised the Kurdistan Regional Government, thereby respecting the autonomy which the Kurds established following the First Gulf War. It also left the door open for the creation of new federal regions in Sunni and Shia areas.

Finally, the interim constitution set out milestones for Iraq's transition to democracy: national elections for a temporary parliament would be held in January 2005; a permanent constitution would be drafted and ratified that summer; and parliamentary elections would be held in December 2005. This process ensured that Iraq's new constitution would be based on elections and national consensus. The Iraqis have since taken each step on this path.

Drafting the interim constitution involved three months of intense negotiations among Iraqi experts and politicians, with the CPA playing an indispensable broker role. It was painful for everyone. The Shi'ites had to understand that majority rule could not be majoritarian rule; minority rights must be respected. The Kurds had to relinquish a measure of the autonomy they had achieved between the First Gulf War and the liberation of Iraq. And the Sunnis had to accept that their days of domination were over. The process did show, however, that it was possible to arrive at complex and enduring agreements with Iraqis from all backgrounds and sects. The document was also useful in achieving a mutually satisfactory accommodation between the Kurds and the central government.

Following the adoption of the interim constitution, the CPA worked with UN Special Representative Lakhdar Brahimi and the Iraqis to establish a broadly representative provisional government to which to transfer sovereignty. This goal was met on 1 June 2004, when a broad-based, largely non-sectarian Iraqi government under Prime Minister Ayad Allawi was established. The Allawi government oversaw preparations for free elections in January 2005. Later that year, again in accordance with the Transitional Administrative Law's framework, Iraqis approved a new constitution, largely based on the transitional law, and elected a parliament which still serves today.

It is fair to ask whether the United States might have followed a different path, with power transferring quickly to an unelected government, as had occurred 18 months earlier in Afghanistan. The administration considered such a course and rejected it in the months leading up to the invasion. Several factors made the Afghan option difficult, if not impossible, to implement in Iraq. First, there was no Iraqi equivalent of the Afghan Northern Alliance, an internal resistance movement that had gained credibility over a decade of conflict, and that controlled most of the population centres by the time the last Taliban stronghold fell in late 2001. In Afghanistan the United States had only to persuade the Northern Alliance leadership to accept a minority admixture of émigré figures into its administration to produce a broadly representative government. In Iraq, at the outset, the CPA had few Iraqis but émigrés with whom to work, and few had much credibility or even name recognition with the indigenous populace.

With the Afghan transition, the United States had secured the active support and cooperation of every neighbouring and regional state. Several of these states, including Pakistan, Iran, India and Russia, exercised great influence in Afghanistan and this they employed, in late 2001, in close coordination with Washington. All of these governments backed the UN- and US-led efforts to broker the emergence of a new government and urged their various Afghan clients to participate in it. In Iraq, the reverse was the case. Among Iraq's neighbours, only Kuwait openly supported the invasion (though Jordan gave important non-public support); even Turkey, a NATO ally, opposed it.

Finally, the UN, not the United States, brokered the Afghan transition, albeit with considerable behind-the-scenes American help. This would have been more difficult to arrange in Iraq. The UN Security Council had declined to authorise the invasion and Washington, in reaction, was initially at least quite averse to giving the UN a major role in determining Iraq's future. Nor, in the light of this history, was the UN particularly eager to assume such responsibility. The UN was also quite unpopular in Iraq. Afghans had associated the UN with humanitarian assistance and efforts to end their long-running civil war. Iraqis, in contrast, saw the UN as an organisation which had imposed sanctions that contributed for more than a decade to their mounting economic deprivation, and that had refused international authority to overthrow Saddam's hated regime. Nevertheless, by summer 2003 a competent UN special representative, Sergio de Mello, was playing a helpful part in support of Iraq's political transformation, and this role might have been enhanced. But de Mello was killed in the August bombing of the UN offices, and the UN regrettably decided to withdraw all personnel from Iraq.

While some critics have argued that power was not turned over to Iraqi leaders soon enough, others have argued that Iraq's elections were held too soon. This position has some merit. In other post-conflict environments, the international community has found it preferable to give sectarian passions some time to cool before moving to national elections. Elections are polarising events even in settled societies, and the 2005 ballot in Iraq had such an effect. Had there been more time, secular Iraqi political parties might have better organised themselves before facing elections. With more time, it might have been possible to hold the vote using single-member districts rather than proportional representation based on party lists. Under such circumstances, non-sectarian parties and unaffiliated local leaders might have stood a better chance against the major sectarian voting blocs into which the resulting parliament was divided.

Elections are polarising events even in settled societies

But the CPA did not have more time. Violent resistance in the Sunni areas of the country was rising, while the Shia leadership, particularly al-Sistani, was insisting on early elections. Further delay was only likely to result in further deterioration of security and complicate or even derail the transfer of sovereignty to an Iraqi government. The ayatollah's support for the political process hinged on the agreement he reached with Brahimi and the CPA that national elections would be held no later than January 2005. While the CPA was aware that elections at such an early date were not ideal, experience had taught that the political process could never succeed in the face of al-Sistani's active opposition. None of the critics of the CPA decision to acquiesce to al-Sistani's demand for early elections has offered a persuasive argument for how confronting the uncontested leader of the Shia community on a matter he considered vital to the interests of Iraq and his constituency would have had any chance of success.

Some critics have argued that the effects of early elections were aggravated by the system under which they were held (a single national list, rather than individual constituencies), which made it more likely that the best-organised parties would dominate the outcome. Such parties in a post-conflict society are usually sectarian- or ethnic-based, as they were in Iraq. These critics have a point, but the CPA was faced with two poor choices. UN officials responsible for organising the elections, and independent experts from the International Foundation for Election Systems (which had overseen elections in scores of countries), repeatedly emphasised to Iraqi and

CPA officials that because of the time needed to create individual constituencies, a system based on national political-party lists was the only way elections could be held by January 2005. Ultimately, the Governing Council and the CPA agreed to proceed because they realised that failing to meet the January deadline would have caused a serious breach with al-Sistani, which could have sent Iraq's Shia majority into open, perhaps violent, opposition to the entire political process laid out in the interim constitution, threatening the formal handover of sovereignty to Iraq by July 2004.

The results of Iraq's first elections showed the dangers of this system for Iraq's future. As anticipated, voting fragmented along sectarian and ethnic lines, though arguably the system did help non-sectarian parties win 40 parliamentary seats. The Iraqi government should be encouraged to move to a system of individual constituencies before the elections scheduled in 2009, as some Iraqi politicians have suggested.

In addition to efforts to complete the political process established in the interim constitution, the CPA took other measures to advance democracy. In a shattered country such as Iraq, this meant building constituencies for representative government throughout civil society. The CPA spent more than $760 million from the Iraqi budget to help establish elements of civil society. The money was used to establish women's centres, democracy centres and human-rights forums in Baghdad and the provinces. The CPA helped Iraqis organise scores of non-governmental organisations and encouraged the formation of professional associations for Iraqi lawyers, doctors and dentists. In a more symbolic arena, the CPA worked with Iraqi athletes to organise and conduct over 500 elections at municipal and provincial club level to produce an Iraqi Olympic Committee, a necessary step for Iraq to be readmitted to the Olympic movement, from which it had been expelled under Saddam.

Had the United States been prepared immediately after the fall of Baghdad to share authority with the UN for managing the political transition, had it convincingly engaged all of Iraq's neighbours on the issue of Iraq's future, and had it scaled back its transformative rhetoric, it is possible, although by no means certain, that a broadly representative interim Iraqi government might have been assembled more quickly. Such a process might have produced a regime not very different from the Allawi government that the UN helped put together a year later. It is unlikely, however, that such a regime would have been any more successful in reconciling the competing Iraqi factions in 2003 than was the one appointed in 2004. The occupation might have been shortened, but the descent into sectarian violence would probably not have been averted, and might well have been accelerated, especially since in that case the Iraqis would be acting in a political environment which lacked the restraining constitutional framework provided by the Transitional Administrative Law.

Those who now argue that an earlier transfer of sovereignty would have been better must consider whether the United States, the coalition and Iraqi authorities would have been better situated to handle a major increase in sectarian violence in 2003 than they proved to be in 2005. On the other hand, an earlier effort to involve the international community and engage neighbouring governments, even if it had not led to an earlier transfer of sovereignty, might have secured more regional and international support for the enterprise.

Reviving the economy

While the scope of Saddam's political brutality was generally known before the war, US authorities were much less well informed about the devastation he (and international sanctions) had inflicted on Iraq's economy. Some Iraqis knew how bad their economy was but the majority, having seen how quickly America achieved military victory, held unrealistic expectations about how quickly the coalition could improve the economy and their material well-being. So did many Americans.

Before the Ba'athists came to power, Iraq was one of the most prosperous countries in the Middle East. But over the three decades of Saddam's tyranny, corruption (fostered by dictatorship) and his belief in state domination of the economy drove it into the ground. The result was spectacular misallocation and outright theft of the nation's resources. In summer 2003, the World Bank estimated that the country had an 'infrastructure deficit' of between $55–75 billion.[28] International sanctions had also contributed to the economy's deterioration, but the overall decline was due to a dysfunctional economic system, chronic economic incompetence and outright corruption. Iraq's per capita GDP had fallen from a level above Spain's in 1980 to one below Angola's in 2002.[29] During those decades, capital formation in Iraq had fallen 90%.[30] Officials at Saddam's Ministry of Planning told CPA leaders in May 2003 that their figures showed that unemployment before the war had been 50%.[31]

In Saddam's last years, Iraq generated less than half the electricity it needed. Saddam used the distribution of electricity as another instrument of control, heavily favouring Baghdad over the provinces. As a consequence, blackouts were endemic, especially in the provinces. Because of electrical outages, water and sewage systems malfunctioned. Iraqis often lacked tap water. Sewage flowed into the streets. During the 1990s Saddam cut health-care spending by over 90%.[32] According to the World Bank, in 2002 Iraq had the shortest life expectancy and highest infant-mortality rates in the region.[33]

Iraq's pre-war economy had been dominated by 192 state-owned enterprises. Almost all of these value-destroying entities produced products without markets, and depended on government funding, subsidised interest rates and artificially favourable exchange rates. Iraq's banks were an arm of the political leadership, extending loans on political, not commercial, criteria. Interest rates were set by bureaucrats. The central bank was subservient to Saddam and his cronies.

Iraq's government budget was grossly distorted by a massive system of subsidies. Every Iraqi family received a monthly 'food basket', a system of subsidised foodstuffs instituted by Saddam in the 1990s. The subsidy cost the government almost $4bn a year.[34] The World Bank and CPA estimated that hidden energy subsidies cost the economy another $5–6bn a year.[35]

Because Saddam had underinvested in refineries and sold fuel at highly subsidised prices, Iraq depended on imported fuels (gasoline, diesel, kerosene and liquefied petroleum gas) even though it sits on one of the largest reserves of oil in the world. These imports cost another $3bn a year and were then sold to the public at highly subsidised prices. For example, in September 2003 figures from the Iraqi Ministry of Oil showed that a gallon of gasoline could be bought in Iraq at less than 1% of what it could fetch across the border in Turkey.[36] To say this encouraged smuggling and corruption is to understate the problem.

Under Saddam, the government budget had been a state secret. The CPA found that Iraqi ministries had very little to say about how government money was spent; over 92% of the budget was allocated directly out of Saddam's office. Iraq's ministries and personnel had little capacity to spend government funds or to manage government programmes.

Under Saddam, the budget was a state secret

Throughout the 1990s, Iraq's budget had been in chronic deficit. Every Friday, the central bank would simply print the amount of new currency demanded by Saddam. Shortly after the CPA was formed, the acting minister of planning told CPA officials that his ministry estimated that inflation at the end of 2002 had been running at an annual rate of 115,000%.

When the CPA was established in May 2003, the country was producing no oil. Electricity production was at less than 10% of the already-inadequate pre-war level. Virtually all the country's state-owned enterprises and banks were closed. Government buildings had been looted and burned all over the country. The cost of the looting was estimated by CPA finance experts at $12bn, equal to half the country's GDP. The economy had ground to a halt. The International Monetary Fund subsequently estimated that the economy contracted 41% in 2003.[37] The CPA faced an economic crisis worse than the American Great Depression in the 1930s and far worse than the US government had planned for before the war. Washington had not prepared itself or programmed the resources to deal with Iraq's multiplicity of economic problems. In June 2003, Rumsfeld asked former Clinton administration Deputy Secretary of Defense John Hamre to travel to Iraq to assess the CPA's challenges. Hamre reported back that 'the CPA is confronting a much more difficult problem than a traditional post-conflict reconstruction challenge. Iraq is also a completely failed economy. The CPA is confronting the equivalent of both a defeated Germany in 1945 and a failed Soviet Union in 1989.'[38] The CPA needed to move fast to stimulate a flat-lined economy and begin the process of opening and modernising it.

Getting the economy moving meant paying government employees, particularly since, in its role overseeing the Iraqi government, the CPA was the nation's largest employer. Millions of Iraqi families depended on civil-service salaries and pensions, which had not been paid for months. Within four days the CPA started paying salaries and pensions from Iraqi government funds. To stimulate employment, the authority set aside hundreds of millions of dollars from the Iraqi budget to start urgent public-works programmes, and it began programmes like micro-credit loans for women to help marginalised Iraqis.

But the authority faced two immediate problems. Since the country's banking system was closed down, and in any case had no system for electronic transfer of funds, government expenditures had to be paid in cash. This cash (some $250m every month) had to be physically moved to all parts of the country. Moreover, most Iraqi government expenses had to be paid in dollars drawn from Iraqi government funds because of a severe lack of Iraqi currency, a large stock of which had been damaged by a flood in the central bank vault. During the looting, the printing presses, plates and paper for printing currency had been stolen.

Within weeks of its arrival, the CPA faced a severe dilemma: Iraq would be inundated by a surge in counterfeit currency of the highest quality, the Iraqi economy would become 'dollarised', or both. The authority undertook an extraordinary task. It replaced the entire currency of a country still in conflict, with a primitive banking and telephone system, and lousy roads. This project was accomplished over a three-month period without serious problems. Since January 2004, when the currency exchange was completed, the new Iraqi dinar has traded freely against all world currencies.

The CPA immediately liberalised trade, the single most important action for quickly stimulating the economy and improving standards of living. Under Saddam, the government had strictly controlled imports. A major source of corruption under the old regime had been providing permits to import, with multiple exchange rates determined by Saddam's cronies. As a result of early decisions by the CPA, today Iraqis can purchase imported medicines, food and appliances such as refrigerators and satellite-TV dishes that they were denied in the past.

Restoring government services was another CPA priority. The authority set a goal of restoring electricity production to (already inadequate) pre-war levels by 1 October 2003, which it missed by only four days. It committed to returning oil production to pre-war levels by the end of 2003, a schedule it beat by three months. Despite regular attacks on the power and oil infrastructure, production in both areas remained at, or near, pre-war levels over the following eight months. The CPA announced a programme to rebuild 1,000 Iraqi schools and print some 72m schoolbooks, expunged of Saddam worship, by the opening of the school year in October 2003. That too was done. By then almost all of the country's 340 bank branches had re-opened, as had all of Iraq's hospitals and public-health clinics. Distribution of pharmaceutical drugs had been increased sevenfold.

On a broader level, the CPA worked to establish modern principles of responsible government. Working with Iraqi ministers, the authority produced balanced government budgets for 2003 and 2004. It introduced principles of monetary responsibility by establishing the independence of the central bank, and freed interest rates to be determined by markets, not bureaucrats. Working with the Governing Council, the CPA repealed Saddam's law forbidding foreign investment, except in the oil industry, a sensitive issue left for an elected Iraqi government to address.

Supported by an able team of Iraqi lawyers, the CPA produced laws designed to help bring Iraq into the modern world economy. While not critical in the short term, these efforts resulted in updated commercial laws in areas such as contracts, banking, bankruptcy and intellectual property. Baghdad's stock market was reopened. It is a mark of the quality of these laws and policies that four years after the CPA was dissolved, none have been changed by the Iraqi government. Indeed, according to Iraqi Deputy Prime Minister Barham Saleh, Iraqi government working groups set up under his direction to re-examine the CPA's main economic orders concluded that they could not improve upon them.

The CPA has been criticised for not tackling the huge subsidies woven throughout Iraq's economy. In an ideal world, it would have been better if the occupying authority could have taken these hard and necessary steps, sparing elected Iraqis from such difficult decisions. But the ideal was elbowed aside by the real. The Iraqi political leaders the authority consulted argued that the growing insurgency and its efforts to capitalise on Iraqi frustrations made it too risky politically to attempt these measures while the CPA was in power.

For the same reason, the CPA did not privatise even those state-owned enterprises that were deemed viable. These 'businesses' were wasting valuable resources in a devastated economy and the CPA had hoped to be able to put some of them on 'hard budget' constraints to face the marketplace. However, the firms employed over half a million people. The political and security arguments against such a course were decisive, so against all economic logic the CPA decided not to privatise the state-owned enterprises and instead to continue paying the employees of the firms, whether they were working or not. These payments continued until the CPA was dissolved, and have continued under successive Iraqi governments.

Because of a lack of pre-war preparation, the reconstruction programme for Iraq took too long to begin, and then had to be rushed. The United States invaded Iraq in March 2003 and committed an initial $2.45bn for reconstruction in April. But the full extent of Iraq's reconstruction needs were not realised until after the CPA was in operation. A World Bank survey of the Iraqi economy in summer 2003 made clear that Iraqi reconstruction would not be self-financing.[39] The administration requested an $18.5bn supplemental budget, which only passed Congress in November 2003, halfway through the occupation. Subsequent bureaucratic obstacles in Washington blocked the actual delivery of these funds for several more months. Moreover, the administration agreed with Congress that this money would be subject to the usual regulations for appropriated funds. This 'business as usual' approach was a mistake, for the rules were far too cumbersome and slow in the midst of a war. As a result, actual funding for reconstruction did not arrive until after the CPA had disbanded; by 30 June 2004 less than 2% of the $18.4bn had actually been spent in Iraq, and half of that amount went to security projects.

The American reconstruction programme for Iraq put greater emphasis upon infrastructure improvement (rather than simply repair) than had most previous post-conflict rebuilding efforts. The supplemental budget approved by Congress in late 2003 focused on large projects, because the programme was designed to address the major infrastructure deficiencies identified by the World Bank study. In hindsight, this emphasis can be questioned. Iraq was no more devastated than, say, Bosnia, Kosovo, Cambodia or Sierra Leone. Nor, obviously, was it as destroyed as Germany or Japan in 1945; the former received no significant reconstruction assistance until three years after the war, and the latter never received any.

In more recent decades, heavy infrastructure improvements have largely been left to the World Bank and other concessional-lending institutions, rather than being covered with bilateral grant assistance. Those international financial institutions have professional experience in structuring agreements which ensure that the improved infrastructure will be maintained and amortised over time. This is something that the United States was unable to assure in Iraq, where the government does not, for example, charge most recipients for electricity, and thus has no dedicated revenue stream from which to maintain and improve its power grid. Bilateral donor assistance more usually goes into sectors such as education, health and government capacity-building. The United States did fund these activities rather heavily, but greater and earlier emphasis would have helped. In any case, the deteriorating security situation soon overwhelmed the reconstruction programme, significantly increasing security costs and causing some projects to be delayed or even abandoned.

Yet criticism of the CPA's stress on large infrastructure projects has overlooked the thousands of small-scale projects that the coalition implemented throughout Iraq. To assist with political and economic development in the provinces, the CPA established Governate Teams in 15 provincial capitals. The teams, usually led by professional Arabic-speaking diplomats from Coalition countries, coordinated with local military commanders and became the model for the Provincial Reconstruction Teams established after the occupation ended. Most projects involved spending modest amounts on high-impact local endeavours such as replacing windows on a school, restoring irrigation systems and providing a generator to a hospital. During its time, the coalition completed almost 28,000 reconstruction projects, more than 65 every day, seven days a week for 14 months.

By the time the CPA was dissolved in June 2004, Iraq's economy had improved remarkably from the situation a year earlier. For almost ten months, oil production, the lifeblood of the economy, had been running at a pre-war rate of 2.3m barrels a day. As a result, Iraqi foreign-exchange reserves rose ninefold during the CPA's tenure. The banking system had begun to recover, with bank deposits up 90% over May 2003 levels.[40]

Iraq's economy had improved remarkably

The month the CPA left, electricity production was 50% above pre-war levels; a significant accomplishment given the constant attacks on power lines and power stations, although still far short of meeting greatly increased demand for electricity. Monthly inflation in June 2004 was only 2%. According to a massive study of Iraqi living standards undertaken by the United Nations Development Programme, unemployment was just 10.5% when the CPA finished its work.[41] A study by the International Monetary Fund found that the Iraqi economy rebounded by 46.5% in 2004.[42]

While the persistence of violence has limited Iraq's economic gains since the CPA's time, the reforms the authority put in place can serve as the basis for a healthy, modern economy as that violence subsides. Iraq was a country in ruins when the CPA was set up, owing to three decades of atrocious economic policies, repeated wars and a decade of sanctions, yet the United States had not made the preparations necessary to rebuild such a country. Although the CPA enabled Iraq to begin what will be a long climb out of the depths to which it had fallen under Saddam, the Iraqi people expected more results, faster than was possible. This contributed to their dissatisfaction with the occupation and, for some (both Sunni and Shia) their susceptibility to militancy. Iraq still faces the fundamental problem of having an economy almost entirely dependent on a single (albeit valuable) commodity controlled by the government.

* * *

In most post-conflict nations, as security improves the economy revives, and as physical and political reconstruction proceeds, peace is further consolidated. As violence goes down, economic activity, confidence in the new order, and hope all climb. This has not been the case in Iraq, where failure to prepare for and contain violence has hindered the building of a new state and economy. As Bush noted on 28 May 2008, 'in Iraq we learned from hard experience that newly liberated people cannot make political and economic progress unless they first have some measure of security'.[43] Had the administration studied with more attention prior nation-building efforts, including those conducted throughout the 1990s, this conclusion might have been reached earlier, and with greater effect.

The CPA's efforts at political, economic and security-sector transformation were frustrated by the difficulties of dealing with al-Qaeda terrorism, a spiralling Sunni insurgency and Shia militancy. Though the CPA helped Iraqis create a new framework for their political life, politics became divided sharply along sectarian and ethnic lines as al-Qaeda pursued its stated goal of igniting a sectarian war. Violence led to more violence as many of the police overtly supported the political goals of some Shia parties. While the Iraqi constitution, based on the Transitional Administrative Law written by Iraqis during the CPA period, is sound and sturdy, legislation on matters such as revenue-sharing has proved hard to pass, in large measure because some of the carefully negotiated compromises in the transitional law were abandoned in the permanent constitution.

The CPA's work to reform and restart the Iraqi economy was set back by the dangers and difficulties of delivering development aid, building capacity, and fostering private enterprise under violent conditions – not everywhere in Iraq, but in those parts of Iraq where such efforts were most needed. Apart from the risks faced by US and allied development workers, the World Bank and UN agencies were unwilling to put people on the ground in such conditions. Now, as violence recedes, economic activity is picking up.

The plan to replace Saddam's security forces and ministries with reliable ones depended on the ability of US forces to secure the country under occupation while such institutions were recreated or reformed, a precondition for any successful post-war reconstruction effort. This in turn demanded that the US-led occupation force be large enough and have the right strategy, one which emphasised public security as soon as the Iraqi army was defeated. Despite repeated urging by CPA leadership, Washington provided only enough troops to topple the old regime, not enough to deter the emergence of violent resistance, or to counter and defeat the resultant insurgency. The United States thus went in to Iraq with a maximalist reform agenda and a minimalist application of money and manpower. The subsequent difficulties encountered owe much to this disjunction between the scope of its ambitions and the scale of its initial commitment.

Politics became sectarian not because of the CPA's approach but despite it. Some de-Ba'athification was necessary and, in any case, inevitable given prior abuses; but its implementation in the hands of Iraqi politicians was too sweeping. Economic reform was generally well conceived, with the possible exception of the heavy emphasis on large-scale infrastructure projects, but hampered by rising violence. Security-sector reform took too long and is only now beginning to yield results. A greater and earlier effort should have been made to prepare ex-soldiers for new jobs and lives. It is notable, however, that the new Iraqi army, built from the ground up, is performing much better than the old Iraqi police, which have been built from the former force with all its imperfections.

Planning for stabilisation and reconstruction for Iraq has been rightly criticised. More importantly, the US was unprepared to assume these responsibilities. Of planning there was a good deal, in the State and Defense Departments and in several military commands. These disparate activities were never fully integrated into a national plan that could have been given to the CPA leadership when it deployed. This meant that the CPA, chronically understaffed, had to create a strategic plan 'on the fly'. The CPA, in any case, lacked sufficient personnel with the right combination of skills to effectively implement any plan.

Contrast the preparations for reconstruction to the planning and preparation for the conventional battle that toppled Saddam. Those plans represented more than a year of intellectual work on the part of the administration's top military and civilian leadership. Of equal importance, the planning process was accompanied by the movement of hundreds of thousands of men and tens of thousands of machines into position for battle, and by the allocation of tens of billions of dollars for its execution. By contrast, the CPA was bereft not just of a plan, but of the money and manpower needed to carry one out.

Throughout its existence the CPA was never more than half staffed. Its senior ranks included top-quality civilian and military professionals, many with relevant experience, but some junior staff lacked qualifications commensurate with their responsibilities, enthusiasm and dedication. Turnover was constant, with many positions vacant and others turning over every few months. In its early months the authority had to fund Iraqi government operations largely with seized Iraqi assets, but the Iraqi economy was broken and those assets were not being renewed.

The CPA was never more than half staffed

In any post-conflict situation, some degree of improvisation is inevitable, no matter how good the pre-war planning. But many of the demands placed upon the CPA in its early months were foreseeable, because American-led coalitions had faced similar situations in Somalia, Haiti, Bosnia, Kosovo and Afghanistan over the previous decade. For instance, all societies emerging from conflict begin with too many soldiers and too few police. Given that the United States had had more than a year to prepare for the stabilisation and reconstruction of post-Saddam Iraq, US plans should have set aside substantial resources and recruited personnel to manage the disarmament, demobilisation and reintegration of excess soldiers into the civilian society and to reform, train and re-equip the police force. Yet both these essential programmes had to be designed, funded and manned only after the CPA was established.

It has been rightly said that no war plan survives first contact with the enemy. It is also true that no post-war plan is likely to survive first contact with the former enemy. The true test of any planning process is not whether it accurately predicts each successive turn in an operation, but whether it provides the operators the resources and flexibility to carry out their assigned tasks. This the planning process for post-war Iraq failed to do.

Not all of the CPA's decisions proved to be optimal, but they were reasonable choices in the light of the circumstances and capabilities at the time. More assets would have given the CPA leadership more options. More options would have probably yielded better outcomes. Adequate coalition force levels and an effective counter-insurgency strategy emphasising public security would have made a big improvement throughout the CPA's time and after.

It is unlikely that American officials will again face decisions exactly like those required of the CPA in spring 2003. Second-guessing those decisions will only take one so far in preparing for future challenges. But it is certain that the United States will once again find itself assisting a society emerging from conflict to build an enduring peace and establish a representative government. Learning how best to prepare for such a challenge is the key to more successful future operations. Iraq provides an object lesson on the costs and consequences of unprepared nation-building.

Notes

1 Unpublished report, Walter Slocombe to Ryan Crocker, 17 April 2003.

2 David H. Petraeus, Testimony before the Senate Armed Services Committee, 22 May 2008, http://armed-services.senate.gov/statemnt/2008/May/Petraeus%2005-22-08.pdf.

3 Unpublished report, Walter Slocombe to Ryan Crocker, 17 April 2003.

4 L. Paul Bremer, III, *My Year in Iraq: The Struggle to Build a Future of Hope* (New York: Simon and Schuster, 2006), p. 55.

5 Bremer, *My Year in Iraq*, pp. 344–81.

6 Multiple oral reports, Walter Slocombe to CPA administrator, April–May 2003.

7 Bremer, *My Year in Iraq*, p. 39.

8 US Department of State, Defense Policy and Institutions Working Group, *The Future of Iraq Project* (Washington DC: US Department of State, 2003), p. 16, available at http://www.gwu.edu/~nsarchiv/NSAEBB/NSAEBB198/index.htm.

9 Unpublished report, Walter Slocombe to CPA administrator, 14 May 2003.

10 Bremer, *My Year in Iraq*, p. 57.

11 Douglas J. Feith, *War and Decision: Inside the Pentagon at the Dawn of the War on Terrorism* (New York: Harper, 2008).

12 US Department of State, *The Future of Iraq Project*, 'Democratic Principles and Procedures', p. 17.

13 Michael R. Gordon, 'Fateful Choice on Iraq Army Bypassed Debate', *New York Times*, 17 March 2008.

14 Walter Slocombe and Dan Senor, 'Too Few Good Men', *New York Times*, 17 November 2005.

15 US Department of State, *The Future of Iraq Project*, 'Democratic Principles and Procedures'.

16 Bremer, *My Year in Iraq*, p. 39.

17 Unpublished report of CPA meeting with SCIRI leaders, 22 May 2003.

18 L. Paul Bremer, backgrounder to press, 16 May 2003;

unpublished memorandum, L. Paul Bremer to Donald Rumsfeld, 22 May 2003.

19 Ali Allawi, *The Occupation of Iraq: Winning the War, Losing the Peace* (New Haven, CT: Yale University Press, 2007).

20 Bremer, *My Year in Iraq*, p. 43.

21 *Ibid.*

22 'Principles for Iraq: Policy Guidelines', unpublished memorandum, Donald Rumsfeld to National Security Council Principals, 8 May 2003.

23 'Oil and Democracy', unpublished memorandum, Donald Rumsfeld to Douglas J. Feith, 21 May 2003.

24 See for example letter from L. Paul Bremer to George W. Bush, *New York Times*, 3 September 2007, and unpublished memorandum, L. Paul Bremer to Donald Rumsfeld, 23 May 2003.

25 Unpublished memoranda, L. Paul Bremer to Donald Rumsfeld, 2 June and 13 June 2003.

26 *Ibid.*; memorandum, Bremer to Rumsfeld, 23 May 2003; unpublished cable, CPA to Defense and State Departments, 19 June 2003.

27 Bremer, *My Year in Iraq*, p. 211.

28 World Bank Study of Iraqi Economy, July 2003 (unpublished).

29 Data from http://www.worldbank.org.

30 Unpublished report, Coalition Provisional Authority Budget Office, 12 August 2003.

31 Personal communication, acting minister of planning to CPA administrator, May 2003.

32 USAID, 'Examples of Quality of Life Baseline Indicators, Pre-conflict Iraq', internal study, 22 April 2003.

33 Bremer, *My Year in Iraq*, p. 35.

34 Iraqi Budget for 2003/04, October 2003.

35 World Bank Study of Iraqi Economy, July 2003.

36 Iraqi Oil Ministry, 'Table of Retail Fuel Prices in Iraq and Adjacent Countries', 30 September 2003.

37 International Monetary Fund, *Iraq: Request for Stand-by Arrangement: Staff Report*, IMF Country Report No. 6/15 (Washington DC: IMF, 2006).

38 Unpublished report, John Hamre to Donald Rumsfeld, July 2003; Bremer, *My Year in Iraq*, p. 114.

39 World Bank Study of Iraqi Economy, July 2003.

40 Unpublished report, CPA Economic Adviser, 8 April 2003.

41 United Nations Development Programme and Iraqi Ministry of Planning and Development Cooperation, *Iraqi Living Conditions Survey 2004* (Baghdad: 2005), p. 104.

42 International Monetary Fund, *Iraq: Request for Stand-by Arrangement*.

43 George W. Bush, Commencement Address at the US Air Force Academy, 28 May 2008, http://www.whitehouse.gov/news/releases/2008/05/20080528-2.html.

Bad Days in Basra

Hilary Synnott

Editor's note

Hilary Synnott was the Coalition Provisional Authority's Regional Coordinator for the four southern Iraqi provinces from July 2003 until January 2004, reporting directly to L. Paul Bremer in Baghdad. His book *Bad Days in Basra: My Turbulent Time as Britain's Man in Southern Iraq* (London: I.B. Tauris, 2008) draws both on his experiences there and on his 30 years as a British diplomat, much of which included dealing with the Muslim world and developing countries, and his prior service in the armed forces. The following extract is reprinted with permission.

I tried hard to convince Baghdad of the importance of agriculture, which employed some 20 per cent of the population and supported a rural population of 7 million souls. A succession of emails remained unanswered so, in mid-October, I decided to put my points personally to the CPA's head of the Agriculture Ministry. The Australian Government had pressed hard to secure this post as a part of their contribution to the Coalition's effort. I had therefore expected to meet someone who was truly engaged in problem solving and helping those provinces where agriculture was an important part of their economies, as was the case in the South.

Perhaps it had been a bad day for both of us, but my encounter with Trevor Flugge, a former chairman of the Australian Wheat Board, was one which caused me to become more angry than at any other time in my stay in Iraq. Judging by the tone of our exchanges, witnessed with open mouths by James

Hilary Synnott is Consulting Senior Fellow at the IISS. He was the Coalition Provisional Authority's Regional Coordinator for the four southern Iraqi provinces between 30 July 2003 and 31 January 2004. As a British diplomat, he had been High Commissioner in Pakistan from 2000 until 2003 and had postings in India, Jordan, Germany and France.

Survival | vol. 50 no. 4 | August–September 2008 | pp. 57–60 DOI 10.1080/00396330802329220

Roscoe, my Private Secretary, and Flugge's own small staff, the feeling was entirely mutual.

I explained to Flugge that, in troublesome Maysan Province, farmers had sold the wheat seeds which they would normally have kept aside for winter sowing because in the summer of 2003 the Coalition was paying unusually high prices for wheat. In the past they would have received a top-up of healthy, treated seeds through Baghdad's central administration. But no such provision was now available. Without the seeds, there would be no sowing, which would lead to massive unemployment. Without the sowing, there would be no winter crop, which would lead to further unemployment and food shortages. The provincial authorities, who were fully conscious of such consequences, were understandably pressing us hard to arrange for supplies. If we did not do this, we would have a major security problem on our hands.

To my mind, which was at one with Graeme Lamb the military commander, the case was incontrovertible. But Flugge did not want to listen. He responded bluntly that the CPA policy was to do away with such subsidies. The Iraqis had to learn to stand on their own feet. They should not have sold their seed grain, so it was their fault if they had no winter crop. As I persisted, making much of the security implications, the temperature rose.

Security was not his concern, yelled Flugge. Well, it should be, I yelled back. We broke away from each other with none of the reconciliatory gestures which are customary with Arabic people after a good argument. This had been a bad one.

In the face of this opposition, I raised my sights and sought assistance from Jeremy Greenstock and Pat Kennedy, Bremer's ever-helpful Chief of Staff. Supplemented by persuasive pressure from Rory Stewart's team in Al Amarah, we secured funding to arrange the purchase of healthy seeds from Mosul, where there was a surplus. This solved the problem, albeit right at the last moment. Rory's team arranged transport and the grains were sold at reasonable market prices, thereby avoiding the additional trap of distorting the market.

I was saddened later to see that the section on agriculture in the official document 'CPA's Achievements' was one of the shortest. In less than a page, it listed just four 'achievements', one-eighth as many as the section on Foreign Affairs which, important though they might be, had little effect on ordinary lives. The four items included the less-than-breathtaking announcement that six Iraqi students had been selected to study agriculture at the University of Hawaii, and a note that the price of wheat in Iraq had risen from $105 per metric tonne in 2003 to $180 in mid-2004. Why this should be regarded as an 'achievement' escaped me. I could not see how such a price rise would benefit ordinary Iraqis, though I supposed that foreign wheat producers and exporters who did business with Iraq might have welcomed it.

... I had one other encounter with the Australian administration. In early autumn of 2003, a ship load of 50,000 live sheep were on their way from Australia to Saudi Arabia when a skin disease called scabby mouth broke out on board. Saudi Arabia declined to receive the sheep and the Australians magnanimously offered to unload them in Iraq for use as part of the rituals at the end of the holy month of Ramadan. Australian diplomats in Baghdad engaged in frantic lobbying. As the Australians' generosity increased and they offered to provide the sheep free of charge, messages became confused.

If the shipment were to land, it would have to be in one of the ports, which were all in the British-led sector. I had told an Australian diplomat who had approached me during one of my visits to Baghdad that, in my view, the Iraqis would take it seriously amiss if they were presented with a consignment of diseased sheep which no one else would accept. But, for some reason, the British military headquarters had come to believe that I had approved such a delivery, which they too opposed. I had to make clear that this was not the case. In doing so, my email pointed out that, anyway, the unfortunate sheep would all first need to be subjected to 'de-baa-thification'. I counted it as a compliment when I heard an Army major at a military briefing some days later recount the same poor joke as if it were his.

The last I heard of this saga was that, unable to slaughter the animals on the high seas and stymied by international quarantine laws, the Australian

Prime Minister had declared that they would be returned to Australia for disposal there. The Australian opposition leader had the final word: 'They went out as lambs … they're coming back as mutton'.

Forum

The Impending Oil Shock: An Exchange

Editor's note

In the April–May 2008 issue of *Survival* (vol. 50, no. 2, pp. 37–66), Nader Elhefnawy argued that oil production is approaching its peak, with consequences that are likely to be dramatic. There will be increased risk of state failure and resource conflict; the economic balance of power among major industrial states will shift according to their relative abilities to adapt to a scarcity of fossil fuels; and oil producers will enjoy greater political power. *Survival* invited two experts on strategic energy issues, Amy Myers Jaffe and Michael T. Klare, to comment on Elhefnawy's essay, and Elhefnawy to respond.

Opportunity, not War

Amy Myers Jaffe

We've heard the argument before: scarcity of future oil supplies is a danger to the global international system and will create international conflict, death and destruction. In 1982, noted historian and oil-policy guru Daniel Yergin wrote that the energy question was 'a question about the future of Western society', noting that 'stagnation and unemployment and depression tested democratic systems in the years between World War I and World War II' and asserting that if there wasn't sufficient oil to drive economic growth, the 'possibilities are unpleasant to contemplate'.[1] His words proved typical prose foreboding the top of a commodity cycle. A year later, oil prices began a four-year collapse to $12 a barrel.

Amy Myers Jaffe is the Wallace S. Wilson Fellow for Energy Studies at the James A. Baker III Institute for Public Policy at Rice University. She is co-editor of *The Geopolitics of Natural Gas* (Cambridge University Press, 2005) and *Energy in the Caspian Region: Present and Future* (Palgrave, 2002). She has a new book on petrodollars coming out next year.

That oil is a cyclical industry is not in question. Since 1861, oil markets have experienced more than eight boom-and-bust cycles. In 1939, the US Department of the Interior announced that only 13 years of oil reserves remained in the United States. In more recent history, Middle East wars or revolutions produced oil price booms in 1956, 1973, 1979, 1990 and 2003. Each time, analysts rushed to warn of doomsday scenarios but markets responded and oil use was curtailed both by market forces and government intervention rather than by war and massive global instability. The question Nader Elhefnawy raises in 'The Impending Oil Shock' is whether this time will be different.

Elhefnawy lays out the traditional Malthusian-style crisis scenario extremely well, with interesting policy implications for the United States. He predicts an impending energy-resources crunch (based on today's geologic facts, in a similar fashion as predecessors have in past cycles) and then lays out why such scarcity will 'have profound implications at the international level' by empowering energy producers, heightening the risk of state failures, and fuelling armed conflicts. The stakes are high, he argues, because the United States, by virtue of the relatively energy-inefficient nature of its economy and high oil dependence, 'could ultimately lose its position as a world power ... just as the UK's position declined along with the age of coal and steam that it [the UK] pioneered'. He concludes that in the oil-scarce world, 'a nation's ability to sustain its economy and preserve its influence will depend less on military capability and more on an ability to insulate its economy from oil shocks'.

Elhefnawy raises several vital facts. First, it is hard to develop a sustainable economy without access to energy. Secondly, key oil producers currently have elevated geopolitical power. And, thirdly, huge benefits could come to countries that pursue energy efficiency and alternative energy. But these three facts do not, in my opinion, coagulate in an end to American power or sweeping global conflict. I would argue that these basic energy facts need to be reorganised to the tune of different concerns: global inequality, climate change and sustainable development. In considering all three, the United States needs to accept more responsibility at home and play a stronger leadership role on the international stage.

As Elhefnawy points out, compared to the Japanese, Americans are certainly wasteful of energy. Americans represent 5% of the world's population but we use 33% of all the oil used for road transportation. By comparison, China, even with its growing economy, consumes only about 5% of global road-fuel production, despite a population more than four times that of the United States.

The American gluttony for oil – combined with OPEC's inability, and perhaps refusal, to provide more affordable energy – is all the more galling in social-justice terms when one considers that many other nations are stuck in abject poverty.

Access to energy services is key to alleviating poverty and an indispensable element of sustainable human development. One-quarter of the global population still has no access to electricity and some 2.4 billion people rely on traditional biomass, including wood, agricultural residues and dung, for cooking and heating. More than 99% of people without electricity live in developing regions, and four out of five live in rural areas of South Asia and sub-Saharan Africa. The health consequences of using biomass in an unsustainable way are staggering. According to the World Health Organisation, exposure to indoor air pollution is responsible for nearly two million excess deaths, primarily women and children, from cancer, respiratory infections and lung diseases, and for 4% of the global burden of disease.[2] In relative terms, biomass pollution kills more people than malaria (1.2m) and tuberculosis (1.6m) each year around the world. As staggering as this situation is, it is not poised to change. The International Energy Agency projects that, under a business-as-usual scenario, by 2030 1.4bn people *still* will not have access to electricity, while the number reliant upon biomass will increase from 2.5bn in 2006 to 2.7bn.

In global environmental terms, US energy use looms large. In 2005, the United States emitted a total of 712m tonnes of carbon, 412m tonnes of which came from petroleum use for road transport. The country emits more energy-related carbon dioxide per capita than any other industrial nation.[3] In the 1990s, the US transportation sector saw emissions of carbon dioxide grow faster than any other major sector of the US economy.[4] The US Department of Energy predicts that the transport sector will generate almost half the 40% rise in US carbon emissions projected for 2025.

Beyond environmental concerns, rising US oil imports to meet soaring national gasoline demand have also been a significant factor strengthening OPEC's monopoly power in international oil markets. US net oil imports rose from 6.79m b/d in 1991 to 10.2m b/d in 2000 while global oil *trade* (that is, oil exported from one country to another) rose from 32.34m b/d to 42.67 m b/d. In other words, the US share of the increase in global oil trade over the period was a substantial 33%. In OPEC terms, the US import market was even more significant – representing over 50% of OPEC's output gains between 1991 and 2000.

Strong US import demand not only enhances OPEC's monopoly power, it has a deleterious long-term impact on the US economy. The US oil-import bill totalled $327bn in 2007 and is expected to top $400bn in 2008.[5] This is an increase of 300% from 2002. The US oil-import bill accounted for as much as 40% of the overall US trade deficit in 2006, compared to only 25% in 2002. This rising financial burden is stoking inflation and creating ongoing challenges for the US economy, challenges one might argue will likely reduce American demand for oil for a time.

Given the large scale of US purchases, incremental US acquisitions of oil affect its overall international market price. Stated another way, the cost of each marginal barrel is higher than the price paid for that barrel, since this additional purchase affects the costs of all oil consumed. From the perspective of the United States, this constitutes an externality.[6]

The US economy is both resilient and blessed with diverse energy

On the other hand, the fact that the United States faces a rising supply curve for oil gives it monopsony power. To the extent that America, or a group of consuming countries on a comparable scale, takes concrete actions to reduce the size of its purchases, it can lower the market price of oil. This can happen by accident (as, in the past, through economic recessions) or by sound public policy, which is the preferable path and the one Elhefnawy advocates.

Still, his doomsday scenario brushes aside too easily the fact that the US economy is both resilient and blessed with diverse energy geography. There is a distinct possibility that the United States and other industrialised nations will not only develop new, even more sustainable energy technologies, but also export them to alleviate poverty in the developing world. Oil giant BP, for example, is already experimenting with a business that markets smoke-free, biopellet stoves to rural households in India, and non-governmental organisations are working to bring small-scale micro-hydro and solar energy to remote areas in Africa and Asia. A multinational effort to increase such programmes would, as Elhefnawy suggests, certainly be valuable.

While the costs of the oil shocks of the 1970s have been widely debated and varied country to country, there is no doubt that the impact was severe, causing years of economic dislocation and stagnation. In the early 1980s, the costs of the oil shocks were estimated at $1.2 trillion in lost economic growth for the seven largest industrial countries.[7] But the lesson of the 1970s oil crises was not that oil-hungry industrial nations went to war. The lesson was that markets can and do adjust without recourse to state violence. In response to the 1970s oil-price shocks, the industrialised oil-importing countries undertook various domestic, bilateral and multilateral efforts. Some worked, others did not; but none, notably, involved the militarisation of energy supplies. The energy efficiency and diversification Elhefnawy praises as better positioning other countries than the United States came about through key policy responses to the 1970s. It was non-military and highly replicable. The stimulus was an oil shortage, so it is hard to see how another shortage that would come with some warning and be known to be permanent would not stimulate even greater and more effective policy and market responses. Today's investors in alternative energy must fear the possibility that cheap oil will re-emerge. Investors in Elhefnawy's world could invest far more capital without any fear that fossil fuels would fight back.

Today, we are better equipped to deal with an oil shock than in the 1970s. We have functioning, transparent global oil-futures exchanges that allow for orderly responses to sudden changes in price. We also have a much wider range of emerging technologies for energy efficiency and alternative fuel. And, most importantly, we have the experience of managing major oil shocks through multilateral institutions for diplomacy and emergency coordination that did not exist in the 1970s. We even have existing international systems for negotiating fair-minded oil rationing through the International Energy Agency emergency systems, were it to come to that.

In sum, there are more alternative pathways and less reason to go to war over oil today than ever before. This is not to say that a major oil crisis couldn't take place or, if it did, that it might not threaten the global trading system. But, surely, a structural realisation that oil will be running out could be planned for, given the fact that the international community has successfully managed unexpected, sudden losses in fuel on several occasions.

Moreover, the United States' experience, while perhaps lacking in comparison to that of some industrialised nations, is nonetheless a promising foundation for launching new, more effective policies. After the oil crises of the 1970s, oil use in several US sectors was greatly reduced through efficiency gains and fuel switching. Around a third of US homes were heated with oil in the early 1970s, compared to around 14% today. Moreover, oil was virtually removed as a fuel for electricity production in the United States. The United States has a wide array of fuels used for electricity generation, including coal, natural gas, hydroelectric, nuclear energy, geothermal, wind, biofuels and solar. We have learned that diversity of fuels creates flexibility, resilience and supplier temperance. This ability to generate electricity without recourse to oil is our greatest asset. The United States, if it embraces technologies to fuel automobiles with electricity, could do much to reduce its dependence on oil, since that electricity can be produced from many other fuels. Israel has already announced a nationwide experiment to embrace a national system for battery-powered cars. The State of California is looking at options to promote similar technology innovation.

Currently, the transportation sector represents more than two-thirds of total US petroleum use and will generate more than 70% of the projected increase in US oil demand. The 2007 US energy bill recognises this, and even its lacklustre regulations for automobile-efficiency standards will eliminate more than 2.5m b/d of oil use by 2020. A technological breakthrough that would allow Americans to get 50 miles per gallon by 2020 would save over 6.6m b/d of oil, according to a study by the Baker Institute.

Elhefnawy's contention that the United States should be doing more to develop and use alternative energy and to enhance its energy efficiency is a good one, even if he should, like many others before him, turn out to be incorrect in his prediction that the world will run out of fossil fuels in short order. The United States needs to forge a better energy policy now and for future generations, even if peak-oil theorists are wrong and we find and recover far more oil than we are currently using.

If other high-population nations, such as China or India, join the United States in its current energy-use practices, with no new breakthroughs in efficiency or alternative technology, the global environmental consequences are unthinkable. Moreover, the global oil system, while providing an economic miracle to support industrialisation in the West and now in parts of Asia, has left a huge swathe of the global population offline. A sustainable planet requires that Americans build a better energy mousetrap, perhaps one that involves distributed energy systems that could have better applicability in the less-developed world.

But the timescale to convert infrastructure is long. The more we delay, the more facilities get replaced with conventional technologies. The International Energy Agency estimates that more than $4.3tr will need to be invested to meet the increase of 30–40m b/d of oil the world will need in 2030 beyond today's demand of 83m b/d.[8] Fifteen percent of that added demand is projected to come from the United States alone and another 24% from China. If the two countries were to get together at the highest political level and develop a concrete joint strategy to eliminate as much of that demand growth as could be reasonably achieved through efficiency and alternative energy technologies, there is no telling how many of the things predicted in Elhefnawy's article could be scoffed at in 25 years.

Notes

1 Daniel Yergin and Martin Hillenbrand, *Global Insecurity* (Boston, MA: Houghton Mifflin Company, 1982).

2 Nigel Bruce et al., 'Indoor Air Pollution in Developing Countries: A Major Environmental and Public Health Challenge', *Bulletin of the World Health Organization*, 2000, pp. 1078–92.

3 John Byrne, Kristen Hughes, Wilson Rickerson and Lado Kurdgelashvili, 'American Policy Conflict in the Greenhouse: Divergent Trends in Federal, State, and Local Green

Energy and Climate Change Policy', *Energy Policy*, vol. 35, 2007, pp. 4555–73.

4 Joseph Romm, 'The Car and Fuel of the Future', *Energy Policy*, vol. 24, 2006, pp. 2609–14.

5 'US Import Bill Set to Top $400 Billion', *Petroleum Intelligence Weekly*, 10 March 2008.

6 See D.R. Bohi and M.A. Toman, *The Economics of Energy Security* (Boston, MA: Kluwer Academic, 1996), pp. 14–15, 44–5.

7 *OECD Economic Outlook*, July 1981; see also Robert Stobaugh and Daniel Yergin, *Energy Future: Report of the Energy Project at Harvard Business School* (New York: Ballantine, 1980).

8 *World Energy Outlook 2007* (Paris: International Energy Agency, 2007).

Sino-American Energy Competition

Michael T. Klare

Nader Elhefnawy provides a rich architecture in which to consider the political, economic and security implications of an eventual contraction in the global supply of petroleum. One need not agree with every aspect of his overall assessment to conclude that a future contraction in supply – whether or not it proves to be as severe as he contends – will have a profound impact on the global security environment.

Elhefnawy acknowledges that there is room for debate in interpretation of the available data on global oil availability, but generally sides with those who believe that an imminent peak in production – to be followed by an inevitable downturn in output – is likely. 'The evidence for a significant, prolonged and continuing contraction in production ... beginning by the 2020s is considerable', he notes. But while this assessment might once have provoked considerable dissent, it is increasingly being viewed as the prevailing norm – especially with crude oil prices exceeding $130 per barrel (as of early June 2008) and the major oil companies reporting both declining rates of output at older fields and few new discoveries to replace them.

Michael T. Klare is Professor of Peace and World Security Studies at Hampshire College in Amherst, Massachusetts, and the author of several books on global resource politics, including *Resource Wars* (2001), *Blood and Oil* (2004), and *Rising Powers, Shrinking Planet: The New Geopolitics of Energy* (2008).

Far more provocative, however, are Elhefnawy's observations on the security implications of an impending contraction in global petroleum supplies. It is here, I suspect, that he will encounter greater skepticism and dispute. These comments are more speculative and, therefore, more subject to criticism. Nevertheless, I believe that many of his findings will survive the test of time. The 'resource curse', for example, is very real, as demonstrated by the current violence in the Niger Delta region of Nigeria; state collapse, a more extreme phenomenon, could well occur in poor countries hit hard by the rising price of oil and food. Other observations might not fare so well, but this remains to be seen; at the very least, he has given us much food for thought.

And yet, for all the valuable insights he provides on the security implications of declining oil supplies, Elhefnawy fails to address the problem I see as the most pressing in this area: the military implications of growing US–Chinese competition for foreign petroleum supplies. Of all the great powers that will be adversely affected by an eventual contraction in the global supply of oil, the United States and the People's Republic of China (PRC) are the ones likely to experience its most severe effects. These nations are the world's leading users of petroleum, jointly accounting for approximately one-third of total world consumption: 28.8m out of a world total of 86.7m b/d, according to the US Department of Energy. The further one looks into the future, moreover, the greater their expected need for oil and the larger their combined share of global consumption: in 2030, predicts the department, their combined usage will have grown to 42.0m b/d, representing 36% of projected world petroleum consumption of 117.3m b/d.[1]

A contraction in global petroleum supplies will have severe consequences for all oil-consuming nations, as Elhefnawy rightly points out. But it will have particularly harsh implications for the United States and China because of the distinctive role oil plays in each. In the United States, oil is the leading source of energy, providing approximately two-fifths of the total supply, and is absolutely essential for transportation, which relies almost exclusively on petroleum-fuelled automobiles, trucks and buses. With its ever-lengthening commute distances and pitifully few passenger-rail services to fall back on, the United States is especially vulnerable to the hardships imposed by dwindling and more costly supplies of oil.

China does not rely on petroleum for as large a share of its net energy supply as does the United States – coal is the leading energy provider in the PRC (with all its attendant environmental problems) – but the government has made petrochemicals and automobile manufacture twin pillars of its industrial expansion and so has generated an ever-growing requirement for oil. According to some estimates, automobile ownership in China is projected to rise from 27m vehicles in 2004 to 400m by 2030, producing a phenomenal increase in petroleum demand.[2] This rise in automobile ownership is not as essential to national transportation as it is in the United States, but it is an important symbol of rising middle-class aspirations and so is something the Chinese leadership has vigorously nurtured, for example, by keeping petroleum prices artificially low. Hence, a contraction in global oil supplies will pose significant political as well as economic problems for Beijing.

All this bears with particular impact on the global security equation because the United States and China are heavily reliant on *imported* oil, and so must compete for access to ever-dwindling overseas supplies. At present, the United States and China are the world's first and third leading oil importers (Japan is number two), obtaining 12.4 and 4.1m b/d from abroad, respectively. But China's oil demand is rising so rapidly that it is soon expected to overtake Japan. By 2030, according to the Department of Energy, the United States will need to import 17.8m b/d and China 11.9m. At that time OECD Europe and Japan will together need to import about 18.5m b/d, so the combined Sino-American import requirement will represent about three-fifths of the total import needs of the world's major economies[3] – a very significant consideration if global petroleum supplies are not growing but rather contracting by that time.

To obtain all of these imported supplies, China and the United States will need to draw upon the same dozen or so major producing countries that possess sufficient petroleum reserves to satisfy their own needs and provide a surplus for export. The list is not long: Algeria, Angola, Libya, Nigeria and Sudan in Africa; Azerbaijan, Kazakhstan and Russia in the former Soviet

Union; Iran, Iraq, Kuwait, Saudi Arabia and the United Arab Emirates in the Gulf region; Venezuela and perhaps Brazil in Latin America. As these suppliers' role in global energy commerce has grown, so, too, has their prominence in the foreign affairs of both the United States and China. Senior American and Chinese officials have made frequent pilgrimages to the national capitals of most of them and invited their leaders to Washington or Beijing for lavish state visits. Typically, these encounters are accompanied by offers of loans, development aid, diplomatic favours or other inducements in return for privileged treatment when it comes to the award of joint ventures or development schemes by these states' national oil companies. Increasingly, however, these inducements also include military packages, and it is in this regard that the security dimension begins to loom large.

Increasingly these inducements include military packages

Looking again at the list of major oil-surplus nations, it is apparent that the governments of many have an obvious requirement for arms and military services, whether to defend against hostile neighbours, to suppress ethnic separatist movements, or to defend themselves against those compatriots who might seek to replace them. It is not surprising, then, that these governments would welcome such assistance from their oil-seeking suitors. And their suitors have, in turn, been more than happy to oblige: as part of their burgeoning ties with these countries, both the United States and China have become major suppliers of arms and military services to many of the countries listed above. The United States, for example, is an arms supplier to Angola, Azerbaijan, Iraq, Kazakhstan, Kuwait, Nigeria, Saudi Arabia and the United Arab Emirates; China is a supplier to Angola, Kazakhstan, Iran, Nigeria, Saudi Arabia and Sudan.[4]

The result is an accelerated flow of arms and military equipment into areas that, in many cases, are suffering from internal or regional friction and conflict. In some cases, this could lead to a greater propensity on the part of central governments to employ force rather than engage in political dialogue when dealing with domestic opposition movements or ethnic separatists, a pattern seen in Sudan and Nigeria. It could also help spark regional arms races. In the Gulf, for example, Chinese and Russian arms sales to Iran have been countered in recent months by stepped-up US military deliveries to Saudi Arabia and other members of the Gulf Cooperation Council. Both phenomena could contribute to the further erosion of stability in the developing world along the lines sketched by Elhefnawy.

The greater danger, however, is that this will lead to increased friction between the United States and China. This will arise as leaders of both countries perceive the respective arms diplomacy of their rival as a threat to their own national-security interests. This perception has, in fact, already begun to take root. Recent editions of the *Military Power of the People's Republic of China*, an annual report prepared by the US Department of Defense, have warned of growing Chinese military ties with key energy and mineral producers in the developing world. 'Securing adequate supplies of resources and materials has become a major driver of Chinese foreign policy', the 2006 edition noted, an impulse that has led Beijing to shower favoured suppliers like Angola, Sudan and Zimbabwe with arms and military technology.[5]

Chinese officials appear to harbour similar concerns about the United States. In particular, Beijing worries about US efforts to establish military ties with the former Soviet republics of Central Asia. These ties were first established during the Bill Clinton administration, when US oil companies acquired substantial production rights in Kazakhstan and pursued similar rights in Turkmenistan. Concerned over the unsettled security environment in the Caspian Sea basin and the risks this posed to the safe transport of Caspian energy, President Clinton oversaw the initiation of US military-aid agreements with Kazakhstan, Kyrgyzstan and Uzbekistan. Following the 11 September terrorist attacks, President George W. Bush built on these relationships to establish US bases in Kyrgyzstan and Uzbekistan, further expanding the US military presence in the area. Now Beijing, working in concert with Moscow and the Shanghai Cooperation Organisation (SCO), seeks to reverse this trend and diminish the US presence in the region. In the most conspicuous expression of this outlook to date, Chinese forces participated last summer in elaborate multilateral military manoeuvres intended to demonstrate the organisation's self reliance. 'The SCO nations have a clear understanding of the threats faced by the region and thus must ensure their security themselves', Chinese President Hu Jintao declared at the time, a clear signal that the United States was not needed – and not wanted – in the region.[6]

These concerns also appear to be guiding the military planning of the two countries. In February 2007, for example, the United States announced the establishment of a new headquarters organisation to oversee US forces operating in Africa, the US Africa Command or AFRICOM. Although not publicly citing Chinese military involvement in the region as a motive for creation of the new command, Department of Defense officials have acknowledged privately that this is a factor. In a PowerPoint presentation at the National Defense University in February, AFRICOM's deputy commander, Vice-Admiral Robert Moeller, indicated that among the key challenges to US strategic interests in the region is China's 'growing influence in Africa'.[7]

For its part, China's growing military assertiveness is perhaps best reflected in the expansion of its deep-sea naval capabilities and its more conspicuous military role in the Shanghai Cooperation Organisation – a point noted by Elhefnawy. In the exercises last summer, for example, Chinese airborne forces engaged in military manoeuvres outside Chinese territory for the first time ever.

These endeavours are likely to gain momentum in the years ahead as both China and the United States become ever more dependent on the oil reserves of Africa, the Middle East and Central Asia and as their competitive drive for access to what remains of these supplies intensifies. It is conceivable that such efforts will lead, in time, to an unintended clash between American and Chinese forces, provoking an international crisis and possibly war. Certainly, at present, with the leaders of all great powers grimly aware of the risks of a major inter-state conflict, the probability of such a confrontation has to be considered very low. This does not mean, however, that US and Chinese leaders are not prepared to devote enormous resources to *preparation* for such an eventuality. In fact, both countries have recently announced significant increases in military spending with heavy emphasis on the sort of forces – advanced air, naval and missile capabilities – one would anticipate using in a future engagement between them. In US budget justifications, moreover, China (that is, a better-equipped and more menacing China of the future) is often cited as a likely future adversary of the United States. One assumes that Chinese budget documents make similar assumptions about the United States, but these are not normally made public.

In the end, it may be the *financial* implications of all this that will prove most harmful. As Elhefnawy rightly concludes, vast sums will be needed to develop climate-friendly energy sources to replace disappearing stocks of petroleum in the coming decades, and much of this largesse will have to be provided by governments. This, in turn, will require an awareness by policymakers that addressing the global energy crisis is a top governmental priority and must entail a substantial mobilisation of scientific, industrial and capital resources. Clearly, the outbreak of a Sino-American arms race will drain both attention and resources away from this sort of mobilisation. It is this outcome that we must fear the most.

Notes

1 US Department of Energy, Energy Information Administration, *Annual Energy Outlook* 2008, Table 20, International Petroleum Supply and Disposition Summary, available at http://www.eia.doe.gov. These figures obviously do not take account of the oil-production declines predicted by Elhafnawy; they do, however, incorporate liquids derived from Canadian tar sands, biofuels and other nonconventional sources.

2 US Department of Defense, *The Military Power of the People's Republic of China 2008* (Washington DC: Department of Defense, 2008), p. 10.

3 US Department of Energy, Energy Information Administration, *Annual Energy Outlook 2008*, Table 20.

4 See Michael T. Klare, *Rising Powers, Shrinking Planet: The New Geopolitics of Energy* (New York: Metropolitan Books, 2008).

5 US Department of Defense, *The Military Power of the People's Republic of China 2006* (Washington DC: Department of Defense, 2006, p. 1.

6 Quoted in the *Guardian*, 17 August 2007.

7 Robert Moeller, 'United States Central Command', PowerPoint presentation, National Defense University, Washington DC, 19 February 2008, available at http://www.ndu.edu/ctnsp/NCW_course/Moeller_08%20 02%2014%20DCMO%20Brf%20v2.pdf.

Response

Nader Elhefnawy

I would like to start by thanking Amy Myers Jaffe and Michael T. Klare for their comments regarding my article. While they agree with many points of my assessment, they also point to a number of items they find problematic. Jaffe argues that I have underestimated the flexibility of the market and the prospects for peaceful adaptation to the new conditions, particularly by the United States. Klare suggests I did not give sufficient attention to the prospects of a Sino-American military competition, to which energy politics is already contributing.

Jaffe observes that 'investors in alternative energy ... in Elhefnawy's world could invest far more capital without any fear that fossil fuels would fight back'. The article focused on long-term energy *security*, rather than financial advice to investors, and therefore warranted a more cautious consideration of the issue, extending to an examination of worst-case scenarios. Nonetheless, Jaffe's characterisation of my position is not entirely inaccurate. The flexibility of markets is not infinite, and natural-resource scarcities remain an important limitation on their capacity for generating solutions.[1] A return to 'cheap oil' (a problematic concept in itself) is no exception. All the signs – the smaller size of newly discovered deposits, the growing shortfall between new discoveries and the depletion of proven supplies, the emphasis on areas where exploration and extraction are more difficult and costly (like offshore fields), the broadly falling energy return on energy invested (EROEI) – strongly indicate a trend toward diminishing marginal returns on investment in oil production. The relatively slow process of enlarging oil production is also a factor, deferring even the hope of a price drop to a point at which this trend will be even more advanced.

Of course, cutbacks in consumption driven by high prices could help in the interim. However, energy consumption is relatively inelastic, and the

---

Nader Elhefnawy currently teaches at the University of Miami. He has previously published on international and security issues in journals including *Astropolitics*, *International Security* and *Parameters*.

energy shortages of the 1970s did not cause consumers to fundamentally reduce their use. Rather, high prices temporarily held down growth in consumption. Substantial, lasting reductions require structural changes like the conversion of infrastructure and vehicle fleets, which tend to be gradual when driven by the market.

Moreover, energy efficiency may also be an area of diminishing marginal returns on investment. While the rise in global energy efficiency in the 1990s (measured in terms of the energy input needed to produce a unit of gross domestic product) kept pace with the progress of the 1970s and 1980s (about 10% per decade), the distribution of the gains of the years 1990–2003 is cause for concern.[2] It was concentrated not among advanced states, but those rated 'lower middle income' by the World Bank – economies which in the natural course of development did away with very easy inefficiencies, rather than pushing the envelope.[3]

In fact, the most efficient among the large states saw their improvement stagnate during these years; the progress of Japan and Italy, in particular, was flat.[4] The more impressive gains of Germany, Britain and the United States are likely due to how far behind they were to begin with – these are 'easy' gains, as in the case of many developing nations.[5] This trend might be attributable to low oil prices affording little incentive to make a greater effort, but that remains speculative. The booms and busts Jaffe mentions as comparable to this decade's should also be examined closely. The 1956 crisis was due to the closure of the Suez Canal. The oil shocks of 1973 and 1979 involved concerted action by the Organisation of Petroleum Exporting Countries (OPEC). The 1990 shock was a result of UN sanctions taking Iraqi and Kuwaiti production offline.

In short, all four shocks were partly attributable to deliberate political decisions regarding oil production, transportation or price, to which the 2003 shock offers no analogue. It is also worth remembering that prices tended to fall through the 1980s and 1990s despite the Iran–Iraq War, sanctions against Iraq and periodic war scares in the Persian Gulf, and reached their low point in 1998, a particularly anxious year where Iraq's relationships with the UN and the United States were concerned. The ongoing war in Iraq and international tensions regarding Iran's nuclear programme therefore seem insufficient to account for the current prices ($138 a barrel), which exceed the earlier 1981 record by over 40% in real terms.

The real issue is that oil producers have less slack for absorbing shocks of all kinds. Rising consumption in Asia is certainly a factor, but still leaves the question of why producers have failed to keep up. That failure can partly be attributed to a fixation on short-term profit-seeking, but also reflecting the diminishing marginal returns that make rectifying the situation more difficult.

This is not to say that oil cannot 'fight back'. Declines rarely follow a straight downward trajectory, but the curve gets much steeper, and it becomes reasonable to expect that those who do fight back will give more and get less. It only muddles the issue to say that prices will at some point go down. A more appropriate question is how much can we reasonably expect them to go down, and for how long before prices start to go back up again. For instance, will prices return to the low of the 1990s, when they hit $10 a barrel – a drop of 90% from today's prices, after adjustment for inflation? Will they even come close?

That seems unlikely. When oil fought back against alternatives in the past, it did so politically as well as through the market. Where renewable energy should have enjoyed the protected status of an 'infant industry' on the grounds of energy independence and ecology, such support was withdrawn in the United States in the early 1980s.[6] While this was done in the name of the free market, renewable energy did not compete on a level playing field but one tilted in favour of fossil fuels, the beneficiary of a long and ongoing history of subsidy.[7] Fossil-fuel-related R&D was funded by the government at four times the level of renewable energy for the 1972–95 period.[8] Such subsidies make the 'cheap' oil to which Jaffe refers illusory in an important sense (even without considering problematic externalities like climate change, which Jaffe rightly raises).

The relative cost of renewable energy has steadily dropped

Despite these disadvantages, the cost of renewable-energy production has steadily dropped relative to oil since the 1970s, so that wind is increasingly competitive. Given recent experience, this trend can be expected to continue (though not indefinitely). A true repeat of the late 1980s and 1990s with regard to the energy markets is thus highly unlikely, barring perverse public-policy decisions.

However, while Jaffe characterises my assessment as a 'doomsday scenario' at which future readers will scoff, the parameters laid down here leave a wide range of possibilities with regard to the speed with which that scarcity develops, the severity of the resulting problems, and the room for manoeuvre actors will have in which to adapt to the new situation. Peaceful, progressive responses are conceivable, and one can point to real achievements. Denmark, for instance, derives a fifth of its electricity from wind energy, and reduced its fossil-fuel use by a comparable margin in the 2001–05 period, all while maintaining one of the highest living standards in the world.[9] Unfortunately, Denmark is the exception rather than the rule; others are proving slow to follow, and even were the propensity to do so greater, not all countries can adapt as easily. Considerable variation exists in this respect among even the advanced industrial countries.

This brings me to the second major point, the case of the United States. As Jaffe notes, America's status as the world's single biggest consumer of energy and oil positions it to have a greater positive impact on the situation than any other single actor. It is also the world's biggest spender on technological R&D, and has enormous potential to produce energy from photovoltaic solar, wind and other renewable sources.[10] All these resources can be mobilised to meet the challenge.

Nonetheless, the United States has further to go than other developed nations, and a number of particularly severe obstacles to overcome. These include the country's overall low energy efficiency, underdeveloped renewable-energy industry, and a 'culture of oil' deeply embedded in national attitudes, consumer habits and physical infrastructure. The US economy may also not be as robust as it appears, and is already suffering the consequences of its de-industrialisation and trade deficits (possibly coming to a head in a currency crisis), which complicate adaptation.

Meaningful action on all these issues will take considerable political will, extending to a fundamental rethinking of the economic legacy of the 1980s.

There is little sign of this as yet, neither at the level of federal policy (though many US states and even localities have been more active), nor in public discourse about the issue, which remains mired in inoffensive platitudes. I am not arguing for economic determinism, but taken together these factors threaten America's position as a global power.

The issue of global-power status, of course, raises Klare's concern over the risk of military competition between the United States and China. I agree that China, along with the United States, will be the major country most adversely affected by contracting oil supplies. China's robust growth, strong currency and heterodox economic policies have, for the time being, constrained the effect of oil-price rises on its economy (just as they constrained the effects of the 1997–98 Asian financial crisis). However, over the long term, deepening scarcity will take its toll.

Klare is also right to note China's support of its energy policy with diplomacy and arms sales in recent years; the resulting frictions with US interests in Central Asia and elsewhere; and the danger not only of an increased risk of a great-power military clash, but the resulting diversion of resources and attention away from more useful investments. Indeed, the pursuit of energy security through military means has already exacted a high price. What might the United States have accomplished if it put even a small fraction of the money spent on securing the Persian Gulf since 1973 into developing alternate energy sources?

Nonetheless, a few qualifiers are in order, particularly where China's position is concerned. The country's wealth, capabilities and prospects are constantly exaggerated. Despite its lengthy investment in military modernisation, China still lacks the power-projection assets of the United Kingdom, let alone the United States. Additionally, while China's relationships with Iran and Sudan rightly raise eyebrows, it is significant that China has become more cautious in pressing its claims in the South China Sea basin since 2001, a situation much closer to home, and where it is far stronger than in the distant Middle East. Indeed, China relies much less on its military resources internationally than the softer power generated by its economic standing and its effective diplomacy, exploiting the desire for a counterweight among those discontented with US foreign policy.[11]

This does not rule out a more militarised and confrontational Chinese policy in the future, but the constraints here are greater than many observers realise. The situation will be slow to change, in part because, energy portfolio apart, China's economy, too, is not as strong as it appears. According to a report issued by the Asian Development Bank last year, the miscalculation of purchasing power parity for China may have led to an overestimate of the size of China's economy by 40%, an assessment now widely accepted.[12] In short, China is several years behind the position the most optimistic estimates have given it, and much else about its economic performance is also called into question by this rethinking.

China's economic progress has also exacted an appalling social and ecological price. The desertification, air pollution and fouling of the Yellow and Yangtze rivers, and the sharp cleavages between regions and classes (manifest in rural unemployed migrating toward the cities), all bode poorly for the sustainability of China's current course. Those who criticise Europe's trend toward an older population would also do well to remember that China is one of the most rapidly ageing countries in the world.

Indeed, China's condition not only invites comparison with the rise of great powers like the United States, but frustrated ascents to superpower status, like the 'Brazilian miracle' of the 1970s, which astonished the world – as China astonishes now – before fizzling out. China's collapse, rather than a lengthy arms race, may in fact be a more likely consequence of its reliance on oil, though these unfortunate paths are not mutually exclusive.

The optimal future is one in which, as Jaffe argues, the United States and China (and other economic powers like the EU and Japan) lead the international community in a project to improve energy efficiency, build up production from already viable and increasingly attractive alternatives, and further develop the technological state of the art in energy production and use, while extending the benefits of these to even the poorest nations. Sadly, however, the rational course is not the only one possible, or even the most likely. There were wide hopes of a similar venture 35 years ago in the wake of the OPEC embargo, but for all the bold rhetoric of the Nixon and Carter administrations, the results of American efforts in particular were dismal. It would be folly to ignore this dismaying precedent, and unfortunately the policy of the United States and China in recent years has not been much more encouraging. A humane and successful response to the problem is well worth working for, but it cannot be taken for granted.

Notes

1 Thomas Homer-Dixon, *Environmental Scarcity and Global Security* (Ithaca, NY: Foreign Policy Association, 1993), pp. 67–8.

2 World Bank, *2006 World Development Indicators* (Washington DC: World Bank, 2006), pp. 158–60.

3 *Ibid.*

4 *Ibid.*, pp. 158–60.

5 *Ibid.*

6 Nader Elhefnawy, 'Toward a Long-Range Energy Security Policy', *Parameters*, vol. 36, no. 1, Spring 2006, pp. 108–10.

7 *Ibid.*

8 Fred J. Sissine, 'Energy Efficiency: A New National Outlook?' *Congressional Research Service Reports*, 12 December 1996, http://www.cnie.org/nle/crsreports/energy/eng-28.cfm.

9 In 2005, Denmark was consuming 20% less oil daily than it was in 2001, and 37% less than in 1981. US Energy Information Administration, 'World Petroleum Consumption', *International Energy Annual 2005*, 6 August 2007, available at http://www.eia.doe.gov/pub/international/iealf/table12.xls. Danish coal and natural-gas consumption have also trended downward.

10 Robert L. Paarlberg, 'Knowledge as Power: Science, Military Dominance and U.S. Security', *International Security*, vol. 29, no. 1, Summer 2004, pp. 122–51.

11 Chris Zambelis and Brandon Gentry, 'China through Arab Eyes: American Influence in the Middle East', *Parameters*, vol. 38, no. 1, Spring 2008, pp. 60–72.

12 See Albert Keidel, 'The Limits of a Smaller, Poorer China', *Financial Times*, 14 November 2007, http://www.carnegieendowment.org/publications/index.cfm?fa=view&id=19709&prog=zch. Between 2007 and 2008, the CIA revised its estimate of China's GDP down from $10 trillion to $7tr. See the 2007 and 2008 editions of the Central Intelligence Agency's *CIA World Factbook.*

Why Europe Leads on Climate Change

John R. Schmidt

In July 1997, five months prior to the Kyoto meeting of the UN Framework Convention on Climate Change (UNFCCC), the US Senate passed a resolution that opposed signing any agreement at Kyoto that did not include commitments from developing nations 'to limit or reduce greenhouse gas emissions'.[1] What made the resolution particularly striking was the fact that the vote was 95 to 0, a degree of Senatorial consensus rarely seen on a substantive issue. The question was not simply one of equity; the Senate feared that forcing US industries to meet Kyoto reduction targets while exempting developing nations would further weaken US competitiveness and hasten the flight of jobs and industry overseas. There were also doubts in some quarters, particularly on the political right, about the reliability of scientific claims regarding climate change.

At the same time, however, on the other side of the Atlantic, the member states of the European Union (EU) were just as unanimous in their approach to Kyoto, but in precisely the opposite direction. Not only were they prepared to exempt developing nations from the Kyoto regime, they were willing to accept reductions in their own emissions even after it became clear that the United States, at the time the world's largest emitter of greenhouse gasses, was unprepared to follow suit. Due largely to European support, the protocol which finally emerged from Kyoto did exempt developing nations.[2]

John R. Schmidt is Senior Analyst for Europe in the Bureau of Intelligence and Research at the US Department of State. The views expressed are his and not necessarily those of the Department of State or the US government.

Survival | vol. 50 no. 4 | August–September 2008 | pp. 83–96 DOI 10.1080/00396330802328990

It was approved by the EU as a bloc, and although eventually signed, was never ratified by the United States.

Although the Kyoto Protocol required the EU to reduce its carbon emissions by 8% over 1990 levels by 2012,[3] the EU was not prepared to leave it at that. In the decade since, it has self-consciously styled itself as the world leader in confronting the dangers of climate change, even to the point of adopting a unilateral successor regime that goes beyond its Kyoto commitments. In March 2007, EU heads of government agreed to reduce emissions by 20% (12 percentage points beyond the targets set for the EU at Kyoto) by 2020, while expressing a willingness to commit to 30% reductions if a multilateral successor regime to Kyoto can be negotiated. The EU also agreed to raise the share of renewable energy in its overall energy consumption from the current 8.5% to 20% and to raise the percentage of its automotive fuel use comprised of biofuels to 10%.[4] On 23 January 2008, the EU Commission released a detailed plan on how to meet these targets, combining member-state reductions tied to per capita GNP with EU-wide reductions in energy allocations to specific industries under the EU Emissions Trading Directive (ETD).[5] Although the plan has already sparked controversy among member states unhappy with their allotted shares, the Commission hopes the plan will be approved by the EU Council and European Parliament no later than the end of the latter's current term in summer 2009.

Most remarkably, perhaps, is that the EU has taken this action unilaterally. Although the United States agreed at the Bali UNFCCC conference last December to participate in negotiating a possible follow-on to Kyoto by 2009, this is far from a guarantee of success.[6] Washington and Brussels continue to disagree on how much should be demanded of developing countries, and the two largest, China and India, continue to resist any limitations on their carbon emissions, despite belief in some quarters that Chinese greenhouse-gas emissions may have already reached US levels.[7] The EU estimates that implementation of its unilateral regime will cost it €60 billion a year through 2020, which it estimates would work out to a reduction of 0.5% in annual European GDP or a tax of €3 per week per person throughout the EU.[8] This unilateral commitment comes in the context of the EU's overall climate-change goal: to avert a global temperature rise of more than 2°C above pre-industrial levels, the point beyond which it believes, on the basis of the assessment reports of the UN Intergovernmental Panel on Climate Change,[9] the 'dangerous anthropogenic interference with the climate system' targeted by Article 2 of the UNFCCC will occur. The EU accepts the UN analysis that this could require an overall reduction of somewhere between 15% and 50% in global emissions by 2050.[10] Since EU emissions currently account for only 14% of the global total (compared to 25% for the United States), the EU's unilateral regime, even if successfully implemented, would only make a very modest contribution toward this goal.

Risky or cautious?

This raises the question of why the EU is prepared to embark on such a costly programme, the ultimate effectiveness of which in combating global warming depends heavily on the active collaboration of others, in the absence of any firm assurance that such collaboration will occur. Although this might appear a risky strategy, with much ventured for potentially little gain, European policy on climate change is in fact grounded on the precautionary principle, whose overarching purpose is the avoidance of risk. Applied to the environment, the precautionary principle holds that when preliminary but not conclusive scientific evidence indicates that human activities might be causing serious harm, society should take appropriate steps to prevent that harm from occurring.[11] This was certainly the situation regarding scientific evidence on climate change during the Kyoto era, and is still largely the case today. Although climatic modelling has substantially improved over the past decade and the evidence for global warming is now largely uncontested, different models continue to predict substantially different degrees of warming and varying (but significant) degrees of harm for a given level of emissions. Nonetheless, Western Europeans were sufficiently concerned about global warming and other environmental problems a quarter-century ago that they inserted the precautionary principle into the founding treaty of the European Union agreed at Maastricht in 1992.[12] While European willingness to go it alone on climate change may suggest a paradox in European thinking, taking a risk to avoid a risk, it also reveals a good deal about contemporary European political culture, the emergence of the EU as a major player on the world stage, and the development of an increasingly distinctive EU approach to global issues based on the institutionalisation of risk.

Activist concern about the environment has never been an exclusively European preoccupation. It developed on both sides of the Atlantic in the 1970s in response to the oil shocks of 1973 and 1979 and the emergence of environmental issues such as acid rain, nuclear power-plant safety and chlorofluorocarbon-catalysed depletion of the ozone layer. Although environmentalism became a significant force for change in both the United States and Europe, in the latter it has come to take on an increasingly institutionalised character. The first use of the precautionary principle in Europe can be found in the 1968 Emission Control Act in West Germany.[13] But it developed into a mainstream political phenomenon only during the early 1980s when West Germany embraced the precautionary principle (*Vorsorgeprinzip*) in response to the perceived threat to German forests from acid rain.[14] Although the harm to forests was palpable, the connection to industrial pollution was suspected but not proven. The founding of the German Green Party in 1980 was both a symptom of, and a spur to, German activism on this and other environmental issues. Germany played a key role in negotiating the 1982 UN World Charter for Nature and in organising the 1992 Rio conference that established the UNFCCC. The UNFCCC Secretariat is itself permanently based in Bonn.

West Germany took the lead

Not surprisingly, West Germany took the lead within Europe in championing the use of the precautionary principle in environmental policy. This was not simply supererogatory behaviour aimed at preserving the larger European environment. Bonn did not want to see its industries suffer competitively within Europe due to higher costs caused by its own implementation of national emission controls to reduce acid rain. This gave it added motivation to convert its European Economic Community (EEC) partners to the cause. The Germans were far from isolated, however. German lobbying coincided with, and was aided by, the rise of Green parties throughout Western Europe. Although Green parties never managed to supplant the largest mainstream political parties, and achieved coalition-partner status in Germany only in 1998, they were disproportionately represented in the European Parliament and exercised an influence on European environmental policy well beyond their numbers. Both European political elites and the general public largely accepted the environmentalist warning that the globe was under threat. By the time Maastricht was being negotiated there was no serious resistance to enshrining the precautionary principle on environmental matters into the founding EU treaty or to subsequently pursuing an activist agenda during the years leading up to Kyoto.

The argument made by supporters of the precautionary principle was that it would be too risky to wait for conclusive scientific proof on global warming before taking action against it. This was the motivation behind European support for Kyoto and for the unilateral successor regime announced by the European Commission on 23 January. This would seem to suggest that Europe is more risk averse on environmental matters than the United States, where there has been much less unanimity regarding the evidence for global warming and the utility of taking precautionary measures against it, particularly if developing nations are exempted or otherwise refuse to participate. But a number of experts on US and European regulatory systems have cautioned against drawing such a conclusion. Jonathan Wiener of Duke University Law School argues that the United States has shown greater precaution than Europe on a host of environmental and public-safety issues.[15] He notes that the United States was far ahead of Europe in taking measures to protect the ozone layer, including banning fluorocarbon aerosols and deciding not to fund a supersonic transport aircraft. The United States also banned lead in gasoline almost a decade before Europe followed suit. The United States has also adopted tougher standards for the approval of prescription drugs and established lower highway speed limits. Weiner contends that these and other examples demonstrate that Europe is no more risk averse than the United States.

It is important to note, however, that a number of the most significant precautionary US regulatory steps, to ban aerosols and lead in gasoline and to lower speed limits, took place during the energy crisis of the 1970s, which was a time of exceptional environmental activism in the United States. Other precautionary measures cited by Weiner, such as tougher US restrictions on teenage drinking and smoking, may reflect more abstemious cultural instincts of the kind that gave rise to Prohibition or, as in the case of more rigorous drug certification, a stronger US reaction to a specific event, in this case the thalidomide birth-defect scandal of the late 1950s which led to significant tightening of the 1938 Food, Drug and Cosmetics Act.[16] The general point is that in the United States regulatory policy on environmental and public-health issues remains subject to the marketplace of political ideas in a way that in Europe it increasingly is not. It is a matter of historical record that some US administrations and congresses are more active on environmental issues than others. This not only affects prospects for adopting additional precautionary legislation but determines how stringently existing regulatory bodies choose to exercise their legislative mandates. In Europe, however, this has become a settled issue. Not only has the precautionary principle been written into the founding treaty of the European Union, in 2000 the European Commission issued a communication that extended its purview beyond environmental issues to all matters of public health.[17] No one then or since has dissented from it. A 2007 Eurobarometer poll showed that 89% of Europeans support the EU taking 'urgent action' to reduce carbon emissions by 20% by 2020 as called for in its proposed unilateral Kyoto successor regime.[18]

The interesting question is why this has become a settled issue in Europe but not in the United States. A large part of the reason lies in the differing political cultures and historical experiences on opposite sides of the Atlantic. While American democracy remains heavily influenced by classical liberalism and its espousal of laissez-faire capitalism, in the years following the Second World War virtually all of Western Europe embraced social democracy and the social welfare state, assuming much greater responsibility for guaranteeing the welfare of its citizens. Between 1950 and 1973 government spending as a percentage of GDP increased from 27.6 to 38.8% in France, from 30.4 to 42% in West Germany and from 34.2 to 41.5% in Britain. The added expenditures, financed by taxes that were both steeply higher and considerably more progressive than in the United States, provided a host of 'cradle to grave' benefits such as nationalised health care, enhanced job security, guaranteed social security and pensions, and subsidised housing.[19]

Such policies prevailed not simply because social democratic parties came to power and implemented them, but because more conservative parties, even when they came to power, did not roll them back. Although the desire to reduce income inequality and improve the fortunes of the least-advantaged members of society was also an essential goal of social democracy, it is hard not to see in social-democratic policies an overarching concern for the avoidance of risk. Nor is it difficult to find the cause. Although social democracy had its roots in Europe well before the Second World War, the unprecedented human suffering brought about by the second catastrophic war in a generation, coming as it did on the heels of the Great Depression, engendered in its survivors a deeply felt need for security, a desire to avoid or minimise risk. Such desires were not simply the province of the left, but spanned the mainstream political spectrum. It is hardly surprising that societies so oriented would want to exercise precaution in protecting themselves against the depredations of global warming once the magnitude of that threat began to fully emerge. The rise of the Greens can be seen in this light, since they were, in essence, persons of social-democratic sensibilities drawn into politics by their overweening concern for the environment.

This post-war pursuit of security did not just manifest itself domestically in the construction of the social welfare state, but in foreign policy as well. Western Europe sought US protection from the Soviet threat through the construction of the NATO Alliance, while at the same time urging caution and restraint on Washington in dealing with the Soviet Union, as in the debate in the early 1980s over stationing intermediate-range ballistic missiles. This desire to avoid confrontation also helps explain the European penchant, noted by Robert Kagan and others, for settling disputes through patient negotiation rather than violence or the threat of violence. It was also a primary motivation, possibly the primary motivation, behind the greatest of all post-war European enterprises, the creation of the European Union, a development which served both foreign and domestic policy interests. On the level of European politics, it aimed to eliminate forever the possibility that the nations of Western European would ever again make war on one another. This would be accomplished by establishing a confederal entity whose members would give up selected aspects of their sovereignty by agreeing to common regulatory mechanisms enforced from a common centre. It is not hard to see in this an effort to institutionalise risk avoidance by building regulatory predictability into the fabric of European governance.

Viewed in this light, it is hardly surprising that once global warming began to loom as a potentially serious threat, Europeans would seek to minimise the risk by incorporating precautionary measures into EU regulatory mechanisms. The European desire to minimise risk through construction of the social welfare state provided the motive, while the creation of the European Union provided the means. Indeed, it can be argued that Europe lagged behind the United States in environmental activism during the 1970s precisely because a mechanism for effectively regulating the environment on a European-wide basis did not yet exist. Agitation, led primarily by Germany and the Greens, during the early 1980s finally culminated in the insertion of Article 25 into the Single European Act of 1986, giving the EEC legislative authority for the first time to establish a European-wide policy on the environment.[20] This was followed by the 1993 entry into force of the Maastricht Treaty, which grounded EU environmental policy on the precautionary principle and gave the EU a mandate to pursue measures at the international level to deal with regional or global environmental problems.[21] Once this 'ever closer Union' became an accomplished fact, the EU was able to move quickly, not only to catch up to the United States, but to build precautionary environmental protectionism into the core of its domestic and foreign policy. Since the late 1980s, the EU has 'erected the most comprehensive and strict body of environmental legislation of any jurisdiction in the world'[22] and been 'a key supporter, if not the chief demandeur, of every major international environmental treaty'.[23]

The creation of the European Union provided the means

The European commitment to the social welfare state also helps explain why Europeans have seemed more prepared to absorb the costs of reducing greenhouse-gas emissions than their US counterparts, even in circumstances where their efforts may prove quixotic. The answer, quite simply, is that Europeans are more used to paying taxes and incurring costs as the price for the security afforded them by the social welfare state. It is no accident that European Commission President José Manuel Durao Barroso, in rolling out the unilateral Commission plan for reducing carbon emissions, broke the costs down into how much each citizen of the EU would have to pay. That cost, €3 per person per week, could then be assimilated conceptually by European publics as just another tax.

What this does not completely explain, however, is why the EU would be prepared to inflict such costs on its citizens with no firm guarantee that others will follow suit. This is a question that the EU has managed to pose for itself:

> The EU cannot decide for the rest of the world. But we are facing a global threat, and the best we can do is to show global leadership by example, and demonstrate that the economy and the community can prosper while fighting to limit climate change.[24]

There is no doubt that the EU believes that the threat from global warming is serious and that someone has to take the lead. But it is also true that ever since the EU was founded, the desire to demonstrate global leadership and, in so doing, enhance EU prestige has been an important driver of EU foreign policy. The ink on Maastricht was barely dry when the EU attempted to take on a leadership role in dealing with the crisis in Bosnia, which at the time was dissolving into civil war. The EU has continued to increase its diplomatic profile, not only in the Balkans but on Iran and other international issues, such as abolition of the death penalty. It has also striven to develop a military defence capability of its own under the European Security and Defence Policy (ESDP) rather than rely exclusively on NATO, and it has used the policy as a vehicle for undertaking peacekeeping missions in the Balkans and Africa. Assuming global leadership on climate change is clearly regarded by European political elites as a prominent feather in the EU's cap.

Given the position Washington has taken on Kyoto, it is hardly surprising that EU efforts to assume a global leadership role on climate change have brought it into conflict with the United States. EU spokesmen and European leaders have frequently criticised the United States for failing to ratify the Kyoto protocol and have been particularly critical of the Bush administration for not taking global warming seriously enough. This contrasts markedly with their much more forgiving attitude toward developing nations that have also refused to participate in the Kyoto regime. As the European Commission put it in yet another communication on climate change:

> The EU has acted on the principle that industrialized nations should take the lead in combating climate change, since those same countries are responsible for the great majority of post-Industrial Revolution emissions, which are at the heart of the global warming problem.[25]

Its position here bears a striking similarity to its stance on the death penalty, the other highly visible issue on which the EU has assumed a global leadership role. Although many developing nations continue to practice capital punishment, the United States has been singled out for special criticism, presumably because the EU believes the United States should know better.[26] This suggests a moralising attitude in EU foreign policy that is also present in its attitude toward combating climate change. This willingness to intrude morality into foreign policy is a relatively new phenomenon for Europeans historically wedded to balance-of-power politics and may reflect an assimilation of America's own moralising proclivities frequently on display during the Cold War, although wedded to a significantly different muse.[27]

The EU believes that the United States, as the richest nation on Earth and historically the largest greenhouse-gas emitter, has a special responsibility to adopt a leadership position on the issue. Developing nations, by contrast, are poor and have the right, endorsed by the EU in numerous policy statements and in documents such as the International Covenant on Economic, Social and Cultural Rights, to develop their economies up to Western standards. Since the cost of reducing emissions could jeopardise or undermine their prospects, the EU believes they should not be asked to do so. Instead, the industrialised nations of the West, the EU and United States pre-eminent among them, have an obligation, presumably a moral one, to shoulder this burden by cutting their own emissions even more than they would otherwise have to. The EU takes the position that in order to achieve the 50% global reduction that may be required to avoid irreversible damage to the global environment, industrialised nations should be prepared to cut their own emissions by 60–80%, making a tough task even tougher.[28] This *noblesse oblige* attitude toward the developing world may also explain why European sympathies on international issues so often rest with the economically disadvantage party, as in the European tendency to support the aspirations of the Palestinian Arabs over Israel.

While the United States has been inclined to see both unfairness and futility in combating global warming without the participation of developing nations, the EU has persuaded itself that Western efforts to reduce emissions will result in more affordable technologies that can be passed on to developing nations, enabling them to successfully reduce their own emissions without sacrificing growth. This tendency to see potential technological benefits in reducing emissions reflects a strain of thinking in the EU that goes back at least to the development of the *Vorsorgeprinzip* in Germany in the early 1980s.[29] Since the EU is particularly dependent on foreign suppliers of fossil fuels, it also sees positive advantage in maximising the percentage of renewable energy it consumes. EU willingness to act unilaterally does have its limits, however. Mindful of the potential competitive disadvantage that European industries could face by unilaterally cutting emissions, the European Commission has proposed levying a carbon tax on those advanced industrial nations who have declined to participate in Kyoto, including pre-eminently, and now that Australia has ratified Kyoto, almost exclusively, the United States.[30] Not surprisingly, Washington has reacted negatively to the threat, charging that the EU is using climate change as a pretext for protectionism.[31]

EU willingness to act unilaterally does have its limits

EU willingness to exempt developing nations from emission-reduction targets can be traced back to the same social-democratic instincts that seek to minimise risk. European support for the right to development is, in essence, a social-levelling policy pitched onto the global stage. This is why the EU is prepared to make larger cutbacks in emissions to compensate for the exemption. The United States, however, qualifies for no such free pass. While the EU hopes that its unilateral effort will demonstrate to Washington that reductions can be accomplished without causing major economic damage, it believes that no such demonstration should be necessary. It is therefore not simply an exercise in prudence but a highly moralistic effort that reflects a willingness to sacrifice while criticising those unprepared to do the same.

Beyond its moral intent, the EU approach to global warming demonstrates the same predilection for enhancing regulatory predictability and avoiding risk that lay behind the creation of the EU itself, although pitched into a global arena. Here the UNFCCC serves as the supranational institutional mechanism for regulating global carbon emissions and, in so doing, reducing the risk of global warming. This is one example of what Robert Kagan has described as the European predilection for establishing a Kantian world order, in which contentious issues are addressed, and potential conflicts resolved, through the establishment of suitably empowered global structures of governance.[32] Kagan construes the establishment of the EU itself as an expression of this tendency. Although Kagan sees in this distinctively European fondness for supranational order a utopian desire for world peace, it is probably more modestly conceived as an effort to manage global risk by recreating the advantages of the social welfare state on a world stage.

Of course, most European nations still behave internationally much of the time as individual nations with individual interests. The widely divergent European responses to the war in Iraq are a prime example of this. Most European foreign policy is still made in national capitals, not in Brussels. Although the same social-democratic proclivities that animate EU regulatory policies are shared by most of its members even when acting as individual nation states, there is no rush to give up national seats at NATO or the OSCE or in the UN. What is true is that on issues like global warming, where the risks involved invite precaution and uniquely or readily lend themselves to institutional regulatory solutions, Europeans are more likely to act in an EU context, pursue global remedies, and in so doing, give expression to their social-democratic roots. As in the EU campaign against the death penalty, the EU approach to global warming says a great deal about how Europeans see the world and what they would like to see done with it.

Notes

1 Byrd–Hagel Resolution, 105th Congress, 1st Session, S. Res. 98.

2 Kyoto Protocol to the United Nations Framework Convention on Climate Change, http://unfccc.int/resource/docs/convkp/kpeng.html.

3 *Ibid.*, p. 20.

4 European Commission, 'Questions and Answers on the European Commission's Proposal for Effort Sharing', http://www.europa-eu-un.org/articles/en/article_7675_en.htm, p. 1.

5 European Commission, 'Boosting Growth and Jobs by Meeting our Climate Change Commitments', http://europa.eu/rapid/pressReleasesAction.do?reference=IP/08/80&format=HTML&aged=0&language=EN&guiLanguage=en.

6 'U.S. Strategy Succeeds in Bali', *Washington Post*, 13 December 2007, p. A24.

7 'A Warming World: China about to Pass U.S. as World's Top Generator of Greenhouse Gases', *San Francisco Chronicle*, 5 March 2007, p. A1.

8 José Manuel Durao Barroso, 'Europe's Climate Change Opportunity', http://europa.eu/rapid/pressReleasesAction.do?reference=SPEECH/08/34&format=html.

9 See, for example, Intergovernmental Panel on Climate Change, *Fourth Assessment Report, Climate Change 2007: Synthesis Report, Summary for Policymakers*, http://www.ipcc.ch/pdf/assessment-report/ar4/syr/ar4_syr_spm.pdf.

10 European Commission, 'Impact Assessment to Limiting Global Climate Change to 2 degrees Celsius: the way ahead for 2020 and beyond', ec.europa.eu/environment/climat/pdf/ia_sec_8.pdf, p. 4. See also parent document at eur-lex.europa.eu/LexUriServ/LexUriServ.do?uri=CELEX:52007DC0002:EN:NOT.

11 European Commission, 'Communication from the Commission on the Precautionary Principle', 2 February 2000, http://ec.europa.eu/dgs/health_consumer/library/pub/pub07_en.pdf, p. 3.

12 'Community policy on the environment ... shall be based on the precautionary principle and on the principles that preventive action should be taken, that environmental damage should as a priority be rectified at source and that the polluter should pay', Treaty on European Union, Article 130r(2), http://eur-lex.europa.eu/en/treaties/dat/11992M/htm/11992M.html.

13 Konrad von Moltke, 'The Precautionary Principle in Environmental Policy', *The Environment Canada Policy Research Seminar Series*, 10 March 2000, p. 1, http://www.ec.gc.ca/seminar/VM_e.html.

14 Andrew Jordan and Timothy O'Riordan, 'The Precautionary Principle in Contemporary Environmental Policy and Politics', prepared for the Wingspread Conference on 'Implementing the Precautionary Principle', 23–25 January 1998, http://www.johnsonfdn.org/conferences/precautionary/jord.html.

15 Jonathan B. Wiener, 'Whose Precaution After All? A Comment on the Comparison and Evolution of Risk Regulatory Systems', *Duke Journal of Comparative and International Law*, vol.13, no. 207, 2003, pp. 207–62, http://www.law.duke.edu/shell/cite.pl?13+Duke+J.+Comp.+&+Int'l+L.+0207. See also Jonathan B. Wiener and Michael D. Rogers, 'Comparing Precaution in the United States and Europe', *Journal of Risk Research*, vol. 5, no. 4, 2002, pp. 317–49, http://eprints.law.duke.edu/1191/.

16 David Vogel, 'The Politics of Risk Regulation in Europe and the United States', *The Yearbook of European Environmental Law*, vol. 3, 2003, p. 11.

17 European Commission, 'Communication on the Precautionary Principle'.

18 European Commission, *Eurobarometer67, Public Opinion in the European Union*, http://ec.europa.eu/public_opinion/archives/eb/eb67/eb67_en.pdf, pp. 161–4.

19 Tony Judt, *Postwar* (New York: The Penguin Press, 2005), p. 361. For another discussion along similar lines see James J. Sheehan, *Where Have All the Soldiers Gone* (New York: Houghton Mifflin Company, 2008), pp. 174–7.

20 David Wilkinson, *Greening the Treaty: Strengthening Environmental Policy in the Treaty of Rome* (London: Institute for European Environmental Policy, 1990), p. 2 (reprinted at http://www.ciesin.org/docs/008-591/008-591.html).

21 David Wilkinson, *Environment and Law* (London: Routledge, 2002), p. 54.

22 R. Daniel Kelemen, 'Globalizing EU Environmental Regulation', paper prepared for conference on Europe and the Management of Globalization, 23 February 2007, Princeton University, p. 2, reprinted at http://www.princeton.edu/~smeunier/Kelemen.doc.

23 *Ibid.*, p. 5.

24 European Commission, 'Questions and Answers'.

25 European Union, Delegation of the European Union to the USA, 'EuFocus, The EU and the Environment', p. 4, http://www.eurunion.org/eu/index.php?option=com_content&task=view&id=55&Itemid=43.

26 John R. Schmidt, 'The EU Campaign Against the Death Penalty', *Survival*, vol. 49, no. 4, Winter 2007–08, pp. 123–34.

27 *Ibid.*, p. 130.

28 European Commission, 'Limiting Global Climate Change ', p. 4.

29 Jordan and O'Riordan, 'The Precautionary Principle', p. 2.

30 Barroso, 'Europe's Climate'.

31 'Carbon Revenues Can Aid Climate Fight – Barroso', Reuters, 21 January 2008, http://www.reuters.com/article/environmentNews/idUSL2160095120080122?pageNumber=3&virtualBrandChannel=0.

32 See section on the origins of modern European foreign policy in Robert Kagan, 'Power and Weakness', *Policy Review*, no. 113, June–July 2002, http://www.hoover.org/publications/policyreview/3460246.html.

Chechnya: Has Moscow Won?

Roland Dannreuther and Luke March

The issue of Chechnya barely featured in the Russian parliamentary and presidential elections of 2007 and 2008. This was in stark contrast with previous elections in which the Chechen conflict was either an embarrassment to be disguised by propaganda or a recognised failure demanding concrete, decisive new action. In 1996, in order to ensure his electoral victory, Boris Yeltsin was all but forced to negotiate a humiliating agreement with Chechen rebel leaders granting them de facto independence. In 1999–2000, the strategic dangers of Islamist extremism and expansionism emanating from a lawless Chechnya were central to Vladimir Putin's presidential campaign. Moscow's subsequent robust military response conferred the mantle of legitimacy on Putin, who had been almost invisible politically a few months earlier. In 2003–04, Putin sought to present his Chechnya policy as an unqualified success, but this meant downplaying ongoing violence, including increasingly cruel terrorist atrocities committed by rebels, which culminated in the horrors of the Beslan siege in September 2004.

By 2007–08, however, things had changed. Certainly, as in previous elections, Russia's state-controlled media poured forth exaggerated claims of success, but this time even respected political scientists were willing to proclaim that:

> the war in Chechnya has ended. We won. The main heroes of this war are its political leaders and also the several thousands of young lads:

Roland Dannreuther and **Luke March** are both Senior Lecturers at the School of Social and Political Studies, University of Edinburgh.

Survival | vol. 50 no. 4 | August–September 2008 | pp. 97–112 DOI 10.1080/00396330802329030

> Chechens, Russians and others, who gave their lives for the territorial integrity of Russia, for the security of the citizens of Russia and for the reduction of the threat of terrorism.[1]

What is more, there was actually some truth in these claims. Although many problems remain in Chechnya, the situation has greatly improved over the last few years. The Russian security forces have had a string of successes in eliminating the most effective and well-known rebel leaders, including Shamil Basaev in 2006, the charismatic 'Che Guevara' of the Chechen resistance. The policy of 'Chechenisation', forcefully promoted by Putin to devolve responsibilities from Russian federal forces to local Chechens, has resulted in the consolidation of President Ramzan Kadyrov's power, and that of his armed formations. Kadyrov might be a brutal ex-bandit, but he has shown sufficient strategic sense and flexibility to win over other former rebels and to gain genuine popular support (albeit mixed with a degree of fear and loathing) from his war-weary population. His public image has also been aided by the fact that substantial federal funds for reconstruction have finally made a marked impact on the ground, and the local economy is showing signs of improvement. The popular appetite for secession has, as a consequence, declined significantly.[2] Russia's success in Chechnya, little recognised in the West, is not just important in itself, but in the way it has structured and legitimated the political changes that Putin has introduced during his presidency. Putin's strategy during the war and the subsequent pacification of Chechnya have helped construct the post-Yeltsin Russian state in a way that has seen the increased centralisation of power and the promotion of authoritarian state structures. Moreover, the policy of 'Chechenisation' and the associated empowerment of Ramzan Kadyrov as Russia's faithful proxy in the North Caucasus, while providing short-term gains, might also have created a political Frankenstein, to use the colourful image of one commentator – Kadyrov's over-zealous loyalty and eagerness to act as Russia's proxy in the North Caucasus has raised wider concerns over an unrequited Chechen expansionist agenda.[3] Further doubts exist about how replicable the 'Chechen model' is in the rest of the North Caucasus, where instability and radicalisation are increasing. Some question whether the broader legacy of the conflict in Chechnya, and its political instrumentalisation by the Kremlin to promote a more authoritarian and self-assertive nationalist state, might have longer-term damaging consequences, not least for the West's relations with Russia.

Putin's Caucasian 'war on terror'

It is no overestimation to say that the North Caucasus defined and moulded Putin's presidency: his democratic legitimacy was indeed 'forged in war'.[4] It was in the North Caucasus that Putin's prestige and popularity were initially grounded, and he reaped the rewards of a military campaign that was deemed by most Russians to be both necessary and successful. Remarkably, his popularity never waned, except briefly after the Beslan hostage-taking incident in September 2004. Putin always understood the critical importance of perceptions of victory and success in Russia's 'war on terror' in the North Caucasus, noting as he came to power that 'my mission, my historic mission – it sounds pompous, but it is true – is to resolve the situation in the North Caucasus'.[5] The fact that in 2007 he and his associates could reasonably declare that victory had been achieved provided a vital source of legitimacy for the distinctly less free and more authoritarian political structures that Putin had constructed in the intervening period.

It is notable that Putin consciously framed his response to the conflict in Chechnya so as to put clear psychological distance between his presidency and that of his predecessor, Boris Yeltsin. For Putin, the North Caucasus was reflective of the larger problems facing post-Soviet Russia – the threat of disintegration, the perceived penetration and subversion by foreign forces, the weakening of state structures as a result of criminality and terror, and Russia's basic inability to stand up for itself and secure its core national objectives. There is no doubt that Putin, whose background was in the KGB, was deeply offended by the chaotic state of Russia in the late 1990s, of which the North Caucasus was the most flagrant example. Yeltsin's unpopularity at this time reflected broader popular revulsion with the state of the nation. The succession of bomb attacks on apartment blocks in Russian cities in September 1999, which caused over 300 deaths, had a traumatic impact on Russians, not unlike that felt by Americans after the attacks of

11 September 2001.[6] This provided the ideal strategic moment to respond with decisive action.

There are certain parallels between Putin's response to the 1999 events and the way in which US President George W. Bush used the 11 September attacks to frame a radical strategic shift in US security policy. Like Putin's implicit representation of the Yeltsin period, Bush sought to characterise the Clinton era as one defined by weakness, indecision, pusillanimity and a lack of moral probity. Instead of meekly appeasing Iraq or lobbing an intermittent cruise missile into the country, as Republicans accused Clinton of doing, Bush launched a full-scale invasion as a part of his 'war on terror'.[7] Putin's 1999 intervention in Chechnya, unlike the earlier Chechen war (1994–96), was similarly defined purely as a counter-terrorist operation.[8] Like the US 'war on terror' that would begin two years later, Russia's second Chechen campaign had new rules of engagement.

Russia's second Chechen campaign had new rules of engagement

First, as a counterpoint to the perceived constant political meddling of politicians in the Yeltsin period, Putin gave the military carte blanche to conduct the war in such a way as to ensure a decisive victory. Compared with the occasionally tragicomic evolution of the first war, the second campaign was far more professional and effective. This helped ease the deep sense of alienation in the Russian military caused by the conviction that politicians had 'pulled the rug from under their feet' and denied them a military victory in the earlier campaign.[9]

Second, the constant mantra of the second war was that there would be no negotiation with the 'terrorists'. Putin resolved any remaining ambiguities on the issue of independence by confirming that it was not open for discussion, and established uncompromising new rules for dealing with major terrorist incidents. During the hostage crises in Budennovsk in 1995 and Kizlyar in 1996, the sight of leading government figures negotiating with hostage-takers, agreeing to their demands and even facilitating their escape presented an image of a Russia abjectly humiliated. When Putin was confronted with similar challenges, most notably the hostage crises in the

Moscow 'Dubrovka' theatre in 2002 and in Beslan in 2004, he brooked no negotiation and was willing to use deadly force (toxic gas in Moscow, flamethrowers in Beslan) to end the sieges, even at the cost of many innocent lives.

A third new rule was that the Chechens were no longer to have the 'oxygen' of media exposure. Unlike in the first war, the international media was given almost no freedom to report on developments in the second. In addition, the Russian government paid little or no attention to international criticisms of their actions. Indeed, Russia's attitude was one of barely disguised contempt, and any criticism was interpreted as further evidence of Western hypocrisy. As Sergei Ivanov, the Russian defence minister, memorably put it:

> to those who recommend that we launch talks with Maskhadov, I always invite them to start talks with Mullah Omar. It's the same thing. Currently on Chechen territory there are around 1,200 to 1,300 active rebels, uncompromising bandits, with whom you can only have one conversation – their destruction.[10]

Probably the most important innovation of Putin's approach to Chechnya was his decision to assume full responsibility for the Chechen campaign. This contrasted with Yeltsin, who habitually sought to devolve responsibility and hide from any unpleasant repercussions emanating from the North Caucasus. It was this decision which, perhaps more than anything else, moulded the popular conception of Putin as a decisive and strong leader. It provided the popular ballast for subsequent decisions made to counter what were perceived as the root causes of anarchy in the region, such as excessive federalisation, the devolution of power and the political prerogatives assumed by the super-rich, resulting in Putin's successive rolling back of regional autonomies and the persecution of the politicised 'oligarchs' by the state and power ministries. (The most famous and notorious of the oligarchs was Boris Berezovsky, whose links to the Chechen separatists made him vulnerable to the claim that he had the blood of innocent Russians on his hands.[11]) Ultimately, the North Caucasus became the crucible in which the authoritarian state structures established by Putin were forged. This was made explicit in the aftermath of Beslan, when gubernatorial elections were abolished and the electoral system was centralised in the name of anti-terrorism.[12] Nevertheless, Putin's highly personalised engagement with Chechnya and the North Caucasus was far from risk-free. There was always the possibility that the conflict would not be successfully ended. Indeed, by 2005 the dominant view among independent analysts was that Putin's Chechen policy had been an unmitigated disaster.[13] While Chechnya was partially subjugated, a succession of deadly mass-casualty terrorist attacks had been unleashed throughout Russia. Similarly, the pacification of Chechnya appeared only to spread the problem of Islamist extremism to the rest of the North Caucasus, and even beyond. Both Western and Russian critics began to talk about a wide-scale 'Islamic threat' to Russia.[14] By the end of 2006, however, such alarmist scenarios had largely faded.[15] The causes of this certainly included some lucky breaks for Russia, of which the killing of both rebel President Aslan Maskhadov in 2005 and Shamil Basaev in 2006 were most notable. The loss of these key rebel leaders undoubtedly depressed the morale of the resistance. Simple war fatigue was also important, as people lost their appetite for secession and increasingly opted for peace and stability. High oil prices and Russia's economic regeneration also played a vital part, providing the funds for reconstruction which were never previously available or which were simply siphoned off. And in 2004 Putin appointed a reasonably competent representative, Dmitry Kozak, to Russia's southern federal district, who succeeded in ousting some of the most corrupt and ineffective leaders of the region and brought some order and transparency, albeit limited, to its clannish, neopatrimonial practices, which had long been the source of much resentment and violence.[16]

Finally, Putin's policy of 'Chechenisation' undoubtedly played a significant role in improving Russia's fortunes in the Caucasus. Central to this policy was the devolution of power to Ramzan Kadyrov.

The 'Ramzanisation' of Chechnya

Although Putin strongly supported the use of military force in Chechnya, he became increasingly aware of its limits. The evidence of the previous war was that military counter-insurgency operations, which inevitably become indiscriminate and cause extensive collateral damage, only exacerbate the situation unless married with a political process and a policy of devolving power and providing 'local ownership' of the political settlement. The problem during the Yeltsin period was that policy oscillated variously between negotiating with the rebels, promoting pro-Russian Chechen leaders who had no popular base, and seeking a purely military solution. In the early part of the second war, Putin faced the opposite problem of potentially too few options, since the military leadership was determined to pursue a purely military strategy. In practice, Putin gave the military free rein until the 2002 Moscow theatre siege, when it became clear that the Russian military lacked the sophisticated counter-terrorist capabilities needed for an efficient military response to a large-scale, mass-casualty terrorist offensive.[17] The only practical alternative was to pursue a political path and localise or de-internationalise the conflict by gaining a genuinely pro-Russian support base within Chechnya. This would require devolving both political and security responsibilities to the Chechens themselves, including those who could be tempted to switch sides from the rebels, a strategy that much of the Russian military opposed.

The choice of Ahmad Kadyrov, the father of Ramzan and former mufti of Chechnya, as the designated pro-Russian leader was astute. Kadyrov had distinguished himself, in comparison to previous 'puppet' leaders promoted by Moscow, by having supported and fought on the rebels' side in the first war. Indeed, it was Kadyrov who as mufti had declared holy war (*gazawat*) against Russia in 1995.[18] However, he had become disillusioned with the rebel movement as it increasingly fell under the influence of Salafist and extremist Islamic viewpoints, which were antithetical to his more traditionalist and Sufi-influenced religious stance. In June 2000 he was appointed by Putin as the republic's head of administration. Power was more seriously devolved in 2003, when there was a (manipulated) referendum on a new constitution, paving the way for presidential elections in 2004, which confirmed Kadyrov's power. There was also a devolution of security responsibilities, first from the Ministry of Defence to the Federal Security Services (FSB) and then to the Ministry of Internal Affairs (MVD).

As federal forces declined in numbers, the local armed formations loyal to Ahmad Kadyrov and his clan, under the command of Kadyrov's son Ramzan, were given increasing powers, including control of a number of the informal but lucrative economic resources and markets of the war economy.[19] This process of 'Chechenisation' was nearly derailed by the assassination of Ahmad Kadyrov shortly after the presidential elections in June 2004. But power was retained by the Kadyrov clan, with Ramzan becoming de facto strongman of the republic despite the election of a new president, Alu Alkhanov. In 2007, even this partial balancing was removed by Putin's decision to force Alkhanov's resignation and promote Ramzan to the presidency. As one commentator put it, 'Chechenisation' had become in practice 'Ramzanisation'.[20] What has this process of 'Ramzanisation' achieved? First, it has been a key point in the narrative of progress and success that has been critical to Putin's consolidation of power. By the time of the 2007–08 elections, Chechnya was consistently presented as a rosy reconstruction site, with official websites such as www.chechnyatoday.com highlighting the miraculous rebuilding of the Chechen capital Grozny under a benevolent Ramzan, and even touting its viability as a tourist destination. Moreover, Ramzan has enjoyed a 'younger son' personality cult analogous to that surrounding the more senior and paternal Putin. Given Ramzan's background, this is an impressive example of what is called 'political technology' in Russia and 'public relations' elsewhere. But Kadyrov is proving to be a more effective and capable leader than his unprepossessing exterior might suggest. The sources of his power certainly include brutality and repression, involving a pervasive recourse to torture, and Chechnya's reconstruction has a definite Potemkin-village element. But unlike earlier Russian-proxy leaders, Ramzan has been reasonably efficient in getting insurgents to switch sides by striking the necessary balance between inducements (encouraging insurgents to join his security forces, the so-called *kadyrovtsy*, and benefit from the associated spoils) and threats (to insurgents' families). Along with the general demoralisation of the resistance, particularly due to the assas-

Chechnya's reconstruction has a Potemkin-village element

sinations of Maskhadov and Basaev, this has markedly reduced the levels of insecurity within the republic.

Russia's faithful client?

There are clear dangers for Moscow, however, in nurturing this enthusiastic proxy in the North Caucasus. The first is that this devolution of power could result in Moscow ultimately losing its influence in the region. Senior figures in Putin's administration, including Dmitry Kozak and Igor Sechin, Putin's deputy chief of staff, have privately recommended replacing Kadyrov and have expressed fear that he might be accumulating too much power.[21] Many *siloviki* (security-forces officials), including FSB head Nikolai Patrushev, are concerned that 'Chechenisation' represents a victory for the rebels, a way of gaining independence through intimating loyalty rather than pursuing rebellion. Traditionally, the Russian security services have sought to prevent such concentrations of local power by classic tactics of divide and rule. In Chechnya, this policy is evident in the two pro-Russian Chechen battalions, *Zapad* and *Vostok*, which are under the control of Chechen family-clans independent of Kadyrov. However, Kadyrov is waging a skilful and relentless campaign to consolidate power and undermine alternative Chechen and federal centres of power. A favoured tactic is to claim that non-Chechen security groups like the *Vostok* battalion (controlled by the Yamadaev brothers), or the notorious investigation unit of the Russian interior-ministry forces, are responsible for human-rights violations and should therefore be disbanded.[22] Assassination and other violent measures supplement these softer tactics. As one Russian commentator has remarked, for Kadyrov, 'the same methods are used for dealing with enemies, fighting with arms, as for unarmed political opponents'.[23] Relations between federal forces in Chechnya and Ramzan's *kadyrovtsy* are understandably hostile. At the same time, Kadyrov is locked in a long-standing dispute with Moscow over the distribution of the revenues from Chechen oil and the location of oil refineries.[24]

Putin's judgement, supported by influential presidential-administration deputy head Vladimir Surkov, was that Chechnya needed a strongman, that Kadyrov filled this requirement, and that the neopatrimonial and personal links between Putin and Kadyrov would ensure his fidelity. Whether this will remain the case under Medvedev's presidency, and whether intra-Chechen resistance to his centralisation can be contained, are open questions. In April 2008, a large-scale gun battle between forces loyal to Kadyrov and the Yamadaev brothers reportedly resulted in 18 dead.[25] And Medvedev allegedly shares with Kozak a distaste for lawless despots. However, Medvedev's warm words to Kadyrov on their first official meeting indicated that Moscow still needs Ramzan, at least for the short term. Ramzan, in turn, has been obsequiously loyal to his Moscow patrons, emphasising that Chechnya's successes result both from Russian and Chechen joint efforts, and Putin's personal input.[26] But even if he remains loyal, Kadyrov still presents a challenge. The key question is whether his clearly expansive ambitions will be satisfied with the territorial limits of the Chechen Republic. The significant resources, both economic and military, which have been dispersed to Chechnya have created a sense that Grozny is becoming the new centre of Russian power in the North Caucasus. There is also a strong belief amongst many Chechens of the legitimacy of a 'Greater Chechnya'. This would incorporate both Dagestan, another Muslim territory that would provide a strategic link to the sea, and Ingushetia, which shares with Chechnya a *Vainakh* heritage, a history of unity during the Soviet period, and a recognition that a combined Chechen–Ingush political force might be better able to resolve the dispute over the Prigorodnyi district in North Ossetia to the advantage of the Ingush. Shamil Basaev, the charismatic Chechen rebel leader, was unabashedly forthcoming about such Chechen ambitions, casting them as an Islamic ideal: 'we are fighting for the proclamation of an Islamic empire and the establishment of a greater Chechen empire in Chechnya, Dagestan and later Ingushetia'.[27] It was not surprising that Kadyrov raised regional hackles when he confirmed that Chechnya's security and law-enforcement agencies were ready to offer whatever help they could to their 'brothers' in Ingushetia, and both Dagestan and Ingushetia have vocally rejected Ramzan's advances. Still, Kadyrov has not hesitated to

Ramzan has been obsequiously loyal to his Moscow patrons

intervene further afield: the Chechen president has 25 official representatives in Russia's regions.[28] However, Ramzan's forays outside domestic politics (such as his closure of the Danish Refugee Council in retaliation for the publication in Denmark of controversial cartoons of the Prophet Muhammad), were viewed in Moscow as exceeding his authority.[29] Many in the liberal intelligentsia remain convinced that Ramzan was involved in the murder of the investigative journalist Anna Politovskaya, one of the most vocal critics of his rule.

Russia: the consequences of success

Russian policies towards Chechnya have succeeded, far more than is generally acknowledged outside Russia, in many of their aims. The republic is now relatively calm, is gradually being rebuilt, and is a loyal member of the Russian Federation. Chechnya's leader Ramzan Kadyrov, although a divisive figure, has succeeded in presenting himself as Russia's most faithful servant in the North Caucasus. Chechnya has ceased to be the constant thorn in Russia's soft underbelly that it was following the collapse of the Soviet Union.

However, the longer-term legacy and consequences of Russia's struggle to reassert sovereignty over Chechnya are not easily predicted. Moscow now finds itself in the curious position of depending on its own appointed proxy for one of its few regional success stories. Moreover, this proxy seems poised to cause trouble for Medvedev. Kadyrov's interventions in regional and even federal policies have done little to smooth relations, while the overspill of the Chechen conflict has contributed to wider regional destabilisation. Whether the Kremlin is capable of removing Kadyrov – assuming it even wants, or dares, to – without reigniting conflict within Chechnya may be doubted, even if he inspires deep distaste in some governing circles.

Elsewhere in the North Caucasus, the 'Chechen model' has not proved easily exportable. The problem with the model is that it depends critically on the effectiveness and capacities of those allies promoted by Moscow and on their ability to recreate Kadyrov's combination of autonomy, local support, guile and sheer brutality. The situation in neighbouring Ingushetia is evidence of the model's limitations: the Kremlin-backed leader, Murat

Zyazikov, is undoubtedly loyal, but is widely viewed as corrupt and weak and lacks local-elite backing. He has struggled to contain the increasing instability and radicalisation within the republic. Despite attempts by regional leaders like Kozak to remove Zyazikov, Putin's personal patronage never wavered, suggesting that Moscow prefers loyalty to effectiveness. This is a risky preference as Moscow increasingly faces an Islamist opposition throughout the North Caucasus which is ever more dispersed, decentralised and uncontrollable, and which has significant mobilisation potential through the exploitation of local dissatisfaction with the lack of socioeconomic and political opportunities.

Against this background, Putin's attempts to use the crises in the North Caucasus to stir up nationalism and reinforce the consolidation of power creates a more diffuse but perhaps an even more intractable set of problems. Not only does increased nationalism raise barriers to the greater integration of Muslim communities within Russia, a focus on external threats and a call for national unity against territorial disintegration denies Russia a sufficiently flexible platform from which to engage with many of the direct causes of its Caucasian headaches, principally issues of political governance and representation. Moreover, the promotion of a defensive nationalist mindset, which interprets local difficulties as proceeding from the deliberate designs of hostile foreign forces, has bred an anti-Western popular sentiment that has made Russia's engagement with its neighbours, such as Ukraine and Georgia, and with the West more generally, considerably more antagonistic and hostile. It is an open question how far Medvedev, whose general outlook appears to be more moderate and more pro-Western, will be able to reign in the forces of nationalism that Putin has unleashed, assuming he even has the autonomy and power to do so.

Moscow currently has two alternatives in the North Caucasus. The first is to appoint several Kadyrov-like strongmen with license to govern their republics autonomously and autocratically. This option offers the prospect of regional pacification but comes with the dangers of increasing corruption and poor governance, consolidating the de facto separation of the North Caucasus from the Russian Federation, driving opposition underground and potentially reigniting terrorist campaigns beyond the region. However, even were the Kremlin to find leaders with the right 'qualities', experiences with Kadyrov are unlikely to convince notoriously control-hungry Kremlin elites to contemplate 'Chechenisation' on a wider scale. Nevertheless, the obvious alternative, greater regional devolution, transparency and democracy is, unless there is a quite astonishing volte-face under Medvedev, off the agenda for the foreseeable future. This leaves the Kremlin with the (quite possibly forlorn) hope that its current policies of ever greater regional subsidies and military presence combined with the occasional rotation of regional cadres will placate the region and not further exacerbate both elite and military corruption and local grievances, as they have so often done in the past.

Notes

1 Sergei Markov, 'Zadachi Ramzana Kadyrova', *Izvestiya*, 19 March 2007.

2 For an overview of these developments see Anna Matveeva, 'Chechnya: Dynamics of War and Peace', *Problems of Post-Communism*, vol. 54, no. 3, November–December 2007, pp. 3–17. For a more critical account, see James Hughes, 'The Peace Process in Chechnya', in Richard Sakwa (ed.), *Chechnya: From Past to Future* (London: Anthem Press, 2005).

3 Pavel K. Baev, 'Has Russia Achieved a Victory in its War against Terror?', *PONARS Policy Memo*, no. 415, December 2006, p. 1.

4 Peter Rutland, 'Putin's Path to Power', *Post-Soviet Affairs*, vol. 16, no. 4, December 2000, p. 326.

5 Quoted in Natalia Gevorkian, A.V. Kolesnikov and Natalia Timakova, *Ot pervogo litsa* (Moscow: Vagrius, 2000), p. 133.

6 For accounts of the impact of the Russian attacks, see Dmitri V. Trenin and Aleksei V. Malashenko, *Russia's Restless Frontier: the Chechnya Factor in Post-Soviet Russia* (Washington DC: Carnegie Endowment for International Peace, 2004), p. 37; and John Russell, 'Terrorists, Bandits, Spooks and Thieves: Russian Demonisation of the Chechens before and since 9/11', *Third World Quarterly*, vol. 26, no. 1, March 2005, p. 109.

7 This became doctrinally encoded in the US National Security Strategy of 2002. For the text of the strategy and commentary on this, see Roland Dannreuther and John Peterson (eds), *Security Strategy and Transatlantic Relations* (London: Routledge, 2007).

8 Pavel K. Baev, 'Instrumentalizing Counterterrorism for Regime Consolidation in Putin's Russia', *Studies in Conflict and Terrorism*, vol. 27, no. 4, April 2004, pp. 337–8.

9 For an interesting memoir containing reflections on this from one of the leading Russian generals, see G. Troshev, *Moya Voina: chechenskii*

dnevnik okopnogo generala (Moscow: Vagrius, 2000).

10 'Interview with Sergei Ivanov, Minister of Defence of the Russian Federation', Agence France Presse, 16 July 2003. For a good general assessment of Russia's Chechnya discourse, see Edwin Bacon and Bettina Renz, *Securitising Russia: The Domestic Policies of Putin* (Manchester: Manchester University Press, 2006), ch. 3.

11 For an evaluation of the claim that Berezovskii was lobbying for separatist Chechen interests see Trenin and Malashenko, 'Russia's Restless Frontier', p. 23. Berezovskii is now based in London and the British government's refusal to extradite him is one of the main causes of UK–Russian diplomatic hostility.

12 Dov Lynch, 'The Enemy at the Gate', Russia after Beslan', *International Affairs*, vol. 81, no. 1, January 2005, pp. 141–61.

13 See, for example, John P. Dunlop and Rajan Menon, 'Chaos in the North Caucasus and Russia's Future', *Survival*, vol. 48, no. 2, Summer 2006, pp. 97–114; Mark Kramer, 'Instability in the North Caucasus and the Political Implications for the Russian–Chechen War', *PONARS Policy Memo*, no. 380, December 2005.

14 See, for example, Gordon M. Hahn, *Russia's Islamic Threat* (New Haven, CT: Yale University Press, 2007); Mikhail Deliagin, *Rossiia posle Putina: Neizbezhna li v Rossii 'oranzhevo-zelenaia' revolutsiia?* (Moscow: Veche, 2005); and I.V. Zhuravlev, S. A. Mel'kov and L.I. Shershnev, *Put' vionov Allakha: Islam i politika Rossii* (Moscow: Reche, 2004).

15 See, for example, Brian D. Taylor, 'Putin's "Historic Mission": State-Building and the Power Ministries in the North Caucasus', *Problems of Post-Communism*, vol. 54, no. 6, November–December 2006, pp. 3–16; and the markedly more optimistic report (compared to the one provided at end of 2005) in Mark Kramer, 'The Changing Context of Russian Federal Policy in the North Caucasus', *PONARS Policy Memo*, no. 416, December 2006.

16 For the best account of neopatrimonial structures of power in the North Caucasus, see Georgi M. Deluguian, *Bourdieu's Secret Admirer in the Caucasus: A World-System Biography* (Chicago, IL: Chicago University Press, 2003).

17 Pavel K. Baev, 'Chechnya and the Russian Military: A War too Far?', in Richard Sakwa, *Chechnya: From Past to Future* (London: Anthem Press, 2005), p. 123.

18 John Russell, *Chechnya – Russia's 'War on Terror'* (London: Routledge, 2007), p. 59.

19 For a discussion of how taking over these markets involved clashes with federal military and interior forces, see Aleksandr Kots and Andrei Rodkin, 'The Ambush', *Komsomolskaya Pravda*, 3 March 2003.

20 Baev, 'Has Russia Achieved a Victory in its War against Terror?', p. 2.

21 Kramer, 'The Changing Context of Russian Federal Policy', p. 4.

22 Andrei Smirnov, 'Ramzan Kadyrov Targets the Yamadaev Brothers', *Chechnya Weekly*, 13 March 2008.

23 Vadim Rechkalov, 'Real'nyi portret Ramzana Kadyrova', *Moskovskii Komsomlets*, 24–29 January 2007.

24 Interview with Ramzan Kadyrov, *Izvestiya*, 13 July 2007.

25 Andrei Smirnov, 'Yamadaev vs Kadyrov: The Kremlin's Quandary with Chechnya', *Chechnya Weekly*, 17 April 2008.

26 *Interv'yu Prezidenta Chechenskoi Respubliki R. A. Kadyrova telekanalu 'Russia Today'*, 1 February 2008, http://www.ramzan-kadyrov.ru/smi.php.

27 *Al-Aman*, 17 September 1999, quoted in Domitilla Sagramoso, 'Violence and Conflict in the Russian North Caucasus', *International Affairs*, vol. 83, no. 4, July 2007, p. 697.

28 N.S. Nukhazhiev, 'Speech at Conference Dedicated to the First Anniversary of R.A. Kadyrov's Accession to the Presidency of the Chechen Republic', www.chechenombudsman.ru/info/8.htm.

29 'Kadyrov, Ramzan', Lenta.ru Lentapedia, http://www.lenta.ru/lib/14161090/full.htm, 18 January 2008.

Separatism and Democracy in the Caucasus

Nina Caspersen

If Kosovo is recognised, Abkhazia will be recognised in the course of three days.

Sergei Bagapsh, president of Abkhazia[1]

Unrecognised states, pseudo states, separatist states or de facto states are entities that have achieved de facto independence, often through warfare, but not international recognition.[2] Examples include Nagorno-Karabakh, Abkhazia, Northern Cyprus, Somaliland, Tamil Eelam and Transdniestr. Although the odds are against them, these entities maintain aspirations for *de jure* independence. However much globalisation, the erosion of the state and the increasing irrelevance of territory dominate international-relations discourse, statehood remains the top prize: it legitimises the struggle for independence, offers protection for inhabitants, and confers prestige and power on leaders. This is because, as Dov Lynch has argued, in the international system, 'there are states and there is little else'.[3] The recent recognition of Kosovo's independence has been followed with great interest in other de facto states whose leaders hope it is a precedent-setting case of recognition of an autonomous province against the expressed wish of its 'parent state'. As the former president of Nagorno-Karabakh, Arkady Ghukasian, put it, 'if the world community is ready to recognize the independence of … Kosovo, I think it will be very hard for them to explain why they don't recognize Nagorno-Karabakh'.[4]

Nina Caspersen is a lecturer in the Department of Politics and International Relations at Lancaster University.

Survival | vol. 50 no. 4 | August–September 2008 | pp. 113–136 DOI 10.1080/00396330802329014

Such statements have been accompanied by a change in the legitimising strategy adopted by the leaders of unrecognised states. In the past, their claims to independence were based primarily on the right to national self-determination, but increasingly this argument has been supplemented by an emphasis on 'earned sovereignty'.[5] Appeals for recognition based purely on national self-determination have always been severely disadvantaged, even in the heyday of rhetorical support for national self-determination following the First World War. Consequently, unrecognised states have from the outset combined self-determination arguments, focused on communal identity and historic continuity, with a claim to a 'remedial' right to secession, based on alleged human-rights violations.[6] Recently, however, these aspiring states have caught on to what they perceive as a normative change in the international arena; they take as their point of reference the 'supervised independence' of Kosovo and the general emphasis on democratisation in, especially, US foreign policy,[7] and conclude from this that recognition might be awarded to entities that have succeeded in building effective, democratic institutions. These entities now argue that they have proven their viability as democratic states and thereby *earned* their sovereignty.

Scott Pegg argues that such a legitimising strategy actually harks back to traditional views of statehood, and that by focusing on their capacity to govern, these entities are 'playing yesterday's game'.[8] The capacity to govern was central to the 1933 Montevideo Convention on Rights and Duties of States, according to which a state should posses (1) a permanent population; (2) a defined territory; (3) a government and (4) the capacity to enter into relations with other states.[9] Pegg's view, however, misses some important differences: the new strategy contains a strong focus on democratisation and values more generally, which is not contained in the traditional view. Through the processes of state-building and democratisation, unrecognised entities are announcing that they share hegemonic international values ('not only are we the victims; we are the good guys, we are like you') and do not, therefore, constitute a security threat.

The internal dynamics of unrecognised states remain under-analysed; most research has focused on relations between the entities and their (*de jure*) parent states. While the issue of state-building has received rudimentary attention,[10] the proclaimed adherence to democratic values, and the accompanying process of democratisation, has not been systematically analysed.[11] What effect has this shift in emphasis had on unrecognised states? Has it affected the internal dynamics of these states, or is it merely a rhetorical ploy to disguise criminalised badlands? Do states have any grounds for hoping that 'earned sovereignty' is indeed an emerging international norm? An analysis of the democratisation process in two specific cases, Nagorno-Karabakh and Abkhazia, does much to reveal the complexities of recent trends in secessionist territories. In the Soviet federal system, Abkhazia was an autonomous republic within Georgia, while Nagorno-Karabakh was an autonomous region with Azerbaijan. Conflicts over the status of these territories have a long history, but outright war was sparked by the collapse of the Soviet Union in 1991. Ceasefires were signed in 1994, and since then a situation of 'no war, no peace' has prevailed.[12] The Abkhaz de facto authorities control the main part of what was the autonomous region of Abkhazia (all territory north of the Inguri River), while the Nagorno-Karabakh authorities control most of the territory of the autonomous region as well as seven surrounding districts. Both entities initially based their claims to independence on the right to national self-determination, but now focus on their self-proclaimed success in building viable, democratic institutions. Their experience calls into question the prevailing image of unrecognised states and shows that while state-building and democratisation is unlikely to lead to international recognition, these processes have had a significant impact on statelets' internal dynamics, presenting an opportunity for conflict resolution and for engaging with these entities.

Outright war was sparked by the Soviet Union's collapse

Criminal badlands?

The image of unrecognised states that dominates in the media, in foreign ministries and in academia is overwhelmingly negative. Unrecognised states are commonly viewed as criminalised, warlord-controlled, ethnic fiefdoms that constitute a risk to individual, regional and perhaps even international

security. Vladimir Kolossov and John O'Loughlin, for example, argue that these entities are 'predicated on criminal or quasi-criminal organisations, frequently specialising in the production and sale of drugs, as well as the illegal traffic of weapons and in the laundering of "dirty money"'.[13] Other analysts add human trafficking and the smuggling of radioactive material to this list of security threats.[14] Such sentiments are echoed by the parent states of these entities, who describe them as little more than criminal badlands: Georgian President Mikheil Saakashvili, for example, asserts that Abkhazia's leaders 'have profited from illegal smuggling and contraband [and] now threaten to draw us all into conflict'.[15] As Lynch argues, unrecognised states are typically dismissed as criminal no-man's-lands or as the likewise criminalised puppets of external states (Russia in the case of Abkhazia and Armenia in the case of Nagorno-Karabakh).[16]

Part of the explanation for this negative image can be found in the framework used for analysing these entities. Much of the literature on unrecognised states has readily adopted the 'greed thesis', as presented by authors such as Paul Collier,[17] who argue that opportunistic elites in these entities have an interest in sustaining conflicts, as this allows them to make considerable sums in the 'shadow economy'. As Walter Kemp puts it, 'in many cases the intractability of these conflicts has more to do with the inability to break vested interests than with the difficulty of brokering a political settlement'.[18]

Moreover, international-relations theory often posits a dichotomy between the rational and the meaningful, as covered by the sovereignty principle, and the dangerous and anarchic,[19] with unrecognised states being perceived as examples of the latter. The dominance of this negative image strengthens the case for non-recognition as, quite apart from the question of the inviolability of borders, de facto states are deemed undesirable entities that constitute a security threat.

There is certainly some truth to this negative image: shadow economies, weak institutions and warlords did play a significant role following the cessation of violence in Abkhazia and Nagorno-Karabakh, and continue to dominate in some areas. For example, the Abkhaz authorities do not fully control all of the territory they lay claim to,[20] and the Gali region in particular is riven by crime and violence.[21] In Nagorno-Karabakh, the former army commander, Samvel Babayan, controlled not only the armed forces but also large parts of the shadow economy until his dismissal in 1999.[22] However, the image of unrecognised states as anarchical badlands is often overplayed: they *are* generally weak, poor and corrupt, but this is not all that different from the countries of which they are formally a part. Pål Kolstø argues that virtually all unrecognised states 'have a large shadow economy, often with intimate links to top state leaders', but this is also true for many of their parent states.[23] The popular image of criminalised badlands may have been a truer reflection of the situation immediately after the cessation of warfare, but developments in the situation of 'no war, no peace' have made it increasingly outdated. Processes of state-building and democratisation in Nagorno-Karabakh and Abkhazia have resulted in significant internal changes which present both constraints and opportunities for negotiators in peace talks.

Of course, building a state, or what looks like a state, is imperative when making a claim to independent statehood. In both Nagorno-Karabakh and Abkhazia, the first priority following the ceasefires was, consequently, the building of state institutions. The proclaimed adherence to democratic values gained prominence only later.

State-building

Considerable disagreement exists over the extent to which unrecognised states have managed to build effective institutions, beyond the more symbolic attributes of statehood. Charles King gives one of the more positive assessments when he argues:

> the territorial separatists of the early 1990s have become the state builders of the early 2000s, creating de facto countries whose ability to field armed forces, control their own territory, educate their children, and maintain local economies is about as well developed as that of the recognized states of which they are still notionally a part.[24]

Pegg similarly argues that these entities do not lack much in terms of the traditional, empirical criteria for statehood: they function, more or less, as effective governing authorities over particular territorial areas.[25] Others, however, are more sceptical and see the entities largely as 'failing states'. Lynch points to Abkhazia, among other cases, arguing that 'they may have the institutional fixtures of statehood, but they cannot provide for its substance'.[26] Kolstø agrees, saying 'the modal tendency ... is deficient state-building'. He argues that the term 'quasi-state' is appropriate, since this is the category most of these states would fall into were they ever to be recognised. [27]

There is undoubtedly great variation within the group of unrecognised states and, of the two cases analysed here, Nagorno-Karabakh has been more successful in building effective institutions. This has been due in large measure to the very substantial financial support provided by Armenia and the sizeable Armenian diaspora. Nevertheless, both Nagorno-Karabakh and Abkhazia can point to some noteworthy achievements. Both have avoided what is referred to as the 'Chechen syndrome' – infighting between rival warlords and military forces – and have also made steps towards overcoming the 'post-war syndrome', or the continued dominance of military forces, including in the political and economic realm. In the first years after the cessation of violence, Samvel Babayan, played a dominant role in the entity's politics, but was dismissed as defence minister in 1999 and was arrested the following year for an alleged assassination attempt against the Karabakh president. Allowing some time to lapse between Babayan's dismissal and his arrest avoided a backlash from the armed forces and put civilian leaders firmly in control.[28] Nevertheless, the army should still be regarded as a veto player when it comes to the future of Nagorno-Karabakh. In Abkhazia, the army has always been weaker and has not taken the same role in internal politics, although the veterans' association Amtsakhara is a powerful player.[29]

The two entities have also made progress in terms of institution building. This has been frustrated by the destruction caused by the war, but aided by the pre-existence of institutions from the Soviet era: not everything had to be built from scratch. Beyond establishing the symbolic attributes of statehood, such as a flag and a national anthem, both states have built the necessary organs of government, such as armed forces, police and a court system, and are able to provide some basic public services, including education and health services.[30] Even Abkhazia, which still struggles to maintain order and provide basic services, has, according to the International Crisis Group, 'taken significant steps to produce a sense of normality' and 'has been establishing the institutions of an independent state'.[31] Some may counter that this state-building is largely confined to the capital, but this is true for the parent states as well.

Thus, unrecognised states are not necessarily 'failed states' in the sense of lacking control over their territory, or failing to provide basic public services. Indeed, some of these entities have all the attributes of statehood *except* external recognition. These unrecognised entities are better functioning than one might expect, and their relative success in state-building is certainly something which is emphasised by their leaders in their claims to independence. Natella Akaba, an Abkhaz leader, when asked why Abkhazia should be recognised, argued that it has 'proved its viability' as a state.[32] The speaker of the Karabakh parliament similarly contends that Nagorno-Karabakh has 'a serious basis for the international recognition of our sovereignty', noting that 'we have held free elections for 16 years, law-enforcement bodies are formed, powers are divided, [and the] army is under civil control'.[33]

Unrecognised states are not necessarily 'failed states'

This emphasis on viability should not, however, obscure the fact that both Nagorno-Karabakh and Abkhazia continue to depend on their 'patron states', Armenia and Russia. Although they have seen some economic regeneration – primarily driven by diaspora investments in the case of Nagorno-Karabakh and by Russian tourism in the case of Abkhazia – both entities remain poor. They continue to receive external military and financial assistance, and neither has its own currency or passport. Russia, for example, provides Abkhazia with passports and pays local pensions, while Armenia assists Nagorno-Karabakh by providing substantial 'inter-state' loans as well as military personnel, equipment and weaponry. The resulting dependence is reinforced by international isolation and a lack of other sources of external support. Consequently, the state-building that has taken place should not necessarily be viewed as demonstrating the viability of Nagorno-Karabakh and Abkhazia as independent states in the present; it does, however, influence internal dynamics which may, in turn, impact on relations with their patron states. If institution building and economic regeneration continue, this will likely increase the autonomy of the entities. This is what happened in the case of the two Serb statelets in war-time Croatia and Bosnia: they gained control of alternative resources and consequently became less dependent on Belgrade.[34]

State-building, therefore, has the potential to change the dynamics of settlement negotiations. It could make it even more necessary to include

Karabakh representatives in peace talks, and Abkhaz leaders might, over time, become less constrained by Moscow. Nagorno-Karabakh is already less dependent on the loans it receives from Armenia,[35] and its leaders are keen to insist on their autonomy,[36] even though the president of Armenia is, in fact, from Karabakh. Links with Russia have become an increasingly salient issue in Abkhazia's internal politics, but so far this seems to have led to increased, rather than reduced, Russian involvement, as evidenced by Moscow's reaction to the defeat of its favoured candidate in the 2004 presidential elections. Russia imposed an economic embargo, cutting off Abkhazia's lifeline, until a power-sharing deal was reached between the two candidates.[37] Increasing tensions between Abkhazia and Tbilisi in the spring of 2008 have further deepened this involvement;[38] Russia is actively using the uncertainty created by Kosovo's recognition to step up its pressure on Georgia.

Democratisation

Abkhazia's and Nagorno-Karabakh's ongoing external dependence has come into conflict with a second, and perhaps more surprising, process of internal change, one of gradual transition away from rule by authoritarian war heroes towards some form of proto-democracy.[39] These processes are not dissimilar to transitional processes seen in their parent states, and in some cases they have indeed gone further.[40] Nagorno-Karabakh has held regular elections since 1995, which have been deemed largely 'free and fair' by international observers, and the entity's leadership continuously emphasises its democratic credentials: 'the democratic process [in Nagorno-Karabakh] is irreversible; Azerbaijan is far behind'.[41] The opposition has yet to gain power through elections at the national level, but an opposition candidate did become mayor of Stepanakert, the Nagorno-Karabakh 'capital', in the 2004 local elections, and the opposition secured victories in 70% of settlements. The Karabakh authorities note that this is unheard of in the South Caucasus.[42]

Pluralism was slower to emerge in the case of Abkhazia, and the authorities there have been more reluctant to loosen their grip on power. The first president of Abkhazia, Vladislav Ardzinba, was unopposed when he ran for re-election in 1999, and the opposition withdrew most of its candidates in the 2002 parliamentary elections in protest over the conduct of the campaign.[43] However, things had changed by 2004, when the opposition candidate won the presidential election despite (or perhaps because of) Moscow's backing for the regime candidate. Previously, the opposition had been weak, but an assortment of civil-society organisations, the veterans' association, businessmen and disgruntled former government ministers managed to wrest power from the incumbent regime. Despite high levels of tension, power was eventually transferred to the winning candidate, although he had to strike a deal with his opponent, who became vice president.

Driving forces and obstacles

National self-determination movements must by definition make claims to popular legitimacy; their leaders claim to speak for the nation. Democratisation could therefore be seen as a natural goal of such movements. There is, however, tension between the political competition entailed by democracy and the nationalist claim to unity and homogeneous interests. Nationalist leaders wish to strengthen internal cohesion to present a united front, rather than highlight the existence of internal divisions. Popular legitimacy has therefore in most cases been demonstrated through referendums on independence, rather than through democratic elections.[44] So what has driven democratisation in Nagorno-Karabakh and Abkhazia, and made their authorities move beyond the usual referendum process? Is it a perceived normative change in the international arena, or are internal dynamics of importance as well? Moreover, what are the obstacles and contradictions facing this process?

Claims to democracy have been found in unrecognised entities before; for example, the constitution of Republika Srpska in war-time Bosnia emphasised that it was a multiparty democracy.[45] However, the emphasis placed on democratisation in Nagorno-Karabakh and Abkhazia is arguably even greater and, unlike in the case of Republika Srpska, appears to have been followed by relatively free and fair elections. There seem to be two main reasons for this, one external and one internal. The perceived importance of an external incentive to democratise is clear in statements made by the de facto authorities. Thus, David Babayan, then adviser to the Karabakh president, argued, 'recognition will not be possible without democracy; we have to be ahead of Azerbaijan'.[46] The president himself stated, 'People who have a very … democratic constitution … have more chances of being recognised by the International Community than others'.[47] In Abkhazia, similar rhetoric is employed, and the authorities can argue that Abkhazia has changed its head of state through a contested election, which is something Georgia has yet to achieve.[48] In the international arena, there is an ever-greater emphasis not only on democratisation but on values more generally – this emphasis is especially prominent in US foreign policy, but also forms an integral part of the EU accession criteria. By encouraging competitive democratisation, Karabakh authorities are implicitly framing their conflict with Azerbaijan as one of values, pitting Karabakh's 'Western' democratic values against Azerbaijan's incompatible 'Eastern' values.[49]

This idea of a link between democratisation and recognition has been strengthened by international policies in Kosovo. The 2003 'standards before status' policy especially caught the interest of Nagorno-Karabakh and Abkhazia; it seemed to suggest that recognition might be awarded to entities that succeed in building effective, democratic institutions. When Kosovo's 'supervised independence' was recognised in February 2008, it raised hopes that a precedent had been set for the recognition of autonomous provinces based, at least in part, on institutional standards.[50] Comparisons with Kosovo are explicitly made by the authorities: the Karabakh leadership argues that in their state, unlike Kosovo, has proved its viability,[51] and the foreign minister of Abkhazia, Sergei Shamba, has similarly argued that the process of democratisation has proceeded further in Abkhazia than in Kosovo.[52] There is a deeply held belief in both entities that democratisation will make recognition more likely.

In addition to this external motivator, there is an internal one: the lengthy existence of these statelets and their relative stability have reduced the role of the military and increased opportunities for political opposition. After the homogenisation caused by, or imposed during, the wars in these entities, pluralism has gradually emerged. This pluralisation has primarily been driven by economic problems and by dissatisfaction with the corruption and war profiteering associated with the authorities. In response to such issues, an opposition emerged and became progressively stronger. In Abkhazia, the nascent opposition was strengthened when the veterans' association Amtsakhara began to criticise President Vladislav Ardzinba's lack of leadership: Ardzinba was ill, and his powers of office had largely fallen into the hands of other members of his clan.[53] Initially, concern was centred on the need for effective governance, but gradually the criticism became focused on the abuse of power associated with the regime and the need for reforms, including the need to curb the power of the president who had previously been regarded as an untouchable war hero.[54] A similar process occurred in Nagorno-Karabakh: in the first years after the war, the opposition was weak and the main opposition party, the Dashnaks, refrained from running in the post-ceasefire elections, reportedly to avoid weakening the state.[55] But over the years, political pluralism and a strengthened opposition emerged, driven by dissatisfaction with the pace of democratisation and the lack of socio-economic progress.[56] The proclamation of democratic values was, moreover, also used by the authorities as a tool in their internal rivalry. Thus, President Arkady Ghukasian described his power struggle with the military commander Samvel Babayan as a struggle between democracy and dictatorship.[57] This argument was all the more powerful because of the perception of external pressure to democratise.

An opposition emerged and became stronger

The strong rhetorical commitment to democracy in these territories should not lead to the false conclusion that the democratisation process is in any way complete in either Nagorno-Karabakh or Abkhazia. Both face problems similar to those experienced by recognised states undergoing transitions: contested election results, weak institutions, limited political differences, and so on. One of the leaders of the Karabakh opposition, in his assessment of the level of democracy in his state, noted, 'We are not suppressed or beaten; there is no violence, no blackmail. The opposition can appear on TV, etc. However, there is the issue of administrative resources.'[58] According to the Freedom House rankings, both Abkhazia and Nagorno-Karabakh are 'partly free', with a score of 5 for both political rights and civil liberties (1 is the best possible score, 7 the worst). In comparison, Georgia is also classified as 'partly free', but with scores of 3, while Azerbaijan is classified as 'not free', with a score of 6 for political rights and 5 for civil liberties.[59] Thus, Nagorno-Karabakh and Abkhazia are ranked in a similar way to other countries caught in protracted post-war transitions.

For unrecognised entities in a situation of 'no war, no peace' there are, however, additional obstacles to democratisation that recognised states can often avoid. Two of these are related to external factors, while three are related to internal structures of power and legitimation. Contrary to other cases of transition, statelets do not receive any international assistance for, for example, the holding of elections or parliamentary development. Financial support or advice is not forthcoming from organisations that usually assist transitional countries.[60] Abkhazia constitutes a partial exception to this, since the European Union and other international organisations have provided humanitarian aid and support for civil-society development. However, there has been little support for the rule of law, a free media or a critical civil society.[61] The involvement of the international community is deliberately depoliticised,[62] with international organisations refusing to engage with Abkhaz authorities so that their involvement can be framed as an issue of human security and grassroots development.

On the other hand, one category of external actors has taken a very active interest in the internal affairs of Nagorno-Karabakh and Abkhazia: their patron states. In the case of Nagorno-Karabakh this does not seem to have been a significant hindrance to democratisation, and Armenia has actually provided some of the assistance that international organisations have withheld. It does, however, mean that an external actor beyond democratic control plays a significant role in internal politics, and the local leadership is, consequently, less accountable.[63] In the case of Abkhazia, such external involvement has had a more direct and negative impact on democratisation, as evidenced by Russia's interference in the election of a new president in 2004.

These external obstacles make it even more difficult to overcome the internal obstacles, which are all in some way related to the 'no war, no peace' situation and the statelets' claim to national self-determination. Firstly, there is the role of the military. Democratisation is not assisted by the predominance of military interests: Nagorno-Karabakh, for example, still operates under martial law. That this should constitute an obstacle to democratisation is, however, vehemently denied by the authorities.[64] When the acting chief of the Karabakh army staff was quoted as saying that the state was not ready for full democracy as long as the war was not over, he was summoned to a special parliamentary session and had to assure the deputies that he had been misquoted.[65] But even if the military does not directly interfere in politics or have any formal influence, its presence as a veto player is bound to influence the terms of political competition.

A related obstacle is the perceived need for unity in the face of external threats, which contradicts the democratic principle of pluralism. Although political debate is allowed, and even encouraged, it remains constrained. Certain issues, such as independence, are not open for public discussion. When Nagorno-Karabakh held a constitutional referendum in 2006, there were no significant voices arguing against the constitution, as this would have been considered tantamount to arguing against the state's existence. Similarly, the Director of Abkhazia's Apsnypress (state press agency) argues that unity is 'unfortunately … often understood as agreement of opinion'.[66]

There is tension between 'ethnos' and 'demos'

Finally, democratisation in the context of a claim to national self-determination runs into the problem of who exactly constitutes 'the people'.[67] There is tension between 'ethnos' and 'demos' – between an ethnic and a civic definition of the people – and the former tends to be favoured.[68] This is most problematic in Abkhazia, where the Abkhaz only constituted 17.8% of the pre-war population, and currently constitute a plurality, but not a majority. As Nicu Popescu argues, 'crucial elements of democracy in Abkhazia … are for only parts of the Abkhaz population'.[69] Armenians and Russians supported the Abkhaz fight for self-determination but are, nevertheless, underrepresented in government structures; they each hold three seats in the 35-seat Abkhaz parliament.[70] However, the main problem is the Georgian returnees in the Gali region. Georgia accuses Abkhazia of having disenfranchised this part of its population, which accounts for roughly a third of Abkhazia's population.[71] Abkhazia's leadership denies this and has become keen to demonstrate that the entity is not ethnically exclusive. Sergei Shamba, Abkhazia's foreign minister, recently stated that 'we are doing everything we can to integrate the Gali population into our society'.[72] This illustrates that the rhetorical struggle for international backing offers a potential mechanism for important internal changes. In Nagorno-Karabakh, the situation is somewhat different since the entity, in its post-war configuration, is almost 100% Armenian, making the ethnic character of its democratisation less obvious. The lack of participation of the entity's pre-war Azeri population is, however, raised both by Azerbaijan and by international organisations.

Impact on possible settlements

Despite growing international emphasis on democratisation, there is little to indicate that 'earned sovereignty' will become a dominant norm. It is true that the conditions attached to the recognition of the former Yugoslav republics in the early 1990s linked democracy and recognition: the first condition established by the European Community's Badinter Commission was that the rule of law, democracy and human rights be respected. However, the possibility for recognition was explicitly limited to republics, and several states chose to recognise the republics *before* the Commission handed down its opinions. Unrecognised states were encouraged by the 'standards before status' policy for Kosovo, but this has now become 'status then standards' under international supervision. Democracy and minority rights were mentioned as part of the reason for Kosovo's recognition,[73] but the uniqueness of this case was persistently stressed, and it was emphasised that a new principle for recognition had not been created. Thomas de Waal has argued that 'events set precedents, whether international leaders like it or not',[74] but if this is indeed the case the precise nature of the precedent remains obscure. Does recognition depend on powerful friends, military superiority, demographic majorities, political and economic viability, or perhaps democratic principles and the protection of minority rights?

The international response to processes of state-building and democratisation in other unrecognised states has been almost uniformly negative:

the legitimacy of elections is routinely denied, no observers are sent and no assistance is provided. The only exception is Somaliland, where the latest elections were monitored by a team of international observers sponsored by the British Embassy in Addis Ababa.[75] The dominant strategy when it comes to unrecognised states is to ignore them.[76] Nevertheless, the shift in the legitimising strategy of these entities affects the possibility for reaching settlements in secessionist conflicts and should, therefore, be acknowledged. State-building and democratisation present new opportunities for compromise and engagement.

If democratisation is not just meant for external consumption, but is also a response to internal pressures, then it contradicts the 'greed argument' that conflicts are driven by unrepresentative opportunists. This necessitates solutions that do not just address the motives of elites and their 'selfish determination' but also popular grievances and fears.[77] If leaders enjoy genuine popular support, this calls for different solutions than if they do not. Furthermore, democratisation, and the changed configuration of power resulting from it, could have a positive impact on stalled peace processes. New forces have gained power through these processes of democratisation, forces that are perhaps more willing to compromise, even if they do not initially say so in public. The new Abkhaz leaders, for example, reportedly acknowledge in private the need for compromise with Georgia.[78]

Democratisation is closely linked to issues of identity, both internally and externally, forcing would-be states to ask, 'Who are we? How does the world see us?' It involves a contestation of identity and has the potential to empower new actors and bring about shifts in an entity's political dynamics, as exemplified by the ongoing, if rather hesitant, attempts to make Abkhazia less mono-ethnic. Secondly, stronger institutions mean stronger, more predictable leadership, which is less constrained by 'men with guns'. This should assist negotiations. Finally, through increased participation and information, the general population will be better prepared for a possible settlement, thereby reducing the risk of a backlash. This is already a recommended strategy for recognised states engaged in peace processes,[79] so why not for unrecognised states as well?

Critics of this reasoning might point to the link between democratisation and conflict and argue that democratisation makes extremism and conflict *more* likely, not less, due to elite competition and weak institutions.[80] Yet the effect of democratisation depends on the starting point, and the risk of radicalisation would not seem to apply in the cases of Abkhazia and Nagorno-Karabakh. Democratisation does not have to coincide with institutional weakening; on the contrary, institutions in these entities have been strengthened. Moreover, it appears unlikely that public opinion should be more susceptible to extremism than the forces that kept the old regimes in power: namely, warlords with a vested interest in ongoing conflict.

The space for compromise, however, remains limited, and with the limits reinforced by the process of state-building. Lynch argues that de facto states are the main reason for the absence of progress in the peace talks,[81] and an entrenchment of their independence, through the building of effective institutions, will consequently make compromise harder. The de facto independence enjoyed by these entities is likely to mean that conventional mechanisms for conflict resolution will not work; autonomy or power-sharing is simply not enough. As King argues, conflict resolution in these cases is 'not so much about patching together a torn country as about trying to integrate two functionally distinct administrations, militaries and societies'.[82] More creative models are therefore needed if a solution short of independence is to be found – sovereignty will have to be fudged. However, state-building has been taking place in Nagorno-Karabakh and Abkhazia since the early 1990s, meaning that de facto independence is already a reality that cannot simply be wished away.

De facto independence cannot be wished away

Democratisation of these entities is not a panacea but it could create fluidity in otherwise stalled peace processes, making room for leaders who are more willing to abandon zero-sum calculations, and populations who are more willing to follow. Such an outcome, however, requires international engagement and a move away from viewing Nagorno-Karabakh and Abkhazia – and entities like them – purely as criminal badlands. Lack of engagement creates a dangerous vacuum which is presently filled by patron states, particularly Russia. Democratisation of unrecognised states, however paradoxical this concept might sound, should be encouraged by negotiators and by the international community more broadly. They should encourage genuine democratisation that moves beyond rhetorical flourish and addresses shortcomings, in particular the ethnically exclusive nature of this process. Such engagement could take several forms: observers could be sent to scrutinise democratic claims; funding could be provided for projects aimed at fostering the rule of law, a free media and a critical civil society; and loans could even be offered, provided certain conditions were met. If the leaders of unrecognised states lack popular legitimacy, or if their power is based on ethnic exclusion, then this can be exposed by holding them to the democratic principles they espouse. Such scrutiny could put them in an uncomfortable position and could even effect changes. The carrot for the entities should not be a promise of independence but rather an end to their current isolation.

* * *

A more nuanced view of unrecognised states is needed, one that moves beyond the common perception that they are little more than criminalised badlands driven by shadow economies and greedy elites. Empirical, or positive, sovereignty can exist without external recognition and, although it presents obstacles, does not render a process of democratisation unfeasible. In fact, non-recognition can serve as an impetus for democratisation. There has been a shift in the strategy for achieving recognition away from national self-determination and grievances to an emphasis on *earned* sovereignty, based in particular on democratic credentials. This is not merely a return to more traditional claims to independence; it reflects an increased international emphasis on democratisation and, more generally, on values. It is an attempt by the leadership of unrecognised states to demonstrate that they share hegemonic values and therefore do not constitute a threat.

The process of democratisation is driven, in part, by the arguably mistaken perception that it will make international recognition more likely. It is reasonable to worry, therefore, that this will lead to a very constrained form of democracy predicated on a siege mentality. Yet the pressures for democracy also come from inside the entities and do not merely reflect a desire to please the outside world. Democratisation has brought actual changes to these entities, changes that can potentially have a positive impact on stalled peace processes. It will not alter the entrenched nature of their de facto independence, but might bring new forces to power that are less driven by military logic and more willing to accept compromises that fudge the issue of sovereignty. For this to happen, however, international engagement is necessary. The de facto leaderships of these entities are adamant that they are legitimate representatives of their populations and adhere to democratic values. These claims should not be taken at face value, but they do provide an avenue for engagement, one which could point a way out of the current, long-lasting stalemates.

Acknowledgements

Research for this article was funded by a grant from Lancaster University's Research Committee. An earlier draft was presented at the ASN Convention, New York, April 2007. Travel costs to this conference were funded by the British Academy.

Notes

1 Quoted in Nicu Popescu, 'Europe's Unrecognised Neighbours: The EU in Abkhazia and South Ossetia', CEPS Working Document, no. 260, March 2007, p. 18.

2 Kolstø defines an unrecognised state according to three criteria: (1) its leadership must be in control of (most of) the territory it lays claim to; (2) it must have sought but not achieved international recognition as an independent state; (3) it must have existed for more than two years. Pål Kolstø, 'The Sustainability and Future of Unrecognized Quasi-States', *Journal of Peace Research*, no. 43, vol. 6, 2006, p. 725–6.

3 Dov Lynch, *Engaging Eurasia's Separatist States* (Washington DC: United States Institute of Peace, 2004), p. 18.

4 Victor Yakubyan, 'Kosovo-Karabakh – Strategic Fork', *Regnum*, 13 November 2006, http://www.regnum.ru/english/737310.html.

5 For a disucssion on 'earned sovereignty' in international law see, for example, Paul R. Williams and Francesa Jannotti Pecci, 'Earned Sovereignty: Bridging the Gap Between Sovereignty and Self-Determination', *Stanford Journal of International Law*, 2004, pp. 1–40; Michael Scharf, 'Earned Sovereignty:

Juridical Underpinnings', *Denver Journal of International Law and Policy,* vol. 31, no. 3, pp. 373–87.

6 Scharf, 'Earned Sovereignty', p. 382.

7 A page called 'Democracy' from the website of the US State Department asserts, 'democracy is the one national interest that helps to secure all the others'. See http://www.state.gov/g/drl/democ/.

8 Scott Pegg, *International Society and the De Facto State* (Aldershot: Ashgate, 1998), pp. 128, 148–9.

9 *Ibid.*, pp. 26–7.

10 See Kolstø, 'The Sustainability and Future of Unrecognized Quasi-States'; Pegg, *International Society and the De Facto State*; Lynch, *Engaging Eurasia's Separatist States*; Charles King, 'The Benefits of Ethnic War: Understanding Eurasia's Unrecognized States', *World Politics*, vol. 53, July 2001, pp. 524–52.

11 For partial, but important, exceptions, see Nicu Popescu, 'Democracy in Secessionism: Transnistria and Abkhazia's Domestic Policies', Center for Policy Studies, August 2006, p. 19, http://www.policy.hu; Oisin Tansey, 'Democratization without a State: Democratic Regime-Building in Kosovo', *Democratization,*vol. 14, no. 1, 2007, pp. 129–50; Laurence Broers, 'The Politics of Non-recognition and Democratization', in Laurence Broers (ed.), *The Limits of Leadership: Elites and Societies in the Nagorny Karabakh Peace Process* (London: Conciliation Resources, 2005).

12 Edward Walker, 'No Peace, No War in the Caucasus: Secessionist Conflicts in Chechnya, Abkhazia and Nagorno-Karabakh', Occasional Paper, Belfer Center for Science and International Affairs, 1998. Available at http://belfercenter.ksg.harvard.edu/publication/3042/no_peace_no_war_in_the_caucasus.html.

13 Vladimir Kolossov and John O'Loughlin, 'Pseudo-states as Harbingers of a New Geopolitics: The example of the Trans-Dniester Moldovan Republic (TMR)', 1998, p. 1, http://www.colorado.edu/IBS/PEC/johno/pub/pseudo-states.pdf.

14 Alexandre Kukhianidze, Alexandre Kupatadze and Roman Gotsiridze, *Smuggling through Abkhazia and Tskhinvali Region* (Tbilisi: Transnational Crime and Corruption Center (TraCCC), 2004), pp. 31, 36.

15 Quoted in Charles King, 'Black Sea Blues', *The National Interest,* vol. 78, no. 5, September–October 2004, pp. 144–47.

16 Lynch, *Engaging Eurasia's Separatist States*, p. 4.

17 Paul Collier, 'Doing Well out of War: an Economic Perspective', in Mats Berdal and David Malone (eds), *Greed and Grievance: Economic Agendas in Civil Wars* (Boulder, CO: Lynne Rienner, 2000).

18 Walter Kemp, 'Selfish Determination: The Questionable Ownership of Autonomy Movements', *Ethnopolitics*, vol. 4, no. 1, 2005, pp. 88–9.

19 Pegg, *International Society and the De Facto State*, p. 230.

20 As Nicu Popescu puts it, 'The Abkhaz de facto state in fact does not reach to many areas it claims its own'. Popescu, 'Democracy in Secessionism,' p. 19.

21 See, for example, United Nations Security Council, *Report of the Secretary-General on the Situation in*

Abkhazia, Georgia, S/2006/435, June 2006, http://www.unomig.org/data/file/843/060626_SG_Report_eng.pdf.

22 Thomas de Waal, *Black Garden: Armenia and Azerbaijan through Peace and War* (New York: New York University Press, 2003), p. 242.

23 Somaliland is a striking example of an unrecognised entity that is actually *better* functioning than its parent state.

24 King, 'The Benefits of Ethnic War', p. 525.

25 Pegg, *International Society and the De Facto State*, p. 50.

26 Lynch, *Engaging Eurasia's Separatist States*, p. 63.

27 Kolstø, 'The Sustainability and Future of Unrecognized States', pp. 725, 727.

28 Interview with Boris Navasardian, Director of Yerevan Press Club, Yerevan, 5 September 2006.

29 Interview with Paata Zakareishvili, political analyst, Tbilisi, 31 August 2006.

30 In Nagorno-Karabakh, the social-services budget doubled between 2000 and 2005. International Crisis Group, 'Nagorno-Karabakh: Viewing the Conflict from the Ground', Europe Report no. 166, 14 September 2005, p. 15. Available at http://www.crisisgroup.org/home/index.cfm?id=4377.

31 International Crisis Group, 'Abkhazia Today,' Europe Report no. 176, 15 September 2006, p. 26. Available at http://www.crisisgroup.org/home/index.cfm?id=4377.

32 Interview with Natella Akaba, via e-mail, 30 August 2006.

33 'Karabakh has serious grounds for international recognition of sovereignty', *Karabakh Open*, 20 February 2008, http://www.karabakh-open.com/src/index.php?lang=en&nid=7849&id=3.

34 See Nina Caspersen, 'Between Puppets and Independent Actors: Kin-state Involvement in the Conflicts in Bosnia, Croatia and Nagorno Karabakh', *Ethnopolitics*, forthcoming, 2008.

35 This money used to constitute around two-thirds of Nagorno-Karabakh's budget, but now represents about one-third. Data kindly supplied by Levon Zourabian.

36 Interview with David Babayan, adviser to the Karabakh president, Stepanakert, 13 September 2006.

37 Inal Khashig, 'Abkhazia Rivals Strike Deal', Caucasus Reporting Service, no. 265, 8 December 2004. The continued influence of Moscow was illustrated in the new governing structures: the Abkhaz defence minister and chief of staff are both ethnic Russians. International Crisis Group, 'Abkhazia Today', p. 14.

38 See, for example, Inal Khashig, 'Abkhazia Cleaves Closer to Russia', Caucasus Reporting Service, no. 443, 7 May 2008.

39 In democratisation literature, external sovereignty is frequently seen as a prerequisite to democracy. Tansey, 'Democratization without a State', p. 131.

40 Democratisation is not unique to the two Caucasus cases; similar changes are seen in other unrecognised states. For example, international observers described the 2003 election in Somaliland as one of the freest and most transparent elections ever staged in the Horn of Africa. Mark Bradbury, Adan Yusuf Abokor and Haroon

Ahmed, 'Somaliland: Choosing Politics over Violence', *Review of African Political Economy*, vol. 97, 2003, p. 475.

41 Interview with David Babayan.

42 *Ibid.*

43 See, for example, Inal Khashig, 'Abkhazia: Government Poll Landslide Contested', *Caucasus Reporting Service,* no. 119, 8 March 2002; Freedom House, 'Abkhazia (Georgia)', available at http://www.freedomhouse.org.

44 Of course, referendums are not always held and may be seriously flawed, making a claim to self-determination, paradoxically, an authoritarian claim.

45 Rajo Kuzmanović, *Konstitutivni akti Republike Srpske* (Glas Srpski: Banja Luka, 1994), p. 60. However, members of the opposition in Republika Srpska vehemently deny that this reflected the reality of the statelet's politics. See Nina Caspersen, 'Contingent Nationalist Dominance: Intra-Serb Challenges to the Serb Democratic Party', *Nationalities Papers*, vol. 34, no. 1, 2006, pp. 51–69.

46 Interview with David Babayan.

47 Stated at a press conference attended by the author, Stepanakert, 11 December 2006.

48 King, 'Black Sea Blues'. See also Popescu, 'Democracy in Secessionism', p. 14.

49 Broers, 'The Politics of Non-recognition and Democratization', p. 71.

50 The day after Kosovo's declaration of independence, the presidents of Abkhazia and South Ossetia announced at a joint press conference that they would shortly apply to the leadership of Russia, the Commonwealth of Independent States, the United Nations and other international organisations to recognise their independence. Kazbek Baseyev, 'We're No Worse than Kosovo Say ex-Soviet Separatists', Reuters, 18 February 2008.

51 'NKR Foreign Minister Georgy Petrossian's Interview to "Demo" Newspaper', 4 February 2008, available at http://www.nkr.am/eng/news/index.htm.

52 Zaal Anjaparidze, 'Kosovo Impedes Settlement of Abkhaz Situation', *Eurasia Daily Monitor,* March 2006, vol. 3, no. 54.

53 Interview with Paata Zakareishvili.

54 *Ibid.*; Interview with Natella Akaba; King, 'Black Sea Blues'.

55 Interview with Artur Mosiyan, president of the Dashnaks, Stepanakert, 13 September 2006.

56 See, for example, 'The Rise and Fall of Samvel Babayan', Armenian News Network, 6 October 2004, http://groong.usc.edu/ro/ro-20041006.html.

57 Interview with Gegham Baghdasarian, deputy for Movement88, Stepanakert, 15 September 2006.

58 *Ibid.*

59 Freedom House, 'Freedom in the World 2008', http://www.freedomhouse.org/uploads/fiw08launch/FIW08Tables.pdf.

60 Interview with Natella Akaba; Interview with David Babayan.

61 Popescu, 'Europe's Unrecognised Neighbours', p. 14.

62 International Crisis Group, 'Conflict Resolution in the South Caucasus: The EU's role', EU Report no. 173, 20 March 2006, p. 18.

63 Broers, 'The Politics of Non-Recognition and Democratization,' p. 69.

64 Interview with David Babayan.

65 'The Rise and Fall of Samvel Babayan', Armenian News Network, 6 October 2004.

66 Manana Gurgulia, 'Democratization in Conditions of a non-Recognized State', paper presented at the conference 'Abkhazia in the Context of Contemporary International Relations', July 2004, http://www.circassianworld.com/Gurgulia.html.

67 Such ethnic exclusiveness is not integral to unrecognised states – Somaliland is, for example, based on 'state sovereignty' rather than 'national sovereignty'. Pegg. *International Society and the De Facto State*, p. 43.

68 Popescu, 'Democracy in Secessionism', p. 19.

69 *Ibid.*

70 Shaun Walker, 'The Phantom Parliament: Abkhazia Votes, but to What End', *Russia Profile*, 21 March 2007. Published in *Georgia News Digest*, 22 March 2007.

71 Popescu, 'Democracy in Secessionism', p. 19.

72 Paul Rimple, 'Gali: A Key Test Case for Georgia's Separatist Abkhazia Region', *Eurasianet*, 5 March 2007, http://www.eurasianet.org/departments/insight/articles/eav030507.shtml.

73 The EU, for example, emphasised that the resolution adopted by the Kosovo Assembly 'commits Kosovo to the principles of democracy and equality of all its citizens, the protection of the Serbs and other minorities'. Council of the European Union, 'Press Release: 2851st Council meeting, General Affairs and External Relations', 18 February 2008, http://www.consilium.europa.eu/ueDocs/cms_Data/docs/pressData/en/gena/98818.pdf.

74 Thomas de Waal and Zeyno Baran, 'Abkhazia–Georgia, Kosovo–Serbia: Parallel Worlds?', *Open Democracy debate*, 1 August 2006, http://www.opendemocracy.net/democracy-caucasus/abkhazia_serbia_3787.jsp.

75 'CIIR's Election Observers Welcome Results of Somaliland Parliamentary Poll,' *The Somaliland Times*, issue 198, 2 November 2005, http://www.somalilandtimes.net/198/15.shtml.

76 Pegg, *International Society and the De Facto State*, pp. 177–8.

77 'Selfish determination' is a term used by Walter Kemp. Kemp, 'Selfish Determination'.

78 Interview with Paata Zakareishvili.

79 See, for example, Laurence Broers (ed.), *The Limits of Leadership: Elites and Societies in the Nagorny Karabakh Peace Process* (London: Conciliation Resources, 2005).

80 See, for example, Edward D. Mansfield and Jack Snyder, *Electing to Fight: Why Emerging Democracies Go to War* (Cambridge, MA: MIT Press, 2005).

81 Lynch, *Engaging Eurasia's Separatist States*, p. 6.

82 King, 'The Benefits of Ethnic War', p. 525.

Missile Contagion

Dennis M. Gormley

In August 2005 Pakistan tested its first land-attack cruise missile, *Babur*, in western Baluchistan province. Intended to achieve a range of 700km, the *Babur* will be capable of delivering a nuclear warhead. But Pakistan seemed most proud of its ability to reach its intended target. Immediately after the successful test, President Pervez Musharraf announced the achievement to a television audience, declaring that 'the biggest value of this system is it is not detectable. It cannot be intercepted.'[1]

Pakistan is not the only new aspirant to long-range land-attack cruise missiles (LACMs).[2] India, together with Russia, is developing the *BrahMos* supersonic cruise missile, which will have the capability to strike targets at sea or over land to a range of 290km. And in the summer of 2007, India disclosed officially that it had at least two other LACMs under development, one similar to the US *Tomahawk* with a range of 1,000km and another co-developed with Israel. Not to be outdone by its rival, Pakistan tested another new LACM, *Raad*, in late August 2007. In East Asia, China, Taiwan and South Korea are rushing to deploy LACMs with ranges of 1,000km or more, while Japan is contemplating acquiring an LACM for 'pre-emptive' strikes against enemy missile bases. In the Middle East, Israel was once the sole country with LACMs, but Iran now appears to be pursuing cruise-

Dennis M. Gormley is a Senior Fellow in the Washington DC office of the Monterey Institute's James Martin Center for Nonproliferation Studies and a faculty member in the Graduate School of Public and International Affairs at the University of Pittsburgh. This essay is drawn from his book *Missile Contagion: Cruise Missile Proliferation and the Threat to International Security.* Reprinted by arrangement with Praeger Security International, an imprint of the Greenwood Publishing Group.

Survival | vol. 50 no. 4 | August–September 2008 | pp. 137–154 DOI 10.1080/00396330802329006

missile programmes for both land and sea attack. Iran has also provided the terrorist group Hizbullah with unmanned aerial vehicles and sophisticated anti-ship cruise missiles, one of which severely damaged an Israeli vessel and killed four sailors during the 2006 war in Lebanon. In April 2005, Ukraine's export agency unveiled plans to market a new LACM, *Korshun*. This missile appears to be based solely on the Russian Kh-55, a nuclear-capable, 3,000km-range LACM, which Ukrainian and Russian arms dealers illegally sold to China in 2000 and to Iran in 2001.

Such developments suggest that the proliferation of LACMs capable of delivering nuclear, chemical or biological weapons and highly accurate conventional payloads is approaching a critical threshold. While India, Iran, North Korea and Pakistan have developed new medium-range ballistic missiles (1,000–3,000km range) since the end of the Cold War, there has been a significant net overall decrease in worldwide ballistic-missile arsenals, largely due to US–Soviet arms-control treaties.[3] Though the range of ballistic missiles has slowly increased, their horizontal spread has been largely kept in check. Yet ballistic missiles, and defences against them, still dominate the missile agenda of defence decision-makers.

Flying under the radar, both literally and figuratively, cruise missiles add a dangerous new dimension to protecting US security interests and preventing regional military instability. Cruise missiles are not destined to supplant ballistic missiles, but if they were employed together, they could severely test even the best missile defences. Perversely, the US quest to sell ballistic-missile defences may be hastening this outcome. Knowing that defences are not nearly as effective against LACMs as they are against ballistic missiles, some states, including China, Pakistan and Iran, are now developing LACMs to complement their ballistic-missile arsenals. Others planning to purchase missile defences, such as Taiwan and Japan, have decided to complement them with much cheaper offensive systems that include LACMs. Worse yet, they are linking LACM use to pre-emptive doctrines. In either case, unintended by-products are likely to include regional arms races and crisis instability.

States have long seen the value of acquiring LACMs capable of delivering conventional as well as mass-destruction payloads, but they faced major hurdles, chief among them designing and building a suitable navigation and guidance system and obtaining an adequate propulsion system. Through the 1980s, only the United States and the Soviet Union had mastered the demanding task of accurately navigating unmanned missiles over long distances to within meters of the intended target area. The advent of the US Global Positioning System (GPS) in 1978 eliminated this hurdle by providing unmanned missiles with precise information about their location, and Europe, China and Russia currently plan similar systems (*Galileo*, *Beidou* and *GLONASS* respectively). The kind of highly efficient turbofan engines that propel American and Russian long-range LACMs well beyond 1,000km still remain beyond the technological grasp of most aspiring missile developers, but LACM aspirants could turn to less highly efficient (but unrestricted by export controls) turbojet engines produced by a broad array of industrial and even some developing countries.

For over 15 years, analysts have been arguing that LACMs were likely to proliferate rapidly. In the first authoritative treatment of the subject, published in 1992, Seth Carus concluded that it appeared 'inevitable that Third World countries will begin to acquire land-attack cruise missiles during the 1990s'.[4] While cautioning that analysts had focused on technology spread at the expense of system-integration challenges, K. Scott McMahon and I concluded in early 1995 that, 'overall, we judge Third World incentives to acquire land-attack cruise missiles to be sufficiently compelling to suggest a threat of some considerable magnitude probably emerging by the end of this decade'.[5] Indeed, several development programmes probably began in the late 1990s, but only now, nearly a decade later, has a series of seemingly small events nudged LACM proliferation toward a tipping point.

Three factors seem instrumental in shaping the spread of LACMs: access to specialised knowledge; *narratives* about reasons for acquiring cruise missiles; and norms of state behaviour relating to non-proliferation policy and defence doctrine. It bears repeating: rather than supplanting ballistic missiles, LACMs may become complementary means of assuring (barring the deployment of advanced and considerably more expensive missile defences) that offensive missiles threaten enemies with a high probability of arriving safely, with increasing effectiveness.

Explicit and tacit knowledge

The prevailing view is that scientific knowledge spreads steadily, aided by globalisation and the Internet, and technology in turn diffuses easily and smoothly into complex systems such as weapons. The Pentagon's Defense Science Board, in a 2006 report on US nuclear capabilities, argued that the desirability of a nuclear-free world was irrelevant because nuclear weapons cannot be 'erased from history'.[6] In effect, the nuclear genie is out of the bottle and can never be put back.

But an alternative view holds that there are actually two kinds of knowledge at work in any complex scientific or technological endeavour: explicit and tacit knowledge.[7] Explicit knowledge consists of information or engineering formulations that can be recorded and easily passed from one place to another, while tacit knowledge is acquired through the laborious and lengthy process of apprenticeship. Tacit knowledge, then, is the product of a uniquely fertile social and intellectual environment composed of mentors and protégés.[8] Obtained under these narrowly bounded circumstances, tacit-knowledge skills are not widely diffused in the same way as explicit knowledge.

To the extent that new design and development work is terminated and tacit skills are not passed on directly to the next generation of designers, it will require a substantial amount of 'reinvention' to recreate any complex weapon system.[9] That states or terrorist groups can easily acquire all the technologies comprising the basic components of a cruise missile does not necessarily mean that they can readily develop militarily useful missile systems. Developing any complex military system depends on a small number of key individuals who possess certain tacit skills, the most important of which involve system engineering or integration. In the case of missile development, system-engineering skills are critical to fabricate, integrate and produce a turbofan engine, or to integrate all the components of a land-attack navigation-and-guidance system so that it can perform consistently and confidently.

Early assessments of cruise-missile proliferation gave insufficient weight to these specialised skills and concentrated instead on export-control shortcomings and the dual-use technologies flooding the marketplace between

1990 and 2000. For example, a colleague and I presented a study to members of the Commission to Assess the Ballistic Missile Threat to the United States (the Rumsfeld Commission) in June 1998, showing how a first-generation cruise missile, the Chinese HY-2 *Silkworm*, could be transformed from a short-range (about 100km) anti-ship missile into a longer-range (about 1,000km) land-attack missile using only commercially available technology.[10] The study was based solely on gathering explicit knowledge; nothing was actually built and tested. Because of this limitation, the study team devoted considerable effort to analysing how long it might take developing countries to accomplish such a feat, including building a serial production capability and integrating a new missile into the existing force structure. The conclusion was that it would take six to ten years, a time that could conceivably be cut in half depending on the extent and nature of foreign assistance, most notably provision of experienced systems engineers. The commission's chairman, Donald Rumsfeld, disagreed, saying that it would take no more than a year. Fortuitously, in searching for Iraq's weapons of mass destruction programmes after the 2003 invasion, the Iraq Survey Group discovered that Iraq had attempted, beginning in June 2002 in a project called *Jinin*, to convert the HY-2 anti-ship cruise missile into a 1,000km-range LACM, intending to complete a development cycle in three to five years. Importantly, Iraq was not starting from scratch. Engineers had devoted years of work to an HY-2 project that extended the missile's range from 100 to 150km, which, noted Survey Group inspectors, directly contributed to the *Jinin* project. In nearly six months of activity, however, little was accomplished aside from computer simulations to test the prospect of integrating a surplus helicopter engine into the missile's airframe. An apparent test of a candidate engine failed to demonstrate sufficient thrust. No work on navigation, guidance and control was even planned until after successful integration of the engine, which Iraqi engineers admitted would be challenging.[11] In arguably simpler unmanned aerial vehicle programmes, Iraqi engineers produced designs that depended heavily on foreign components (including engines and guidance components) but achieved only modest progress in most cases, over

Iraq was not starting from scratch

as much as seven years of development work.[12] In short, even the three- to five-year estimate for Iraq's HY-2 conversion programme seems overly optimistic.

The kinds of specialised knowledge that Iraq would have needed help explain the recent spike in cruise-missile proliferation. For example, Chinese fingerprints are all over Pakistan's *Babur,* while Russian engineering is known to have enabled China to produce a workable propulsion system for its own new LACMs. Russian technical assistance, formalised in a joint production agreement, has helped India to produce and deploy its *BrahMos,* and Israeli assistance is manifest in New Delhi's subsonic LACM programmes. Iran's three cruise-missile programmes reportedly depend heavily on foreign-trained engineers who honed their skills in France, Germany, Russia, China and North Korea.[13] And even though the United States has apparently sought to forestall Taiwan's cruise-missile ambitions diplomatically, Taiwan has already obtained critical US cruise-missile technology and is working to convince its patron (without any reported success) to provide a more advanced turbofan engine to extend its missile's range. Thus, while a flow of technology is necessary, it is not sufficient to enable cruise-missile proliferation without the critical support of a small and exceptionally skilled group of engineers in an equally small number of industrial countries. This is the good news. If states can more effectively control the spread of these 'black arts', there is hope that the worst features of the contagion can be checked.

Proliferation narrative

Just as the specialised knowledge of a small number of engineers can help foster the spread of LACMs, a seemingly inconsequential event can embellish the narrative associated with LACMs and their consequent appeal. During the 2003 Iraq War, five crude Iraqi LACMs managed to evade otherwise successful US missile defences. Because it did not produce any casualties, or derail coalition military operations, Iraq's surprise use of LACMs was generally viewed as a footnote to a swift and successful military campaign. But to specialists within the US government and elsewhere, the chief lesson was that ballistic-missile defences alone cannot address the threat of low-flying cruise missiles. And because they are significantly less expensive than missile defences, LACMs, alongside existing ballistic-missile arsenals, will make defending against all types of missile threats an increasingly daunting and costly challenge.

Since the launch of the first operational German V-2 rocket in 1944, ballistic missiles have given their owners the cachet of military sophistication, not to mention the confidence that comes with possessing a long-distance weapon capable of arriving reasonably close to its target without prospect of interception. Against Germany's slow, high-flying V-1, the ancestor of today's LACMs, Britain had managed by war's end to greatly improve its defences. By the last week of attacks, Britain's air defences intercepted 79% of incoming V-1s. Still, roughly 21,000 V-1s were launched against the Allies during the war, causing more than 18,000 casualties in London alone.[14]

Modern low-flying LACMs offer more attractive options. Compared with ballistic missiles, LACMs are expected to be much more accurate (by a factor of at least ten), less costly (by at least half) and, because of their aerodynamic stability and larger footprint, substantially more effective in delivering chemical and biological agents (conservatively enlarging the lethal area for biological attacks by at least ten times).[15] They provide more flexible and survivable launch options from air, land and sea platforms than larger ballistic missiles, while offering easier maintenance in harsh environments. And surely the success of American *Tomahawk* cruise missiles in the 1991 and 2003 Iraq wars burnished their appeal. Nevertheless, until recently the symbolic and psychological power of ballistic missiles trumped LACMs' superior efficiency and effectiveness. As long as ballistic missiles were not seriously threatened by effective missile defences, they maintained this apparent advantage over cruise missiles no matter how problematic their true military utility proved to be.

By 2003, circumstances had changed. US missile defences performed poorly against Iraq's ballistic missiles during the 1991 Gulf War (the Government Accountability Office generously attributed to them a 9% interception rate), but greatly improved *Patriot* missile defences intercepted all nine of the ballistic missiles Iraq launched in 2003. That the *Patriot* batteries failed to detect or intercept any of the five primitive Iraqi LACMs only bolstered the cruise missile as a difficult-to-defeat delivery system. In fact, the addition of LACMs to the Iraqi missile threat sowed such confusion among US forces that it contributed to a number of friendly-fire casualties: *Patriot* batteries erroneously shot down two friendly aircraft, killing three crew members, while an American F-15 crew destroyed a *Patriot* radar, in the belief they were being targeted.[16] That a mere handful of primitive LACMs could achieve such an impact seems to have sunk in quickly. 'This was a glimpse of future threats. It is a poor man's air force', the chief of staff of the 32nd US Army Air and Missile Defense Command told the *New York Times* shortly after the fall of Baghdad. 'A thinking enemy will use uncommon means such as cruise missiles and unmanned aerial vehicles on multiple fronts.'[17]

Patriot batteries shot down two friendly aircraft

During the 1990s, when many of the cruise-missile development programmes were launched, the LACM narrative rarely, if ever, fixed on the appeal of surviving missile defences. But in the aftermath of 2003's events, a new narrative began to adhere to virtually every new cruise-missile programme. Musharraf's characterisation of Pakistan's new missile as undetectable and incapable of intercept seemed intended for Indian ears. It came less than a month after Washington had reportedly agreed to permit New Delhi to acquire Israel's *Arrow* missile-defence system.[18] Pakistan repeated this emphasis in the aftermath of its 22 March 2007 test launch of its *Babur* LACM, when it announced that '*Babur* ... is a terrain hugging, radar-avoiding cruise missile, whose range has now been enhanced to 700km. It is a highly maneuverable missile with pin-point accuracy'.[19] Iran, too, confronted with Israel's substantial investment in ballistic-missile defence, appears to view a cruise-missile arsenal as an efficient way to increase the return on investment in its *Shahab* ballistic-missile programme.[20] China, on the other hand, has steered clear of boasting about using its cruise missiles to penetrate missile defences. Instead, the low cost of cruise missiles relative to defending against them (Chinese planners believe in a 9:1 cost-ratio advantage applies here) figures heavily in the Chinese narrative.[21] This may explain a report from the People's Liberation Army *Military Digest* in May 2007 that China is transforming more than

1,000 retired *Jian-5* fighters into cruise missiles, the cost of which, according to a Taiwanese analyst, would be roughly $100,000 each. The assured penetration narrative has even crept into South Korea's otherwise reticent discussion of their four LACM programmes, where they have begun to refer to their cruise missiles as difficult to defend against – despite the absence of any notable North Korean defences.[22]

Shifting norms

Norms against missile proliferation do not have anywhere near the robustness or legal standing of those pertaining to the proliferation of nuclear, biological and chemical weapons, yet there have been recent attempts to strengthen them.[23] In 1999, the 34-nation Missile Technology Control Regime, a supplier cartel launched in 1987 by the United States and its G7 partners to curb missile proliferation, initiated work that led to the adoption in November 2002 of the Hague Code of Conduct against Ballistic Missile Proliferation. Open to all states and meant to complement the regime's supply-side restrictions on the transfer of technology and missiles, the Hague Code established a broad international norm against the spread of ballistic missiles. As of February 2008, 128 nations had subscribed. Despite the fact that the regime covers both ballistic and cruise missiles, its members regrettably left cruise missiles out of the Hague Code's normative content. In so doing, they inadvertently contributed to an epidemic of LACMs.

Three months prior to the launch of the Hague Code, the George W. Bush administration issued a new National Security Strategy emphasising pre-emption. The doctrine moved policy away from deterrence and containment toward attacking enemies before they could attack the United States. From the purely military point of view, there are obvious advantages to decisive and successful pre-emption, but from the policy point of view there is equally the danger that brandishing such an aggressive strategy will establish a precedent and generate unwanted instability during regional crises.[24] Indeed, it is worrisome to see emulation of the US pre-emption doctrine interact with weak missile non-proliferation norms to make cruise missiles the 'first strike' weapon of choice in several volatile regions.

Shortly after the US invasion of Iraq, Russian President Vladimir Putin said his country retained the right to launch pre-emptive strikes to defend its interests. Israel, too, cited US pre-emption doctrine when it attacked an alleged terrorist camp in Syria in October 2003. North Korea announced that 'a preemptive strike is not the monopoly of the United States'.[25] The Indian external affairs minister avowed that India had a more persuasive case to launch pre-emptive strikes against Pakistan than did the United States against Iraq.[26] In October 2004, a Japanese Defense Agency panel report stipulated a requirement for launching pre-emptive strikes against enemy ballistic-missile launch installations with a ballistic missile of its own.[27] Under pressure from its coalition partner, the Liberal Democratic Party decided to drop the ballistic-missile study plan, but it was later revealed that Japanese planners had turned instead to considering LACMs. According to Japanese defence officials, they anticipate fewer obstacles, both inside and outside Japan, to acquiring cruise missiles than ballistic missiles.[28] Moreover, the high cost of purchasing US land- and sea-based missile defences, particularly in light of the ever-growing size of the Chinese and North Korean offensive-missile arsenals, is an economic and strategic justification for acquiring LACMs. Cheaper offensive-missile options allow the Japanese to mimic the US military's doctrinal preference for 'attack operations', or counterforce strikes to reduce the enemy's capacity to overwhelm missile defences.[29]

Elsewhere in Northeast Asia, the United States has long sought to curb the missile ambitions of South Korea and Taiwan. Worried about a North–South arms race and keen to avoid suspicion in Tokyo and Beijing of a South Korean missile build-up, Washington persuaded Seoul to accept a 300km range/500kg payload limit on ballistic missiles as a condition of South Korea's entry into the Missile Technology Control Regime in 2001. Yet, despite the regime's equal treatment of ballistic and cruise missiles, Washington gave Seoul the go-ahead to develop LACMs regardless of range, so long as the payload was under 500kg.[30] Shortly after Pyongyang's October 2006 nuclear test, South Korean military authorities leaked the existence of four LACMs under development, with ranges between 500 and 1,500km. The South Korean press took immediate note that both the whole of North Korea as well as neighbouring countries such as Japan and China would be within the range of these missiles.[31] Almost simultaneously, the South Korean military rolled out a new defence plan involving pre-emptive use of 'surgical strike' weapons, including LACMs, against enemy missile batteries.[32] For cost reasons, South Korea has rejected America's offer to sell them its most advanced *Patriot* missile-defence system (the *Patriot* Advanced Capability-3).[33] Offensive solutions are clearly winning out over missile defence in South Korea.

A similar story is unfolding in Taiwan. Since the mid 1970s, Washington has pressured Taiwan to steer clear of ballistic-missile development, while allowing Taipei to pursue a short-range anti-ship cruise missile. To cope with China's relentless build-up of ballistic missiles facing Taiwan, Washington preferred that Taipei purchase *Patriot* missile defences. Taiwan finally did so in the mid 1990s, but has thus far baulked at purchasing the latest American 'hit-to-kill' missile defences due to their high cost and the realisation that they would not suffice against China's new LACMs. Taiwan now appears headed, increasingly openly, toward emphasising offensive missiles as its best option. In early 2005, Taiwan test-fired its first LACM to a range of 500km, but with the intention to extend it to 1,000km and to deploy 500 on mobile launchers.[34] Taiwanese military analysts also spoke of a 'preventive self-defence' strike option, entailing early pre-emptive use of cruise missiles to sow confusion in China's strike plans.[35] The US State Department has pressured Taiwan to terminate its LACM programme, but with few signs of success. In fact, Washington's long-standing policy against Taiwan's acquisition of ballistic missiles is showing signs of failure, too. Taiwan told a visiting US delegation in April 2007 that it is converting its *Tien Kung* air-defence interceptor into a ballistic missile to complement its growing LACM ambitions.[36]

Offensive solutions are clearly winning out

Nor is South Asia immune from the contagion. In early 2004, the Indian military rolled out a new offensive strategy, called 'Cold Start', involving the capacity to conduct lightning strikes across the Line of Control in Kashmir followed by withdrawal before Pakistan had a chance to react.[37] Precision, long-range strikes, including India's new *BrahMos*, would feature heavily in such a strategy. But Indian strategists have reacted to Pakistan's

Babur, which has a substantial range advantage over *BrahMos* (currently 400km), by suggesting that India approach its missile partner, Russia, to obtain certain 'restrictive technologies' to match or exceed *Babur*'s range. Such an expansion of *BrahMos*'s capabilities is seen as feasible because, unlike India's ballistic-missile programmes, the *BrahMos* is 'not under the global scanner'.[38] The discrepancy in missile norms also came into play after Pakistan's surprise test launch of the *Babur* in August 2005. Only a few days earlier, Pakistan and India had agreed in principle to notify each other before missile tests. But the agreement, like the Hague Code, dealt only with ballistic missiles.

Implications

Ballistic missiles have dominated the missile-proliferation scene. They symbolised ultimate military power during the Cold War. Iraq's use of modified *Scud* ballistic missiles during the 1991 Gulf War mesmerised the public with lasting images of duels between Iraqi *Scuds* and US *Patriot* missile defences. Ballistic missiles based on *Scud* technology have spread widely to potential American adversaries and, as a potential means of nuclear-, biological- or chemical-weapons delivery, they are a significant impediment to US force projection and a potent means of future coercive diplomacy. An epidemic of cruise-missile proliferation would aggravate matters gravely. If the use of large numbers of LACMs becomes a major feature of military operations in the future, a combination of cruise- and ballistic-missile attacks, even with conventional payloads, could make early entry into regional bases of operation increasingly problematic. Nuclear or biological payloads would produce catastrophic consequences.

By fixating on the familiar threat of ballistic missiles, strategic planners and non-proliferation specialists are in danger of overlooking the broader implications of parallel cruise- and ballistic-missile proliferation. Writing in a Foreword to a 1995 monograph I co-authored that addressed the need to control the expected spread of LACMs, the late Albert Wohlstetter wryly warned of the tendency of decision-makers to view so-called lesser-included cases – in this regard, the anticipated spread of LACMs – as merely problems that could readily be handled by larger policy thrusts. As he put it: 'the dog that could deal with the cat could easily handle the kitten'.[39] In December 1996, a congressionally mandated independent review panel chaired by Robert Gates, former director of the CIA (and currently secretary of defense), chided the intelligence community and, by implication, policymakers for 'an inconsistency in ... its treatment of ballistic and cruise missiles'.[40] While the Gates panel found ample reason for concern about cruise-missile threats to the American homeland, it disclosed that the intelligence community had dismissed LACMs, despite their technological feasibility, largely because it could not imagine reasons and scenarios for their use. The US intelligence community has since sought to treat missile threats with greater balance, but evenhandedness is far less evident in non-proliferation policy and missile-defence planning.

Faulty non-proliferation policies need urgent attention. The second-class treatment of cruise missiles will not change until the Hague Code gives the same normative status to ballistic and cruise missiles. A more progressive approach to addressing missile proliferation within the Missile Technology Control Regime is also required to curb the LACM epidemic. Given the cardinal importance of specialised knowledge in enabling indigenous development of LACMs, particularly those skills transferred through direct, face-to-face engagement between skilled practitioners and novice engineers, much better thinking is needed on ways and means of preventing, or interfering with, such intangible technology transfers.

Practices that encourage US cooperation with Russia and China would make dampening intangible technology transfers easier. One important priority for the next US administration would be greatly increased transparency measures vis-à-vis both Russia and China in regard to US defence programmes, particularly on ballistic-missile defences, the US nuclear posture, and growing US reliance on conventionally armed global-strike concepts. Working closely with Moscow on developing joint ballistic-missile defence and early-warning systems would eliminate a source of great tension between the two countries over the past two years.

The United States points the finger at Russia and China (not a formal Missile Technology Control Regime member but an avowed adherent to its principles) for their inconsistent export practices. Most notably, China's suspected support for Pakistan's new LACM programme, if true, egregiously violates regime principles. On balance, however, it would be better to have China operating from within the regime than as a mere adherent, but only on the condition that Beijing adjust its behaviour, particularly in regard to changes in the regime since 1993 that improve its treatment of cruise-missile and unmanned aerial vehicle transfers. Regime members should also encourage Russia to ignore Indian requests for technological assistance to help develop strategic-range LACMs in response to Pakistan's new cruise missile. And Russia should exercise extreme caution in selling the *BrahMos* to interested countries in Latin America and Southeast Asia, among others.

US export behaviour warrants adjustment as well. Unless the United States decides to add cruise missiles to the Hague Code, normative change is doomed. Washington should also reverse course in regard to its reported wish to loosen rules governing the sale of both large unmanned aerial vehicles and missile-defence interceptors, and possibly remove interceptors altogether from consideration. Though the Bush administration has grand plans for global missile defences and views unmanned aerial vehicles as tools that allow for precision delivery of conventional weapons rather than nuclear weapons, it is foolish to view interceptors or large unmanned aerial vehicles as purely defensive systems, incapable of offensive use. The latter can deliver nuclear payloads or large quantities of biological or chemical agents, and the Soviet-era SA-2 interceptor has been widely used as a basis for building offensive ballistic missiles. In the end, incautious missile defence and unmanned aerial vehicle exports could accelerate rather than abate the LACM epidemic.

While improved defences against short- and medium-range ballistic missiles have made LACMs more attractive offensive options for several states, cruise-missile defence programmes remain stalled. Fighters equipped with advanced detection and tracking radars will eventually possess some modest capability to deal with low-volume attacks. But existing US programmes are underfunded, while interoperability, doctrinal and organisational issues discourage the military services from producing joint and effective systems for defending US forces and allies in military campaigns. Homeland defence is even more sadly lacking: an August 2006 Pentagon assessment identified nine 'capability gaps' that may not be rectified until 2015.[41] However, cruise-missile defences needed for safely projecting force over great distances ought to take priority over very-low-probability, high-consequence threats such as terrorist employment of ballistic or cruise missiles from sea.

Looming large in any missile-defence debate is the question of affordability. During the height of the Reagan-era Strategic Defense Initiative, defence strategist Paul Nitze, no critic of missile defences, argued that they should be 'cost effective at the margin', meaning that it should be less expensive to make incremental improvements to missile defences than it would be to achieve offensive gains. Whereas such a proposition always seemed dubious with respect to ballistic missiles, it appears inconceivable when large arsenals of relatively cheap cruise missiles are added to the mix. In a new era in which denying one's adversaries their military objectives has superseded mutual assured nuclear destruction as a strategic imperative, the missile-defence challenge will stiffen immeasurably if LACMs spread. At the very least, the United States, as the predominant if not exclusive purveyor of missile defences globally, should carefully remind its friends and allies of what its missile defences can and cannot be expected to accomplish against current and prospective missile threats, ballistic and cruise missiles alike.

Though new weapons do not inherently increase the risk of conflict, when coupled with pre-emptive doctrines, advanced weapons that are difficult to detect and could allow for a surprise attack (especially those capable of producing decisive results with conventional warheads) may tempt states to take risks. Past wars in the Middle East come readily to mind, as does China's increasing reliance on a doctrine espousing 'actively taking the initiative' to catch the enemy unprepared.[42] That Taiwan, South Korea and Japan, driven by the high costs of missile defence and the perceived benefits of cruise missiles, have also turned to pre-emptive strike notions, ought to be a matter of great concern. By tying precision conventional-strike weapons to truly offensive war doctrines, a number of states, including several great powers, may inadvertently be moving closer to lowering the vital threshold between peace and war. These developments suggest the urgent need for the United States to cut a path back to strategic stability by toning down, if not entirely eliminating, the pre-emption option.

Notes

1 'President Musharraf Compares Babur Missile with India's BrahMos', Islamabad PTV World in English, 11 August 2005, Foreign Broadcast Information Services [FBIS] transcribed text.

2 Land-attack cruise missiles (LACMs), like the US *Tomahawk*, are distinguished from widely proliferated anti-ship cruise missiles (ASCMs), 75,000 of which are now deployed by over 70 countries. LACMs generally have substantially longer ranges (300–3,000km) than ASCMs and fly over land to their intended target, while ASCMs are employed generally against ships at sea from comparatively shorter ranges (75–300km). Unmanned air or aerial vehicles comprise a third category. Relegated, until recently, largely to reconnaissance and target-drone roles, vehicles like the US *Predator* have been adapted to deliver munitions, with some important success in Afghanistan and Yemen in attacking al-Qaeda targets. Armed vehicles such as *Predator* are distinguished from LACMs and ASCMs in that they can be re-used. A fourth category consists of unmanned combat air vehicles, which are essentially high-performance aircraft flown by a ground operator (like *Predator*) and capable of performing various lethal and non-lethal missions. Unlike ballistic missiles which, for the most part, operate outside the atmosphere, cruise missiles, unmanned aerial vehicles and unmanned combat air vehicles are fitted with aerodynamic surfaces that furnish lift to keep them airborne, within the atmosphere, during their entire flight. See Dennis M. Gormley, 'New Developments in Unmanned Air Vehicles and Land-Attack Cruise Missiles', in *SIPRI Yearbook 2003* (Oxford: Oxford University Press for SIPRI, 2003), pp. 409–32.

3 Joseph Cirincione, 'The Declining Ballistic Missile Threat', Carnegie Endowment for International Peace, 25 January 2005, http://www.carnegieendowment.org/static/npp/Declining_Ballistic_Missile_Threat_2005.pdf.

4 W. Seth Carus, *Cruise Missile Proliferation in the 1990s* (Westport, CT: Praeger, 1992), p. 3.

5 K. Scott McMahon and Dennis M. Gormley, *Controlling the Spread of Land-Attack Cruise Missiles* (Marina del Rey, CA: American Institute for Strategic Cooperation, 1995), p. 26.

6 *Report of the Defense Science Board Task Force on Nuclear Capabilities, Report Summary* (Washington DC: Office of the Under Secretary of Defense for Acquisition, Technology, and Logistics, December 2006), http://www.fas.org/irp/agency/dod/dsb/nuclear.pdf.

7 For the classic treatment, see Michael Polanyi, *Personal Knowledge* (London: Routledge and Kegan Paul, 1958). As it applies to missile technology, see Donald MacKenzie, *Inventing Accuracy* (Cambridge, MA: MIT Press, 1990).

8 Donald MacKenzie, 'Theories of Technology and the Abolition of Nuclear Weapons', in Donald MacKenzie and Judy Wajcman, eds, *The Social Shaping of Technology* (Philadelphia, PA: Open University Press, 1999), pp. 425–9.

9 Donald MacKenzie and Graham Spinardi, 'Tacit Knowledge, Weapons Design, and the Uninvention of Nuclear Weapons', *American Journal of Sociology*, vol. 101, no. 1, July 1995, p. 44.

10 While the Rumsfeld Commission was formally tasked by Congress only to evaluate the threat of ballistic missiles to the United States, the commission's final report did note that 'cruise missiles have a number of characteristics which could be seen as increasingly valuable in fulfilling the aspirations of emerging ballistic missile states'. Besides my and Gregory DeSantis' unclassified presentation, delivered on 3 June 1998, my separately delivered unclassified working paper, 'Transfer Pathways for Cruise Missiles', was also appended to the commission's full final report. For the Rumsfeld Commission's executive summary see http://www.fas.org/irp/threat/bm-threat.htm.

11 *Comprehensive Report of the Special Advisor to the DCI on Iraq's WMD*, Vol. II (Washington DC: Central Intelligence Agency, 2004), pp. 39–41.

12 *Ibid.*, pp. 42–56.

13 'Focus on Iran', Geostrategy-Direct, 18 October 2005.

14 Dennis M. Gormley, *Dealing with the Threat of Cruise Missiles*, Adelphi Paper no. 339 (Oxford: Oxford University Press for the IISS, 2001), pp. 9–10.

15 *Ibid.*, p. 9. These advantages notwithstanding, possession of even a short-range ballistic missile puts a country on a path toward developing a much longer-range delivery system, including one of intercontinental range. Today's longest-range LACMs are limited to roughly a range of 3,000km.

16 Dennis M. Gormley, 'Missile Defence Myopia: Lessons from the Iraq War', *Survival*, vol. 45, no. 4, Winter 2003–04, pp. 61–86.

17 Michael R. Gordon, 'A Poor Man's Air Force', *New York Times*, 19 June 2003.

18 Dana Milbank and Dafna Linzer, 'U.S., India May Share Nuclear Technology', *Washington Post*, 19 July 2005. Such permission is required because of the significant presence of US technology in the *Arrow* system.

19 'Pakistan Test Fires Nuclear-Capable Cruise Missile', 22 March 2007, Agence France-Presse, FBIS in English.

20 'Iran Seeks Cruise Missile to Support Shihab', *Middle East Newsline*, 10 June 2004.

21 Mark A. Stokes, *China's Strategic Modernization: Implications for the United States* (Carlisle Barracks, PA: Strategic Studies Institute, US Army War College, 1999), p. 81.

22 Kim Min-seok, 'Seoul Has Longer-range Cruise Missile', *JoongAng Ilbo* (Internet version, in English), 21 September 2006.

23 For a useful treatment, see Dinshaw Mistry, *Containing Missile Proliferation* (Seattle, WA: University of Washington Press, 2003), 15–40.

24 Ariel E. Levite and Elizabeth Sherwood-Randall, 'The Case for Discriminate Force', *Survival*, vol. 44, no. 4, Winter 2002–03, pp. 89–90.

25 Steve Andreason and Dennis Gormley, 'Edging Ever Closer to a Nuclear Death Row', *Minneapolis Star-Tribune*, 29 March 2006.

26 S.M. Hali, 'Exercise Vajra Shakti', *The Nation*, 19 May 2005.

27 'Preemptive Strike Ability Said Necessary for Japan', *Japan Times*, 2 October 2004.

28 Interviews with Japanese defence officials in Tokyo, March 2005.

29 Joint Publication 3-01.5, *Doctrine for Joint Theater Missile Defense* (Washington DC: US Government Printing Office, 1994).

30 Sources differ over the precise payload weight, with Korean news reports stating for the most part that in regard to cruise missiles there is no restriction on range as long as the payload is under 500kg.

31 'S. Korea's Cruise Missile Program Revealed', *Chosun IIbo* (Internet version, in English), 25 October 2006, http://english.chosun.com/w21data/html/news/200610/200610250007.html.

32 Chin Tae-ung, 'Military Works on Nuclear Defense Plans', *Korea Herald* (Internet version, in English), 28 October 2006.

33 Instead of purchasing expensive American *Patriot* missile defences, Seoul has turned to Germany to discuss buying a modest number of older, surplus *Patriots*. See Jin Dae-woong, 'Korea, Germany Discuss Patriot Missile Deal', *Korea Herald*, (Internet version, in English), 13 March 2007.

34 Wendell Minnick, 'Taiwan Tests "Brave Wind" Cruise Missile', *Defense News*, 12 March 2007, http://www.defensenews.com/story.php?F=2610742&C=asiapac.

35 Chang Li-the, 'Taking a Look at Taiwan's Cruise Missile Requirements and Capabilities – A Report on the Successful Test-Firing of the Hsiung-Feng 2E', *Defense Technology Monthly*, July 2005, FBIS report in Chinese, 3 October 2005).

36 Wu Ming-Chieh, 'Publicizing Cruise Missile Meant to Pressure United States into Exporting Technology', *Taipei Chung-Kuo Shih-Pao* (Internet version, in Chinese), 27 April 2007, FBIS translated text.

37 I am grateful to Sharad Joshi, on whose PhD dissertation committee I served, for drawing my attention to Indian interest in pre-emptive strategy. See Sharad Joshi, *The Practice of Coercive Diplomacy in the Post 9/11 Period*, unpublished PhD dissertation, Graduate School of Public and International Affairs, University of Pittsburgh, December 2006. Also see Walter C. Ladwig III, 'A Cold Start for Hot Wars? The Indian Army's New Limited War Doctrine', *International Security*, vol. 32, no. 3, Winter 2007–08, pp. 158–90.

38 'No Time to Lose', *New Delhi Force* (Internet version, in English), 9 March 2005, FBIS transcribed text.

39 K. Scott McMahon and Dennis M. Gormley, with a Foreword by Albert Wohlstetter, *Controlling the Spread of Land-Attack Cruise Missiles* (Marina del Rey, CA: American Institute for Strategic Cooperation, 1995), p. v.

40 'NIE 95-19: Independent Panel Review of "Emerging Missile Threats to North America During the Next 15 Years"', December 1996, http://www/fas.org/irp/threat/missile/oca961908.htm.

41 John Liang, 'DoD Finds Cruise Missile Defense "Gaps"', InsideDefense.com NewsStand, 17 August 2006.

42 James C. Mulvenon et al., *Chinese Responses to U.S. Military Transformation and Implications for the Department of Defense* (Santa Monica, CA: The Rand Corporation, 2006), p. 50.

The California Consensus: Can Private Aid End Global Poverty?

Raj M. Desai and Homi Kharas

Foreign aid from private sources is changing the landscape for international development assistance. Since 1998, international giving by US-based corporate and independent foundations has doubled, and they now contribute, along with non-governmental organisations (NGOs) and charities headquartered in the United States, over $30 billion to international causes annually. The World Bank, in comparison, disburses about $20bn in loans, credits and grants.[1] Some have traced the beginning of the new era of global philanthropy to 1997, when cable-TV mogul Ted Turner pledged $1bn to the United Nations – and challenged wealthy 'skinflints' to do likewise.[2] Two years later the world's richest man, Bill Gates, poured $16.5bn into his foundation to help pay for a campaign to improve health care for the world's poor. Bill and Melinda Gates have since pumped $31bn – over two-thirds of their current net worth – into their foundation, making it the world's largest. With Warren Buffett's promise to contribute an additional $31bn, the Gates Foundation promises to become the largest, most rapidly growing foundation of all time.

This growth in private aid is being seen at all levels: community foundations are growing faster than 'mega-charities' such as the Gates, Ford and

Raj M. Desai is Associate Professor of International Development at the Edmund A. Walsh School of Foreign Service at Georgetown University, and a visiting fellow at the Wolfensohn Center for Development at the Brookings Institution. He has served as a consultant to the World Bank Group, the Asian Development Bank, the United Nations Development Programme and other international organisations. **Homi Kharas** is a Senior Fellow at the Wolfensohn Center for Development at the Brookings Institution and a member of the Working Group for the Commission on Growth and Development. He previously worked at the World Bank, serving as Chief Economist for the East Asia and Pacific region, and as Director for Poverty Reduction and Economic Management, Finance and Private Sector Development.

Survival | vol. 50 no. 4 | August–September 2008 | pp. 155–168 DOI 10.1080/00396330802328982

Hewlett Foundations.[3] Meanwhile, NGOs distribute more development aid than the entire United Nations and multilateral system, excluding the European Community. Large NGOs such as CARE, Oxfam, Médecins Sans Frontières and Save the Children, each with annual budgets exceeding $500 million, now deliver essential services and public goods that poor-country governments cannot. Over the next decade, this expansion in private giving to international causes will continue.

Charitable organisations and philanthropies, of course, have long found fertile soil in the United States. John Winthrop's sermon 'A Model of Christian Charity', best remembered for its invocation of the 'city on a hill', argued that the wealthy had a holy duty to look after the poor. And Alexis de Tocqueville commented in *Democracy in America* on the American disposition to organise and join voluntary associations which, among other things, provided relief to those in need. Modern philanthropy emerged between the 1880s and 1915 when multimillionaires sought practical ways of disposing of their immense wealth. The cornerstone of charitable giving – domestic and global – was Andrew Carnegie's set of guidelines for 'scientific philanthropy': investigating the causes of poverty and influencing the morals of the poor by personal involvement. Similarly, private giving for international causes can trace its roots, primarily, to the United States, where nineteenth- and early twentieth-century international charity was closely tied to American missionary work around the globe. Both the Rockefeller Foundation (1913) and Ford Foundation (1936), for example, had partnerships with religious missions in India among their first programmes in developing countries.

Early twentieth-century global philanthropy focused primarily on health and disease, including the eradication of yellow fever, the professionalisation and training of public health workers, and the spread of Western medicine to non-Western lands. Post-Second World War philanthropy, on the other hand, broadened to encompass educational needs, birth control, maternal health and agriculture.

Private development aid may soon eclipse official aid, a development that many of those disappointed with the spotty performance of such assistance would welcome: 'Turn all foreign assistance over to the private sector' trumpeted a *Wall Street Journal* article in July 2007.[4] Development activists (and an alliance of left-leaning NGOs, conservative groups, and other aid critics) have long argued that the global 'foreign aid' regime is ineffective – even harmful – and increasingly irrelevant given the needs of the poorest around the world. These claims are supported to some extent by official-aid statistics. Of the more than $100bn in official foreign aid disbursed by rich countries to poor ones in 2005, over $60bn was used for debt relief, technical cooperation, emergency or humanitarian relief, and food aid. Of the remaining $40bn directed at actual development projects and programmes, perhaps half reached its intended beneficiaries, the rest being spent on administrative costs, side payments to politicians or local elites in recipient countries, or routine bribes to bureaucrats. In other words, only $20bn actually reached the poor. Of that, a mere $5–6bn was allocated for the poorest continent, Africa.[5]

In response to such deficiencies, the global foreign-assistance regime is rapidly changing. Traditional donors are splintering into many specialised agencies. Some, like the Millennium Challenge Corporation, only select well-performing countries. Others target their resources in places where they determine the need is greatest. The Global Fund to Fight Aids, Tuberculosis, and Malaria, for example, focuses its activities in those countries where the burden of these diseases is heaviest. Countries like China, India, Venezuela, Russia and Saudi Arabia are setting up their own foreign-aid programmes with their own approaches to development cooperation.

Meanwhile, a new form of global philanthropy has emerged, exemplified by the Global Philanthropy Forum. Established in 2001, the forum considers itself a 'community of donors and social investors committed to international causes'. More generally, it promotes a new philanthropy that is increasingly global, aims to reduce poverty through flexible and innovative initiatives, and sits at the intersection of the private and non-profit sectors. It is also closely tied to the US information-technology sector – many of the forum's members derive their wealth from high-tech and IT ventures. Thus, their initiatives largely reflect their experiences in starting companies and securing capital, customers and markets, and they are focused on innovative, small-scale projects in which there is often significant donor involvement. Their approach – what has been called 'venture philanthropy', 'philanthrocapitalism' or 'social entrepreneurship' – emphasises the 'scalability' of innovative, small-scale projects (that is, the extent to which the number of beneficiaries can be quickly expanded). In contrast to earlier philanthropic approaches, the new global philanthropy has moved away from programme-based grant-making to a more open, flexible architecture in which donors are typically heavily involved in beneficiary projects. And there is an emphasis on blurring the line between 'non-profit' and 'for-profit' approaches, as the new philanthropists seek to invest in income-generating activities. Google.org (a for-profit charity aiming to address issues of global health, disease, poverty and climate change) and the for-profit Omidyar Network are prime examples. Rather than funding a medical clinic, for example, the new philanthropists invest in biotech companies working on tropical diseases. Rather than fund the distribution of drugs, the new philanthropists seek to invest in and create incentives for drug companies to operate in poor regions.

Private aid is less susceptible to 'leakage'

Many of these newer foundations, charities and non-profit organisations have reached something of a consensus on their potential role in reducing global poverty. Reflecting the Silicon Valley dot-com boom that created much of the wealth of these new philanthropists, this 'California consensus' holds an abiding faith in the capacity of innovation, technology and modern management methods to solve problems of extreme poverty. Indeed, the strength of the new private-aid movement stems from the 'power of many', the notion that the thousands of international NGOs, tens of thousands of developing-country NGOs and hundreds of thousands of community-based organisations in developing countries provide a network of knowledge and resources that can be tapped in powerful new ways. Private aid is less susceptible to 'leakage' due to corruption and bribes, and because it usually avoids governmental recipients and is transferred directly to front-line NGOs and development projects, it avoids the thorny problems associated with poorly functioning public sectors in developing countries. Smaller portions of private aid are spent on overhead and administrative costs, and on technical assistance and other purposes that typically fund contractors, advisers and consultants in rich countries.

How much private aid?

Most of the world's charitable activity takes place in the domestic rather than the international sphere. Out of 100,000 foundations worldwide, fewer than 1,000 conduct activities that affect developing nations. Moreover, although the United States is by far the largest source of global private aid, only about 11% (18% when the Gates Foundation is included) of US foundations' grant-making has gone to international development, and most of that money has been channelled through international institutions such as the International Committee of the Red Cross or the World Health Organisation rather than going directly to developing countries.[6]

Nevertheless, the amount of private aid dedicated to international development is rapidly growing. Estimates for the United States suggest a fourfold increase in international giving in the 1990s, and, after a dip in 2002 following the stock-market crash, steady growth since. In 2005, private giving from the United States to developing countries, excluding remittances, was estimated at $33.5bn.[7] Sources of American giving comprise foundations, corporate donations, private voluntary organisations, NGOs, educational scholarships and religious organisations (see Table 1). Moreover, this giving is broad-based: some 65% of all households with annual incomes of less than $100,000 contribute to international charitable causes.[8]

US philanthropic giving represents between 49 and 58% of the global total annually.[9] If US private international giving, excluding humanitarian aid and emergency relief, is about $21.4bn per year, then global

Table 1. Sources of US Private International Giving, 2005

	US$bn
Foundations	2.2
Corporations	5.1
Voluntary and non-governmental organisations (NGOs)	16.2
Higher education	4.6
Religious organisations	5.4
Total	**33.5**

Source: *The Index of Global Philanthropy*, Hudson Institute, 2007

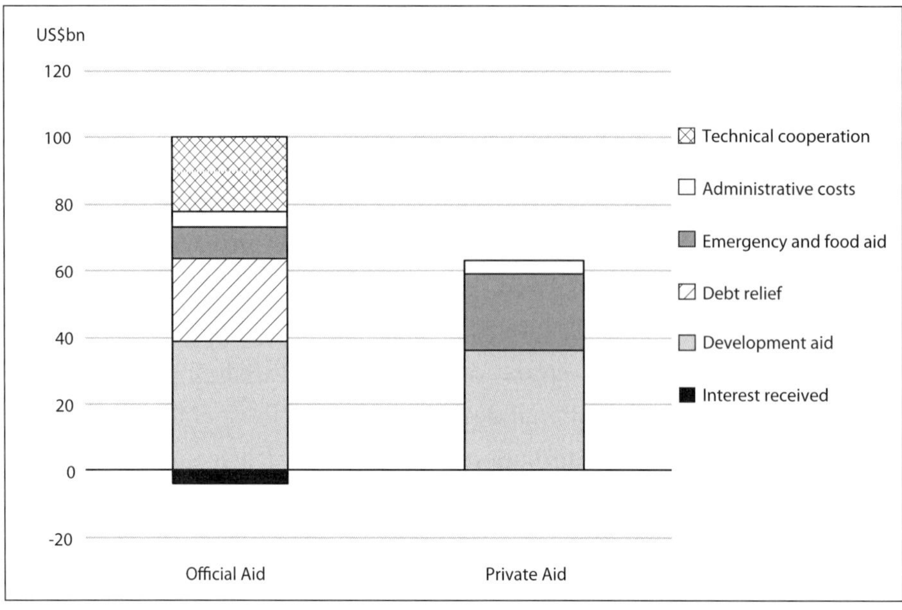

Figure 1. Breakdown of International Aid Spending, 2005

private giving for international development might total around $37–44bn per year. However, not all of this is available for development projects. In the United States, administrative overhead and fundraising consume roughly 11% of NGO expenditures.[10] Applying this percentage to all private-aid organisations yields an estimate for private giving in the range of $33–39bn per year. This is less than official aid from rich countries, which totals $61bn, plus $6.7bn in new developing-country bilateral aid programmes. But one-third of this ($23bn) pays for technical cooperation and is not available for development projects and programmes. Moreover, $6bn in bilateral funds is channelled through private NGOs, and when these are counted, private service delivery may be as large as, or even larger than, official aid in terms of the money actually reaching the poor. Figure 1 shows that comparable amounts of official and private aid are allocated for development work. It also shows that charitable organisations and NGOs have been generous in mobilising funds for emergency operations. In the United States, humanitarian aid and relief work is estimated to represent 36% of total private assistance, much more than is the case for official aid.[11]

The destination of private aid is more difficult to assess, but general trends suggest a focus on Africa and Asia. Among prominent international NGOs and US foundations, Africa and Asia are clear areas of intense activity. But US-based organisations give Latin America nearly twice the attention Africa receives, suggesting a propensity to send aid to projects closer to home in geographic, cultural and religious terms.[12]

How effective is private aid?

The 'California consensus' view is that private aid is more effective than official development assistance for numerous reasons. Freed from the complex decision-making structures of official aid agencies and the sensitivities of maintaining bilateral relationships, international philanthropies are assumed to be cost-effective, nimble institutions that adapt well to local environments.[13] Overhead costs are lower: foundations and charitable organisations typically lack a (costly) network of field offices with international staff, and instead tend to rely on local staff and partnerships with frontline NGOs. NGOs, in turn, find their public image is bolstered by keeping overhead costs low.[14] Very little private-aid money is funnelled back to consultants and contractors in rich countries, leaving more for beneficiaries in developing countries. And while official donor allocations are influenced by, among other things, political coalitions, policy concerns and colonial ties, NGO allocations are assumed to be influenced by need. Finally, because international philanthropy does not fund public sectors in recipient countries, NGO resources are said to suffer from less leakage (in the form of bribes and other transfers to public officials) than official aid.

There are certainly reasons to believe that private aid is more cost effective, and that larger portions of private aid than official aid actually reach the poor. But in contrast to the extensive evaluation of official-aid effectiveness, there is very little evidence for or against the argument that private aid is more cost efficient. To be sure, self-evaluations of NGOs are overwhelmingly positive, but these are rarely conducted according to accepted standards of reliable evaluation. NGOs raise billions of dollars each year from individuals, private- and public-sector donors, and charitable foundations, but there are no commonly accepted benchmarks for evaluating the effectiveness of NGOs in their stated missions, and NGOs are not subject to the same standards of budgetary and governance oversight as official aid agencies.

Of the thousand or so NGOs operating internationally,[15] a tiny portion has been evaluated. The available evidence is mixed. One study of several European NGOs found that NGO aid per capita had a limited effect on infant mortality and female illiteracy in recipient countries.[16] An examination of Swedish NGOs found that the selection of potential recipients was less affected by policy considerations than was the case with official aid, but that the funds did not outperform official Swedish aid.[17] A study of leading NGOs from the Netherlands, Germany, Norway and the United States concluded that NGOs tend to cluster in 'favourite' recipients, allowing them to take advantage of networks of other NGOs and aid workers.[18] Thus, NGOs complement official aid, concentrating their efforts in the same countries as official donors. This means, however, that NGOs and official donors often make similar allocation decisions; it also means that NGOs are able to spread the blame for failure among many partners.

The history of charitable giving is replete with scandals

Some sceptics of private development aid believe that aid allocation is influenced by considerations unrelated to the needs of the poor in recipient countries. In particular, they assert that increased competition among NGOs for funding has prompted these groups to capitalise on the misery of the world's poor in order to perpetuate and fund themselves. As a result, NGOs hop from crisis to crisis, forever seeking the next development cause or humanitarian disaster that will draw funding. A study of NGOs, however, found no evidence of 'faddishness' in aid allocations.[19]

While there are reasons to believe that NGOs may be less vulnerable to corruption, some notes of caution are necessary. First, the history of charitable giving is replete with scandals involving misappropriation of funds and theft. High-profile incidents include the misuse of children's-aid funds by US-based groups in the late 1990s, the American Red Cross's use of donations in response to the 11 September attacks for other causes, and a series of questionable land deals by the Washington DC-based Nature Conservancy in 2003. A study by Harvard University's Hauser Center for Nonprofit Organizations listed 152 incidents of misconduct by US non-profits between 1995 and 2002, including 104 cases of criminal activity.[20] These may be no more alarming than recent cases of corporate wrongdoing, but as NGOs operate more and more like businesses, there will inevitably be a greater need for tighter rules and enforcement.

Second, many high-profile NGOs are now closely involved with managing official aid programmes and may be susceptible to the same sorts of pressures that traditional implementing agencies face, including the temptation to adopt corrupt practices to speed up implementation. Between 1990 and 2005, official aid grants and funds channelled through NGOs more than tripled, rising from $1.7bn to $5.4bn in constant 2005 dollars. Programmes executed by NGOs now constitute between 5 and 6% of total official development aid, up from 2% in 1990.[21]

Third, unlike official aid agencies, which have the backing of recipient governments, NGOs often find themselves at odds with the governments of countries in which they work. Governments may deny them access to those in need; officials or warlords may demand payoffs; and local violence may threaten the safety of field personnel. This kind of harassment, unfortunately, is often a way of life for NGO workers. In extreme cases, recipient governments see NGOs as Trojan horses for Western governments. When international aid workers die in the field, it is more likely to be from intentional violence than from any other cause, including illness and vehicle accidents. In the vast majority of cases, aid workers have been deliberately targeted.[22]

Moreover, accountability with respect to private aid raises a host of additional difficulties. Global regulation is mixed at best. The United States and United Kingdom have fairly rigorous reporting requirements for charitable organisations, but in many other countries there is virtually no control. While many large NGOs have strong internal rules, NGOs as a class are generally much less transparent than either business or government.[23] Large and small NGOs, the beneficiaries of their activities, and their donors are increasingly aware of the importance of ensuring that the work of international charities is transparent and subject to oversight. But in practice even those who think that NGOs should be accountable cannot agree on how to accomplish that goal. Should donors or recipients judge success? Should achievement be measured by those within the organisation or by an independent watchdog? And what exactly should be measured: short-term improvements or harder-to-assess long-term investments?

Another criticism is that NGOs are too small and fragmented to make a real difference on a large scale. By this argument, private aid organisations can alleviate the worst forms of poverty by providing 'band-aid' assistance, but this does not mean they are effective in attacking the root causes of poverty that are often to be found in the ineffective – or downright harmful – operations of the public sector in poor countries.[24]

Finally, private aid can exacerbate the growing fragmentation and volatility that characterise the international-aid architecture. The costs of fragmentation and volatility are well known: multiple donors will make requests for studies and for individual meetings with country officials; these donors will establish separate project-management units and multiple procurement practices for the same products; and they will be unable to coordinate to identify and propagate best practices. With the multiplicity of groups now involved in the delivery of aid, and especially as amounts increase, it is common for aid recipients to see high volatility in their year-to-year disbursements. This translates into large swings in a recipient's domestic expenditures, especially recurrent spending which is difficult to adjust.

Breaking the official aid cartel

If the new milieu of international aid is fragmented and volatile, it is also one in which private aid will continue to represent an ever-larger share of total assistance. With traditional multilateral and rich-country bilateral aid agencies still expanding, developing-country aid agencies proliferating, and private aid from large and small foundations (and individuals) growing all the time, 'harmonisation' will be harder to achieve. Recipients who once faced a choice between loans and grants now have a vast repertoire of instruments from which to choose. Under these conditions, how can the growth in private aid improve the overall architecture for assistance to poor countries?

A competitive market for aid – in which experimental and innovative ideas are matched with donors – has historically faced several obstacles. Official aid to most places has typically been determined by political alliances, geopolitical considerations and national security rather than need. For many years, private aid was too small to make a difference. Accurate information about donor performance was often difficult to come by, preventing recipients from making informed choices. And the lack of rigorous evaluation prevented donors from understanding the prospects for success and failure of different programmes.

Competition should be embraced by official aid agencies

The oligopoly that characterises official aid can be broken only by its regulators: the political powers that govern their boards. The governance structure of most official aid agencies encourages them to harmonise activities, diffusing accountability. As is often the case with oligopolies, 'buyers' (recipients seeking help) are usually forced to deal exclusively with a particular official bureaucracy on matters of project design, appraisal and evaluation, and are prevented from getting second opinions from non-official sources.[25] Instead, competition should be embraced by official aid agencies. They should be encouraged to be transparent about the costs of their programmes and open to contracting with those who can provide the same poverty-reduction services for less.

Also, the focus of private donors must shift to programmes that can be replicated and enlarged. Traditional donors have long claimed that they can 'scale up' programmes more effectively than private-aid suppliers, but this is because they have been entrusted with far more resources. The availability of resources would be less of a constraint for private-aid givers if they could demonstrate their ability to reduce poverty and improve public services for the poor. But too often, private aid programmes mix several objectives – providing fair wages, minimising environmental impacts, changing mindsets – in a way that reflects the preferences (and zeal) of their founders. This may be admirable, but it often produces short-term projects. The history of private global philanthropy is filled with plenty of 'success stories' with little follow-up.

Finally, private donors need to intensify efforts to better gauge their own effectiveness. Information, coordination and planning are becoming harder as more players deliver aid. In well-functioning markets, trade associations and other bodies monitor market conditions, set standards and define regulations that force a certain degree of transparency. Private-aid givers need to do more to provide good statistical data on their activities so as to permit others to identify key gaps and overlaps. That is the minimum level of accountability they owe the countries in which they operate, and the poor they claim to serve.

* * *

Private aid that is above political influence, that is assiduously evaluated, and that can clearly demonstrate effectiveness could catalyse competition in aid giving. It could allow recipients to judge donor performance according to benchmarks based on comparisons between private and official aid. And it could encourage public and private donors to deliver services and public goods to underserved areas in innovative ways. Such a revolution is possible because private aid is offering new business models and transformative technologies. The provision of better information to the poor on matters such as microbanking and health services through mobile telephony, for example, has already improved the effectiveness of several types of antipoverty programme. There is reason to believe that future innovations will drive similar improvements, but only if certain conditions prevail. Global philanthrocapitalism, as with any other kind of capitalism, will only yield results if there is a market for the goods it offers, if the prices of its products convey accurate information, and if there is true competition between multiple providers of similar goods.

Acknowledgements

The authors express their gratitude to Lael Brainard and the participants of the Brookings Blum Roundtable (2007) and the Global Philanthropy Forum (2007). They also thank Joshua Hermias for invaluable research assistance. All views expressed are the authors' own.

Notes

1 The World Bank, *Annual Report* (Washington DC: The World Bank, 2007), p. 55.

2 John A. Byrne, 'The New Face of Philanthropy', *Business Week* 2 December 2002, pp. 82–6.

3 Loren Renz and Josie Atienza, 'International Grantmaking Update', Foundation Center, October 2006, http://foundationcenter.org/gainknowledge/research/pdf/intl_update_2006.pdf.

4 Rob Katz, 'Privatize Foreign Aid?', *The Wall Street Journal*, 7 July 2007, http://online.wsj.com/article/SB118376061378259540.html?mod=most_viewed_opinion24.

5 Homi Kharas, 'The New Reality of Aid', in Lael Brainard and Derek Chollet (eds), *Global Development 2.0*, (Washington DC: Brookings, forthcoming), p. 58.

6 Total giving in the United States, both domestic and international, was estimated at $295bn in 2006. *Giving USA Annual Report* (Bloomington, IN: The Center on Philanthropy at Indiana University, 2006), p. 7.

7 *The Index of Global Philanthropy* (Washington DC: Hudson Institute, 2007), http://gpr.hudson.org/files/publications/IndexGlobalPhilanthropy2007.pdf. In arriving at this figure, best estimates have been used to eliminate the double counting that can arise from the simple summing of all private-source giving. For example, if the Soros Foundation gives money to the Open Society Institute (OSI), then counting both Soros and OSI contributions would lead to an overestimate of what ultimate beneficiaries really receive. The Soros contribution must be netted out; its value will show up in the OSI contribution.

8 *Giving USA Annual Report*, p. 8.

9 Data are from The Comparative Nonprofit Sector Project, Center for Civil Society Studies, Johns Hopkins University, 'Comparative Data Tables', 2005, www.jhu.edu/cnp/research/compdata.html. Their figures include both domestic and international giving and show that private giving from the US accounts for 49% of giving from all OECD Development Assistance Committee (DAC) countries combined. The DAC itself reports on private giving, but in a very partial way. It reports that US private giving reached $8.6bn in 2005, compared to total of $14.7bn from all DAC countries. This implies that the United States accounts for 58.5% of the global total. See Homi Kharas, 'Trends and Issues in Development Aid', Wolfensohn Center for Development, Working Paper no. 1, November 2007, p. 13.

10 Janelle A. Kerlin and Supaporn Thanasombat, 'The International Charitable Nonprofit Subsector: Scope, Size, and Revenue', Urban Institute Policy Brief No. 2, September 2006, http://www.urban.org/UploadedPDF/311360_nonprofit_subsector.pdf.

11 *Ibid.*

12 Homi Kharas, 'The New Reality of Aid', p. 66.

13 Organisation for Economic Co-operation and Development, *The*

Role of Non-Governmental Organizations in Development Co-operation (Paris: OECD, 1983).

14 Ian Smillie, 'NGOs and Development Assistance: a Change in Mind-set?', *Third World Quarterly*, vol. 18, no. 3, 1997, pp. 563–77.

15 This figure does not include community-based organisations, which are generally thought to number in the hundreds of thousands.

16 Nadia Masud and Boriana Yontcheva, 'Does Foreign Aid Reduce Poverty? Empirical Evidence from Nongovernmental and Bilateral Aid', IMF Working Paper, WP/05/100, May 2005.

17 Axel Dreher, Florian Mölders and Peter Nunnenkamp, 'Are NGO's the Better Donors?', Kiel Institute for the World Economy, Working Paper 1383, October 2007.

18 Dirk-Jan Koch, Axel Dreher, Peter Nunnenkamp and Rainer Thiele, 'Keeping a Low Profile: What Determines the Allocation of Aid by Nongovernmental Organizations', Kiel Institute for the World Economy, Working Paper 1406, March 2008.

19 Solomon Major et al., 'The Allocation of Private Development Aid: Empowering Recipients or Advancing Donor Interests', American Political Science Association conference paper, August 2006, http://www.allacademic.com/meta/p150437_index.html. The authors find that aid allocation from the largest NGOs is more likely to be based on GDP per capita than measures of public or media awareness.

20 Marion R. Fremont-Smith and Andras Kosaras, 'Wrongdoing by Officers and Directors of Charities: A Survey of Press Reports 1995–2002', Hauser Center Working Paper No. 20, September 2003, available at http://www.ksghauser.harvard.edu/publications/working_papers/workingpaperlist.htm.

21 Organisation for Economic Cooperation and Development, *International Development Statistics*, Table 1, available at http://www.oecd.org/dac/stats/idsonline.

22 Abby Stoddard, 'Increasing Risks to Aid Workers?', *The Globalist*, 10 January 2007, http://www.theglobalist.com/storyid.aspx?StoryId=5893.

23 The *2007 Global Accountability Report* looks at 30 of the world's most significant international-aid players and finds that NGOs generally do less well on transparency measures than their official-aid-agency counterparts. Robert Lloyd, Jeffrey Oatham and Michael Hammer, *2007 Global Accountability Report* (London: One World Trust, 2007), http://www.oneworldtrust.org/documents/OWT_GAR_07_colour_lo-res.pdf.

24 On the consequences of private donors' involvement in global disease-specific projects rather than those aimed at improving public-health delivery systems, for example, see Laurie Garrett, 'The Challenge of Global Health', *Foreign Affairs*, vol. 86, no. 1, January–February 2007, http://www.foreignaffairs.org/20070101faessay86103/laurie-garrett/the-challenge-of-global-health.html.

25 See, for example, William Easterly, 'The Cartel of Good Intentions', *Foreign Policy*, no. 131, July–August 2002, pp. 40–9.

Review Essay

Misreading Russia

Rodric Braithwaite

The New Cold War: How the Kremlin Menaces both Russia and the West
Edward Lucas. London: Bloomsbury, 2008. £18.99/$26.95. 352 pp.

Edward Lucas is a consummate entertainer, in the best British tradition of the stand-up artist in the music hall. He recently held a London audience spellbound as he painted an alternative history. Imagine, he began, a Germany, post-Hitler but still Nazi, ruled by President Waldemar Putoff and his ex-Gestapo cronies, prepared to regret but not to repudiate the Holocaust, and still showing a distressing tendency to bully its neighbours. Why, he wondered, were we all so willing to give President Vladimir Putin – that apologist for the Soviet past – the benefit of the doubt, when we would not have touched President Putoff with a barge pole?

His written style is equally brilliant – colourful, energetic, lucid, passionate, manic – a pyrotechnic display of cutting polemic, dubious historical analogy and solid erudition. For Lucas knows his stuff. He has lived and worked in Russia, Poland and the Baltic states. He has deep knowledge of the East European peoples and a profound sympathy with the appalling historical traumas they have suffered. You can rarely fault him on the facts.

His argument boils down to this: under Putin, Russia has reverted to brutal authoritarianism and predatory imperialism, to which is now added

Rodric Braithwaite, whose diplomatic career included postings in Jakarta, Warsaw, Rome, Brussels and Washington, was British ambassador in Moscow from 1988 to 1992. He has written two books on Russian affairs and is preparing a third, *Afghantsy*, about the Russians in Afghanistan.

economic blackmail. Western governments do not understand what is happening, or are too greedy, pusillanimous or supine to do anything about it. 'The West is losing the New Cold War, while barely having noticed that it has started. Mr Putin and his Kremlin allies have seized power in Russia, cast a dark shadow over the eastern half of the continent, and established formidable bridgeheads in the main Western countries' (p. 13).

So Lucas has set himself the task of arousing the sleepers and denouncing the appeasers. A former Estonian Prime Minister goes so far as to compare the book to Churchill's 'Iron Curtain' speech at Fulton in 1946[1] – but that was in the publisher's blurb, and authors cannot be blamed for the way their books are puffed. Certainly, the book is great fun to read. But the flood of tendentious rhetoric undermines its value as a serious contribution to the debate. It is not exactly dishonest, but many formulations are inaccurate, the language is often loaded, and arguments contradict one another from chapter to chapter.

Take, for instance, the title. Lucas seems unable to make up his mind about whether we really face a 'New Cold War' or not. The real Cold War was a 40-year confrontation between two nuclear powers, each capable of obliterating the other. It was a worldwide competition between two ideologies, democracy and communism, fought not only in the field of ideas, but also on the bloodiest of battlefields in Korea, Vietnam, Afghanistan, Africa and Latin America. Twice – in the autumn of 1962 and again in the autumn of 1983 – the world came close to Armageddon.

Lucas tells us that 'The New Cold War' is his shorthand for something rather different. Russia today is a nasty, authoritarian place. Even though there is no worldwide confrontation, Russia uses its diminished military forces, its growing financial power and its dominance of the energy market to impose its will on its small neighbours and beyond. This behaviour is guided by a 'new ideology', the ideology of Putinism. To counter the threat, Lucas proposes a kind of 'neo-confrontation'. This would be based on Atlantic solidarity, and bring Russia's small neighbours into the European Union and NATO.

Lucas's book is seeded with interesting facts, enlightening phrases and surprisingly balanced judgements. In the end, however, it is a sadly missed opportunity. However disagreeable the present relationship between Russia and the West, to suggest that it amounts to a 'New Cold War' in any way comparable with the old one is a damaging misuse of language.

The fall and rise of a Great Power

Let us look more closely both at the Russia which Lucas describes reasonably accurately – when he is not spinning colourful and prejudicial phrases – and at some of the policy issues he raises.

Politics everywhere is coloured and directed by historical memory and historical myth. For Russians, the defining memory today is of the trauma and humiliation of the collapse of the Soviet Union and its aftermath. Most of them do not attribute that collapse to the innate weakness of the system, but to the intrigues of foreigners and the machinations of domestic traitors. Western policy in the 1990s was not ill-intentioned. But it was a damaging mixture of incompetence and opportunism as Westerners tried to impose their own views and policies on the Russians at a time when they were weak. In May 2001 an article in *Atlantic Monthly* even proclaimed that 'Russia is Finished'.[2]

So much for prophecy. The oil price took off, and Russia was back, a European Great Power once again, of a rather nineteenth-century kind.

It is fashionable these days to argue that the world is no longer a nineteenth-century place. Today globalisation and the 'obligation to intervene' have replaced the old order, in which nation-states laid claim to absolute sovereignty and created spheres of influence. Looking around, however, it is not immediately clear that the conflict-ridden twenty-first century differs in fundamental ways from the somewhat less conflict-ridden nineteenth century. The principle that 'might is right' still, for the most part, governs the relationship between states and the way they conduct their domestic affairs.

Perhaps only the European Union has found a formula by which to transmute centuries of conflict into a laboured collaboration over a wide range of what used to be called domestic business. To a remarkable extent, its smaller members, previously the victims of the machinations of the Great Powers, can now deal with them almost as equals. Europe, as Danish Foreign Minister Uffe Ellerman-Jensen once said, has become safe for small countries.

This new Europe is widely praised for its ability to build democracies out of nations with little or no relevant historical experience. There is nothing mysterious about the process. All members have to conform to a dense network of Union policy, law and regulation which can only work if they share common standards of democracy, and in particular if they all equally accept the common rule of law.

Lucas wonders if this can last. Some of the new members from Eastern Europe, he thinks, show 'a sharp disregard for what Western Europe sees as the elementary values of a liberal society at home and abroad ... The old EU ... felt united by a common purpose that now seems to be lacking'. The whole thing could unravel as 'the halo effect of proximity to rich stable Europe evaporates' (pp. 205, 208). How then can the Union bring in the West Balkans, Ukraine, Moldova, Georgia, Belarus? Lucas makes no attempt to resolve the dilemma.

Where do the Russians fit into this European enterprise? European countries share some elements of a common geography and history and a culture based on the Classical-Judaeo-Christian heritage. But though they may prate a good deal about them, many countries' experience of the 'European' values of democracy, human rights and the rule of law is neither long nor deep. By these standards, the Russians too can claim to be European, even though they themselves are divided on the matter.

The debate is unimportant in practice. What is important is that – 'European' or not – Russia is Europe's largest neighbour, and is linked to Europe in numerous, growing and inescapable ways. This is something European policymakers cannot ignore.

The Russians themselves barely understand the European Union. They show no sign of wanting to submit to the disciplines of membership. They take the thoroughly nineteenth-century view that it is for the Great Powers to settle the big issues, and for the small countries to conform. They find it absurd that common mechanisms enable the minnows to frustrate the intentions of major countries like the United Kingdom, France or Germany. They find it particularly galling when, as they see it, Union policy is biased against them by the 'anti-Russian' prejudices of new members which were formerly their vassals.

Nor do they do take seriously the Union's pretensions to be a Great Power. As Stalin famously said of the Pope, the Union has no divisions. Its Common Foreign and Security Policy cuts no ice in Moscow. And so the Russians do what the United States or any sensible third party does. They deal with Brussels when they have to, with capitals when they can, and do their best to divide and rule in the meantime. We Europeans cannot reasonably criticise them for this: it is ourselves we have to blame.

When the Union has agreed on formal common policies, when it has forced itself to act together, then it is indeed a formidable international player not to be underrated. Microsoft and Honeywell learned this, to their (literal) cost, when they fell foul of the EU's Competition Policy. Even the United States and Japan find that they cannot easily shift the Union on trade issues. The Russians were unable to bully Lithuania – thanks to its EU connection – into accepting a one-sided visa and transit regime to their exclave of Kaliningrad. The Union backed the Estonians as a matter of course when the Russians cut up rough in spring 2007 over the Soviet war memorial in Tallinn.[3]

But where there are no binding common policies – for example, in the matter of energy – the Union is always vulnerable to divisive tactics. Lucas points out that Russia largely depends on energy revenues from Europe to prop up its lopsided and vulnerable economy, and emphasises the risk – both to the Russian economy and to us – that Russian energy production will fail to keep up with domestic and foreign demand. He nevertheless believes that the Russians deliberately use their dominance in Europe's energy market as a political weapon. If that is what they are doing, however, they are not very good at it: 'Like the Kremlin's other tactics', says Lucas, 'the energy weapon so far has proved not only blunt but ineffective' (p. 188).

But whatever Russia's motives, the European Union needs to pull itself together. It needs a Common Energy Policy with teeth, so that neither the Russians nor anyone else can pick off its members one by one. Before that can happen there will be serious disagreements to overcome within the Union. But the Union has risen to such challenges in the past and can do so again.

Rattling the sabre

So what about Russia as a global military threat? Putin has gone some way towards reviving the demoralised remnants of the Soviet armed forces. But Russia still spends less than one-twenty-fifth of what America spends on defence. Russian published figures for defence expenditure are opaque,[4] but the Russian government has repeatedly stated that it will not allow defence expenditure to drag down the economy as it did in the Soviet period. This is one lesson Russia's leaders really do seem to have learned from the past.[5]

Lucas reluctantly recognises this. 'On the face of it', he says, 'Russia is still an intimidating military power. It has one of the world's largest armies, excellent special forces and some remarkable modern weapons' (p. 247). But he admits that Russia is still too poor and weak to do more than posture. 'Russia [is not] a global adversary, despite its increasingly assertive presence on the international stage. Indeed, it often looks like a partner' (p. 13). In a striking and apt phrase, he goes on: '[Russia] is too weak to have a truly effective independent foreign policy, but it is too disgruntled to have a sensible and constructive one' (p. 267). But if this is so, what is all the fuss about?

Of course, on a lesser scale the Russian armed forces can and do act against ill-armed insurgents and threaten their small neighbours: they have not yet learned that you are no longer supposed to do this. Lucas believes that the answer is to bring Russia's neighbours into NATO. The Russians – who were assured in 1991 that NATO would not expand beyond Germany – have threatened nameless countermeasures if NATO extends still further into their back yard. Perhaps we can live with that. But NATO is heavily engaged – possibly beyond its capacity – in Afghanistan and elsewhere. It has a residual role in the defence of its existing members. Can it extend *effective* security guarantees to such a large country as Ukraine, or to such a distant one as Georgia? If not, does the proposal to make them members have a primarily political purpose? And what is it?

As for Putin's nationalist 'ideology', which echoes the Tsarist slogan 'Orthodoxy, Autocracy, Nationality', it has no appeal beyond Russia's borders and cannot be used, as the Soviet Union used communism, as an instrument of Russian policy abroad. Nor, even in its domestic arrangements, does Russia resemble the Soviet Union. 'Those determined to tangle with the authorities risk trouble, but people can largely say what they like and read what they like', Lucas admits (p. 5). Russians live in increasing prosperity. They can travel and work abroad in large numbers. Many Russians have never had it so good.

What is to be done?

Like Vladimir Lenin, Lucas reserves his particular scorn for 'the useful idiots' – the woolly-minded Western liberals who spend their time trying to understand and apologise for Russian behaviour. The idea that Russia would become liberal, he says, 'always seemed optimistic, but now it looks downright fanciful; those who still advocate it are deluding themselves, and those who listen to them.' He goes on: 'Many of the most sophisticated foreign policy thinkers in Western Europe saw the collapse of communism not as a triumph, but as a tragedy' (pp. 8, 204). Many of them? Really?

Once again, he exaggerates. Despite the unattractive things going on in Russia today, quite sane people can sustain a reasonable argument that Russia – in the great fullness of time, and after many fits and starts – can become a recognisably democratic and law-bound society. The opposite argument – that the Russians have autocracy in their genes – is historically illiterate. After all, for a century the Germans were regarded as irremediably militaristic: had they not been so since the time of Tacitus? Now we cannot even get them to fight in Southern Afghanistan.

Perhaps, in the short term, none of this really matters. We cannot know for sure what Russia will be like tomorrow. But our policies have to be robust for today – and more sophisticated than the neo-containment based on Atlantic solidarity with which Lucas would like to fight the New Cold War. And this means two things. First, we should not delude ourselves that we can have much influence on Russian domestic developments. Second, the numerous political, commercial, economic, security and personal links between Russia and its neighbours mean that Europeans at least must deal with the place as they find it, not as they would like it to be. They need to cooperate with Russia where they can and block it where they must. What this means in practice will always require tricky choices by the policymakers. Luckily for him, these are choices that Edward Lucas does not have to make.

Notes

1 Mart Laar, a historian by profession, was prime minister of Estonia from 1992 to 1994 and from 1999 to 2002. He is credited with having brought about Estonia's economic miracle.

2 Jeffrey Taylor, 'Russia is Finished', *Atlantic Monthly*, May 2001.

3 Lucas' account of the dispute (pp. 198–201) is well balanced. Both sides had understandable grievances. The Estonians were not very clever in their handling of the dispute, but that does not excuse the gross Russian overreaction.

4 The International Institute for Strategic Studies nevertheless estimates that, allowing for inflation, Russian defence expenditure has remained static at around 2.5–2.8% of GDP. Russian GDP is growing rapidly and defence expenditure has increased in proportion.

5 The International Institute for Strategic Studies (IISS), *The Military Balance 2008* (London: Routledge for the IISS, 2008), p. 210.

6 The Russian Health and Social Development Minister claimed in spring 2008 that the number of Russians with incomes under the minimum subsistence level had gone down by 23% (about 6 million) over the last two years and that real incomes had grown by 25% over the same period. *RFE/RL Newsline*, April 2008, http://www.rferl.org/newsline/2008/04/1-rus/rus-250408.asp.

Review Essay

Ancient Lessons for Today's Soldiers

H.R. McMaster

The Warrior Ethos: Military Culture and the War on Terror
Christopher Coker. Abingdon: Routledge, 2007. $39.95. 170 pp.

Military Honour and the Conduct of War: From Ancient Greece to Iraq
Paul Robinson. Abingdon: Routledge, 2006. £75.00/$150.00. 218 pp.

Stoic Warriors: The Ancient Philosophy Behind the Military Mind
Nancy Sherman. Oxford: Oxford University Press, 2005. £9.99/ $15.95. 242 pp.

Prior to the wars in Afghanistan and Iraq, much of the debate over the nature of future armed conflict focused on the military application of emerging technologies. Many analysts believed that new communications, information, surveillance and precision-strike technologies had generated a 'Revolution in Military Affairs' (RMA). The RMA, some argued, would permit technologically advanced military forces to wage war rapidly, decisively and efficiently. Since 2001, the experiences of soldiers and military units in protracted conflicts in Afghanistan and Iraq have revealed important continuities in warfare that RMA advocates overlooked. As John Keegan observed in *The Face of Battle*, his classic 1976 study of combat across five centuries:

H.R. McMaster is a US Army Colonel and Consulting Senior Fellow to the IISS.

 DOI 10.1080/00396330802329071

> What battles have in common is human: the behaviour of men struggling to reconcile their instinct for self-preservation, their sense of honour and the achievement of some aim over which other men are ready to kill them. The study of battle is therefore always a study of fear and usually of courage; always of leadership, usually of obedience; always of compulsion, sometimes of insubordination; always of anxiety, sometimes of elation or catharsis; always of uncertainty and doubt, misinformation and misapprehension, usually also of faith and sometimes of vision; always of violence, sometimes also of cruelty, self-sacrifice, compassion; above all, it is always a study of solidarity and usually also of disintegration – for it is toward the disintegration of human groups that battle is directed.[1]

Keegan was obviously sensitive to the social and psychological dimensions of combat, but he argued against turning the study of war over to sociologists or psychologists. Keegan contended that understanding war and warriors required an interdisciplinary approach and a 'long historical perspective'.

Consistent with Keegan's recommendation, three recent books – Paul Robinson's *Military Honour and the Conduct of War: From Ancient Greece to Iraq*, Nancy Sherman's *Stoic Warriors: The Ancient Philosophy Behind the Military Mind*, and Christopher Coker's *The Warrior Ethos: Military Culture and the War on Terror* – take interdisciplinary approaches to understanding warriors and the warrior ethos in contemporary Western armed forces, which the authors endeavour to place in broad historical perspective. Drawing on history, literature and philosophy, as well as memoirs and accounts of combat experiences, Robinson, Sherman and Coker deepen our understanding of modern Western military culture as well as the human, psychological, ethical and sociological dimensions of war. Their perspectives are complementary and their analysis seems particularly relevant as Western militaries engage in conflicts in which uncertainty about the nature of the enemy and the environment, combined with the persistent danger of operations, create a degree of stress that threatens to erode military professionalism and the moral character of soldiers and units.[2] A reading of their books fosters comprehension of the values and ethical precepts that have guided military thinking and behaviour for centuries, but which are often misunderstood by the governments and societies that armed forces serve.

Military honour

The military value with which Paul Robinson, a lecturer in Security Studies at the University of Hull, is most concerned in his book is honour. In Robinson's view, 'honour and war are inseparable' because, since the time of Achilles, ideas of honour have influenced the causes, conduct and termination of wars (p. 1). His analysis traces the evolution of ideas of honour and their influence on warfare in ancient Greece and Rome, medieval Europe, Elizabethan England, nineteenth-century America, the age of British Imperialism, the post-Second World War era and present-day Iraq. In each chapter, Robinson examines the interaction between honour and the causes of war, the motivation for fighting, rewards offered for excellence, death, the enemy, war termination and women.

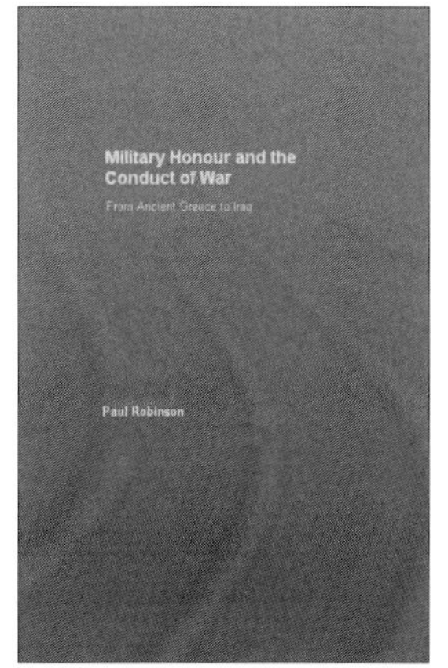

Robinson casts honour in an Aristotelian light as the 'reward for virtue'. He differentiates between 'external honour' bestowed upon an individual through reputation and prestige and 'internal honour' earned through personal integrity and bestowed by one's own conscience. Although Robinson argues that the virtues from which Western society derives its sense of honour have evolved since the time of Achilles, he observes that 'people continue to go to war to defend their honour; that honour still determines how they fight, and the manner in which they treat enemies; and matters of honour still affect the way in which wars are brought to an end' (p. 185). Robinson defines the 'unchanging core' of military honour as military prowess, loyalty and truthfulness; other virtues, such as obedience, discipline, duty and prudence, are also important.

However, Robinson does not view military honour as an unqualified good. For example, he argues that military prowess must be combined with courage and loyalty to achieve honour. He also notes that the pursuit of honour can run counter to society's interest: while notions of honour can limit excess in war, they can also *encourage* excess. The effect of defeat on a nation's or a leader's honour can also provide a significant disincentive for avoiding or terminating destructive armed conflicts.

Robinson's exclusive focus on honour is both a strength and limitation of his study. He is most persuasive in arguing that honour plays an important role in the conduct of war, and is least persuasive in arguing that honour is both the principal cause of armed conflicts and the main impediment to ending them. His contention that, in the ancient world, 'ideas of precedence and individual honor carried over into inter-state relations' and led to 'near constant wars, most of them rather pointless' (p. 32), seems to overstate the matter. Similarly, on the basis of nothing more than public statements that leaders used to mobilise popular support, he identifies honour as driving the decision to invade Iraq in 2003 after a 'southern takeover of U.S. policy' associated with the administration of President George W. Bush. Robinson's argument that war termination is particularly difficult because of nations' determination to defend their honour likewise neglects other strategic and political factors. A broader view consistent with Thucydides' observation that nations go to war because of interest and fear as well as honour might have prevented this overextension of his argument. The benefits of Robinson's consistent focus on honour, however, outweigh these disadvantages as he defines and contextualises the concept of military honour, a concept that might otherwise remain platitudinous without his comprehensive and insightful analysis.

Mild stoicism

Like Robinson, Nancy Sherman is concerned with the interplay between ancient ideas – in her case, Stoic philosophy – and contemporary military culture. She begins with a summary of Stoic moral thought and then applies Stoicism to the prisoner-of-war experience of Admiral James Stockdale (who used the Stoic philosophy of Epictetus to endure physical and mental trauma), the military's focus on physical fitness, the importance of discipline, the impact of fear and anger on soldiers and military units, the importance of comradeship, and the need to grieve the loss of fellow soldiers. Sherman views the influence of Stoic ethics on soldiers and military institutions as both a blessing and a potential curse. The benefits of the Stoic lesson that emotions are subject to cognitive control seem clear in connection with the fortitude and resilience that combat requires. Sherman argues, however, that soldiers must preserve their capacity for anger over inhumanity and the ability to grieve the loss of comrades. She warns that aspiring to an unfeeling state would also retard the development of unit cohesion and undermine the maintenance of soldiers' mental health under traumatic conditions. She concludes that modern-day warriors would benefit from an ethos based in a mild form of stoicism that cultivates humanity and balances emotion and reason.

In addition to illuminating Stoic philosophy, Sherman, who held a chair in ethics at the United States Naval Academy from 1997 to 1999, also provides practical advice for military and defence leaders. She quotes Roman statesman Cicero that leaders should 'show severity while avoiding abusiveness' and observes that leaders can best command respect by showing respect (p. 57). She argues that a leader's emotional demeanour matters because example is a powerful means to inspire courage as well as respect and empathy among soldiers for fellow human beings – she views respect and empathy as the principal bulwarks against abuse and inhumane treatment in combat. Sherman quotes Roman Emperor and Stoic philosopher Marcus Aurelius to make the point that 'respect becomes concrete through empathy', and again quotes Cicero to support her argument that a soldier's respect must extend to the enemy and civilians: 'we ought to revere, to guard and to preserve the common affection and fellowship of the whole of humankind' (pp. 170–1).

Sherman uses two well-known ethical failures, the 1968 My Lai massacre and the 2004 Abu Ghraib prisoner-abuse scandal, to demonstrate the relevance of these ancient writings to contemporary military affairs. She argues that the Abu Ghraib scandal might have been prevented if the soldiers who committed the abuses were equipped to control their anger and were conscious of their common humanity with the prisoners. Sherman cites Roman philosopher Seneca, who attributed wartime atrocities to anger and a failure to remember that the human community is bound together by 'supreme laws'. But while Sherman warns about the debilitating effects of anger and rage, she uses the example of helicopter pilot Hugh Thompson (who took bold action at My Lai to prevent the murder of innocents) to argue that some forms of anger, such as indignation over moral violations, are appropriate and necessary. Sherman relates the well-known story in Homer's *Iliad* of how Achilles' desire for revenge and preservation of his own honour manifested itself in unrelenting fury and contributed to the death of Achilles' comrade Patroclus. She argues that while 'an Achilles-like spirit of vindictiveness and frenzy are precisely the emotions that a warrior needs to restrain', she cautions that 'Stoic aspirations for the warrior to treat anger as an enemy are extreme and unrealistic' (pp. 98–9).

Throughout *Stoic Warriors*, Sherman advocates a balance between empathy for human suffering and the Stoic drive to cultivate resilience. She emphasises the positive Stoic point that 'well being depends on a sense of control and agency, a sense that even in the most constrained circumstances we are not entirely powerless', but argues that soldiers should not endeavour to suppress completely emotions such as anger and grief (p. 126). Sherman describes both the means by which soldiers cope with combat trauma as well as what society and military institutions might do to protect soldiers from the potentially damaging psychological effects of sustained combat. She cites Achilles' rage and survivor's guilt after the loss of Patroclus to illustrate that post-traumatic stress disorder (PTSD) is not a new phenomenon. The author provides a useful summary of cognitive behavioural therapy, particularly cognitive restructuring, which seeks to 'revise automatic and erroneous thoughts that ground traumatic symptoms' (p. 128). She highlights the importance of comradeship in insulating soldiers from the negative effects of combat stress as well as facilitating recovery from PTSD. She suggests a combination of Sigmund Freud's psychotherapeutic 'unlocking of the demons' and the Stoic approach of 'building walls' to protect against unwanted or damaging emotions (pp. 98–9). She highlights the importance of Stoic decorum for leaders, but also warns against stifling the natural expression of grief.

Sherman's insights into how military leaders might inoculate their soldiers against the debilitating effects of combat trauma through effective leadership, realistic training and comradeship appear particularly prescient. In applying Stoicism to contemporary conflict, she identifies tension between the Stoics' emphasis on individual strength and self-reliance and the need for social and emotional support from others, concluding that, in the modern military, self-sufficiency is necessarily social. 'The motivation to fight hangs in no small part on solidarity, and ideally on a respect that travels upward to the commander in chief and downward to the lowest grunt' (p. 151). Unit cohesion and a soldier's confidence in himself and the other members of his team can help achieve the degree of agency or control that the Stoic philosophers advocated. Sherman also stresses the importance of professional military education and realistic training to help reduce the uncertainty and anxious anticipation that contribute to combat stress. Even the emphasis in basic military training on decorum, rituals and drill is identified as a means of coaxing 'inner change' and introducing recruits to the warrior ethos (p. 63).

Warrior ethos under fire

In *The Warrior Ethos*, Christopher Coker, Professor of International Relations at the London School of Economics, reinforces Sherman's emphasis on agency and comradeship as well as Robinson's focus on military honour. Coker argues that soldiers preserve agency through self-trust. Consistent with Robinson's definition of internal honour, Coker describes the military profession as the only profession with altruism at its core. Observing that 'the problem of philosophy since Plato has been the need to harness the desire for recognition in a way that would serve the political community as a whole', he argues that the state harnesses the warrior's desire for what Robinson defines as external honour by 'making the warrior an instrument of its own purposes' (p. 93). Coker links these two points by observing that 'when we are valued by others we value ourselves', noting that 'it is this fusion of inner and outer worlds which gives the warrior ethos its appeal' (p. 14). Ultimately, it is the warrior ethos that permits soldiers to see themselves 'as part of an ongoing historical community', a community that sustains itself through 'sacred trust' and a covenant that binds them to one another and to the society they serve (p. 133). The warrior ethos forms the basis for this covenant and is comprised of values such as honour, duty, courage, loyalty and self-sacrifice. The warrior ethos is important because it makes military units effective and war 'less inhumane'.

Coker relates that he wrote *The Warrior Ethos* 'to show how the warrior ethos has been increasingly hollowed out in recent years and why this matters, or should matter, to the rest of us in whose name warriors fight' (p. 146). Coker argues that contemporary warriors' actions and thoughts are increasingly 'patrolled' and that the 'warrior myth' is being undercut in a way that threatens the warrior ethos. Coker is concerned that the Western warrior is becoming separated from the societies he is meant to defend; this separation is consequential because soldiers must be respected for what they do in order to maintain their agency and self-respect. His analysis is pessimistic:

> Warriors are unhappy today because they are increasingly alienated from a society which won't allow them to be themselves, which patrols their thoughts as well as actions. They are alienated from a military that asks them to conform to what instrumental reason demands. And they are alienated from a world which no longer grants them the glory they once took for granted. We have cut war down to size; and in downsizing its heroic dimensions we have diminished those who fight. No wonder so many warriors are unhappy. Unhappiness inheres in the condition. If we become what we sing, today we sing in minor key. The muse is beginning to fail us (p. 15).

Coker concludes that the 'western warrior is in trouble', due mainly to three challenges: the erosion of the warrior myth, the judgement of civil society in which sacrifice is not in fashion and courage is not celebrated, and new technologies that threaten to strip warriors of their sense of agency.

Coker argues that popular culture has watered down and coarsened the warrior myth. This is troubling, because Coker argues that myths are 'destiny defining': a soldier is shaped, in part, 'by the myths that echo in his heart' (p. 36). Our 'visual culture' spurns the literature and poetry that provide windows into the warrior's soul. Hollywood is ill suited to communicate to audiences 'the significance of the warrior's calling or his station, or what compels him to tap into his heroic potential, to live more intensely than the rest of us' (p. 42). The entertainment industry 'is much more interested in warriors than it is war; it makes them larger than life but it often renders them lifeless at the same time' (p. 39). The warrior myth is difficult to capture on film because film lacks the necessary psychological depth. The Hollywood version of history is comic and its message is one-dimensional. Perhaps most importantly, Hollywood cannot communicate sacrifice and has difficulty making sense of death.

Coker sees the warrior ethos as increasingly disconnected from societies that do not understand, let alone encourage, sacrifice and risk. Because Western societies are increasingly risk averse, it is difficult for people to understand why soldiers enter a profession that involves such extreme risk or to appreciate men and women who want more out of life than security. This gap in understanding between soldiers and society has fostered a view of soldiers 'not as the authors but as the victims of their circumstances' (p. 95). Coker argues that 'the heroic norm now encompasses the passive sufferer rather than the hero – or heroine – who actively courts danger or takes risks on behalf of others' (p. 97). Coker observes that 'war becomes soulless when it is more life defying than life affirming' (p. 95). He sees contemporary America as a 'culture that knows how to honour the casualties and the dead, but not the strength and prowess of its warriors' (p. 102).

Coker may overestimate the harmful effects of new military technology on the warrior ethos. He contends that the United States in particular has 'instrumentalised' war almost entirely, so that opportunities for displaying the traditional warrior virtue of courage are diminishing. While some RMA advocates predicted that technology would change the character of war in this way, countermeasures to Western technological capabilities and the intermingling of enemy combatants with civilian populations have limited the effect of new capabilities and meant that combat on the ground has continued to predominate in Iraq and Afghanistan. There, Western forces, typically alongside indigenous forces, fight the enemy at close quarters every day. Indeed, soldiers in those conflicts consistently exhibit extraordinary courage and take extraordinary risks, ones that often involve forgoing firepower advantages to protect civilians among whom terrorists and insurgents fight. It may be that courageous actions have become so commonplace in Afghanistan and Iraq that the small, cohesive, all-volunteer forces engaged in those conflicts regard as unremarkable actions that others would describe as heroic. Yet Coker's underestimation of the opportunities for courage afforded by ongoing conflicts bolsters his argument: the actions of soldiers in combat today go largely unreported and are arguably underappreciated by the societies those soldiers serve.

Bridging the gap

The gap between the warrior ethos and Western societal values is not a new phenomenon. More than 50 years ago, Samuel Huntington was inspired to write *The Soldier and the State* because he was concerned that a Western liberal society would prove unable to sustain a professional military establishment necessary to counter the threat of the Soviet Union.[3] While the threat to international security today is different, the challenges to civil–military relations remain largely the same: the twin dangers that societal values incompatible with military requirements will undermine the effectiveness of military institutions, or that military institutions will become disconnected from their societies and governments.

These dangers remain consequential because, as Coker points out, society's expectations permit warriors to imagine their social existence and help establish the expectations they have for themselves and for each other. If military forces become insulated from their societies, this unhealthy condition might erode civilian control of the military or rend the covenant between soldiers and the societies in whose interests they fight. Additionally, if society is disconnected from and unsympathetic to the warrior myth, it will become increasingly difficult to recruit soldiers, and governments might not appreciate the fundamental requirements of military effectiveness. Understanding warriors and their culture is necessary if societies and governments are to make sound judgements concerning military policy.

Some who equate the warrior ethos with militarism might argue that the military should bridge the civil–military gap by simply conforming to civil society's values. This is a dangerous proposition, however. Soldiers must view war as a challenge and as their duty, not as trauma. Moreover, soldiers must embrace risk not only to accomplish objectives over which others are prepared to kill them, but also to protect innocents, especially in today's 'wars amongst the people'. Perhaps most important, as Coker emphasises, soldiers must remain willing to sacrifice for the mission and for each other.

Scholars of civil–military relations have recommended several ways to reduce the gap between soldiers and the civilians they serve, including increasing civilian understanding of military affairs.[4] It is here that Robinson's, Sherman's and Coker's works have particular value. The authors provide insights into military values and military culture, and also demonstrate, through their scholarship, that developing knowledge of military affairs does not require military service.

But the military must also work to understand and preserve its own values and do so in a manner consistent with its place in a democratic society. The need to preserve ethical conduct under the complex and trying conditions of counter-insurgency operations has inspired a renewed emphasis on the warrior ethos in the professional military-education curricula of the armed forces of the United States, the United Kingdom and other nations. Military leaders recognise that the warrior ethos is critical to accomplishing missions and preserving the military's professionalism and sense of honour. For example, the US Army's and Marine Corps' values aim, in part, to inform soldiers and marines about the covenant between them, their institutions and society.[5] The 2006 Army and Marine Corps counter-insurgency manual states that 'the Nation's and the profession's values are not negotiable' and that 'violations of them are not just mistakes; they are failures in meeting the fundamental standards of the profession of arms'.[6] The seven US Army values of loyalty, duty, respect, selfless service, honour, integrity and personal courage are consistent with Aristotelian virtue as well as the ancient philosophy of Cicero. It is easy, for example, to identify the similarity between the Army's definition of respect as beginning 'with a fundamental understanding that all people possess worth as human beings' and Cicero's exhortation in *On Duties* that 'we must exercise a respectfulness towards men, both towards the best of them and also towards the rest'.[7] The US Army's values have obvious implications for moral conduct in counter-insurgency, especially in connection with the treatment of civilians and captured enemies. Nancy Sherman points out that 'soldiers are not philosophers, but philosophy helps us understand soldiers' behaviour and base motivation' (p. 104). It might also be said that philosophy helps soldiers understand their own ethos and values and how important it is to maintain them. Coker, Sherman and Robinson make philosophy accessible to soldiers just as they make the warrior ethos accessible to both students of philosophy and general readers.

Those charged with introducing new soldiers to the warrior ethos and professional military ethics should read these books. Applied-ethics indoctrination for new soldiers is perhaps even more important today than in the past because of the need to differentiate between society's and the professional military's views on the use of violence and to help soldiers maintain ethical standards in the face of enemies that do not adhere to those standards. As Coker points out, in much of the media to which young soldiers are exposed – including action films, video games and gangster-rap music – violence appears justifiable as a means of advancing personal interests or demonstrating individual prowess. Some might argue that terrorist tactics justify a relaxation of the counter-insurgent's ethical and moral standards.[8] However, as the US counter-insurgency manual points out, the insurgent often hopes to provoke the excessive or indiscriminate use of force:

> One of the insurgents' most effective ways to undermine and erode political will is to portray their opposition as untrustworthy or illegitimate. These attacks work especially well when insurgents can portray their opposition as unethical by the opposition's own standards. To combat these efforts, Soldiers and Marines treat noncombatants and detainees humanely, according to American values and internationally recognized human rights standards. In [counter-insurgency operations], preserving

> noncombatant lives and dignity is central to mission accomplishment. This imperative creates a complex ethical environment.[9]

Beyond the utilitarian need to maintain ethical standards, if Western soldiers compromise their standards (and the standards of the societies they represent) when confronting terrorists, it may be argued they have already lost. Values education can ring hollow unless it is pursued in a way that provides context and demonstrates relevance. Robinson's *Military Honour and the Conduct of War*, Sherman's *Stoic Warriors*, and Coker's *The Warrior Ethos* provide that context and demonstrate the relevance of ethics to war, warriors and the societies that warriors pledge to serve.

Notes

1 John Keegan, *The Face of Battle* (New York: Viking Press, 1976), p. 83.

2 A response to these conditions can be seen in the December 2006 US Army and Marine Corps counter-insurgency manual, which directs leaders to 'establish and maintain the proper ethical climate of their organizations' and 'ensure that the trying counterinsurgency environment does not undermine the values of their Soldiers and Marines'. The manual further enjoins soldiers and marines to 'remain faithful to basic … standards of proper behavior and respect for the sanctity of life'. United States Army and United States Marine Corps, *Field Manual 3-24, Counterinsurgency*, December 2006, p.7-1. Available at www.usgcoin.org/library/doctrine/COIN-FM3-24.pdf. Similarly, the British Army urges its soldiers to 'act properly under the law and maintain the highest standards of decency and a sense of justice at all times, and to all people, even in the most difficult of conditions'. See 'The Values and Standards of the British Army', www.army.mod.uk/servingsoldier/usefulinfo/valuesgeneral/values/ss_hrpers_values_comd_w.html.

3 Samuel P. Huntington, *The Soldier and the State* (Cambridge, MA: Belknap Press of Harvard University Press, 1957).

4 See, for example, Peter Feaver and Richard Kohn, eds, *Soldiers and Civilians: The Civil–Military Gap and American National Security* (Cambridge, MA: The MIT Press, 2001).

5 For a discussion of US Army values, see www.goarmy.com/life/living_the_army_values.jsp. For comprehensive analyses of the Army profession and military ethics, see Don Snider and Lloyd Mathews, eds, *The Future of the Army Profession: Revised and Expanded Edition* (New York: McGraw-Hill, 2005).

6 *Field Manual 3-24, Counterinsurgency*, p. 7-1.

7 Marcus Tillius Cicero, *On Duties*, ed. and trans. M.T. Griffin and E.M. Atkins (Cambridge: Cambridge University Press, 1991), p. 39.

8 For example, some French Army officers made this argument during the War of Algerian Independence. See Lou Dimarco, 'Losing the Moral Compass: Torture and the *Guerre Revolutionnaire* in the Algerian Civil War', *Military Review*, Summer 2006, pp. 70–2, www.carlisle.army.mil/usawc/parameters/06summer/dimarco.pdf.

9 *Field Manual 3-24, Counterinsurgency*, p. 7-5.

Review Essay

Responsible Intervention

Mary Kaldor

Humanitarian Intervention
Thomas G. Weiss. Cambridge: Polity, 2007. $19.95/£12.99. 176 pp.

The Impossible Mandate? Military Preparedness, the Responsibility to Protect and Modern Peace Operations
Victoria K. Holt and Tobias C. Berkman. Washington DC: The Henry L. Stimson Center, 2006. $20.00. 241 pp.

Development, Security and Unending War: Governing the World of Peoples
Mark Duffield. Cambridge: Polity, 2007. £18.99. 280 pp.

Those of us who favour humanitarian intervention, that it is to say the use of military force in another state in order to prevent a humanitarian catastrophe,[1] tend to assume that the international community can play God. We tend to treat the new multilateral phenomenon we call the 'international community' as if it were, like Hegel's state, the embodiment of universal values. The reality is that the international community is a complex network of self-interested, inefficient and sometimes corrupt nations, international institutions and non-governmental organisations (NGOs) that often leave the places where they intervene in more of a mess than before. So are we wrong to favour humanitarian intervention? Can we push the international community towards a more universalist and effective performance?

Mary Kaldor is Director of the Centre for the Study of Global Governance at the London School of Economics and Political Science.

 DOI 10.1080/00396330802329055

Humanitarian Intervention by Thomas Weiss and *The Impossible Mandate?* by Victoria Holt and Tobias Berkman start from the premise that the international community can indeed play God, even if it has not succeeded so far. Weiss was the research director of the International Commission on Intervention and State Sovereignty (ICISS), which produced the influential report that translated 'humanitarian intervention' into the 'responsibility to protect'.[2] He has written a clear and straightforward account of the changing meaning, history and practice of humanitarian intervention, which offers an invaluable introduction to the subject. He discusses a number of new concepts, such as the changing meaning of sovereignty, and traces the way in which the 'responsibility to protect' paradigm has emerged. The development of new forms of warfare involving the deliberate targeting of civilians, a very high level of population displacement, and a war economy financed through criminal activities, combined with the post-Cold War international political context, set the stage both for greater interest in humanitarian intervention and the reconceptualisation of the term. Francis Deng, who was the representative of the United Nations secretary-general for internally displaced persons between 1994 and 2004, was the first to develop the notion of sovereignty as responsibility. The doctrine

> stipulates that when states are unable to provide life-supporting protection and assistance for their citizens, they are expected to request and accept outside offers of aid. Should they refuse or deliberately obstruct access to their displaced or other affected populations, and thereby put large numbers of them at risk, there is an international responsibility to act.[3]

Along with responsibility, the other key element of the new humanitarianism is an emphasis on protection. According to Weiss, the responsibility to protect shifts the terrain from the rights of the interveners to the rights of the victims.

The ICISS report came out in 2000. The concept of the responsibility to protect was taken up in 2005 by the High Level Panel on Threats, Challenges and Change, appointed by then Secretary-General Kofi Annan, as well as by Annan's own report, *In Larger Freedom*.[4] It was adopted by the United Nations General Assembly at the 2005 World Summit, even though the wording still requires United Nations Security Council approval. All this happened against the backdrop of the 'war on terror'. To some, it might seem like progress, but Weiss ends his book by asking, 'so what?' Even if the concept of the responsibility to protect has been formally taken up, do not the wars in Iraq and Afghanistan discredit notions of humanitarian intervention? It is a question he leaves largely unresolved.

Doing the impossible

The great merit of *The Impossible Mandate?* is its focus on implementation. Most studies of humanitarian intervention tend to deal with the 'why': when it is justified and on what grounds, and how it should be authorised. This book deals with the 'how', the ways in which the responsibility to protect can be implemented on the ground. The book makes the important point that what the authors call 'coercive protection' is different both from traditional peacekeeping, which aims to separate sides and maintain ceasefires, and from war fighting, in which the aim is to defeat an adversary. Protection of civilians is often a secondary or indirect goal for both peacekeeping and war fighting, but not the primary mission. The book provides a diligent and systematic investigation into the extent to which nations and international institutions have introduced the protection of civilians into military doctrine, training or the definition of capabilities. (It is a pity the book does not have an index, as it could be a very useful reference work.) It is clear that the protection of civilians has increasingly entered the security lexicon, particularly for the United Nations. Even for the UN, however, the authors are only able to identify one Standardised Training Module that deals directly with protection.[5] For most individual nation-states that contribute to UN and other multilateral operations, protection is not seen as the main goal, although many nations do refer to it, particularly Canada and the United Kingdom. As one US officer quoted in the book notes, 'while eighty per cent of US missions are civilian-related, eighty per cent of training requested is for combat' (p. 147).

The book includes a fascinating case study of the United Nations Mission in the Democratic Republic of the Congo (MONUC). It shows how the UN found itself having to respond to developments on the ground by upping the level of troops, strengthening the mission's mandate and eventually learning by doing in order to increase its capacity to protect. Since 2005, UN forces have acted more aggressively in disarming Congolese militias and protecting civilians, especially in the Ituri and Kivu provinces. It has established a protection framework and set up joint working groups. Military protection activities include:

> removal of threats against civilians by a 'cordon-and-search operation and/or disarmament of individuals threatening the civilian population', the establishment of 'buffer zones between combatants' and safe areas 'with adequate military protection', utilization of an 'area domination' strategy through frequent patrols, overflights, and 'mobile temporary operations bases', escorting humanitarian and human rights actors to areas, and evacuating populations out of danger zones. (p. 174)

For example, the book describes how the 3,700-strong Pakistani brigade in South Kivu introduced some innovative techniques, partly derived from experience on the Afghan–Pakistani border. The brigade's *Operation Night Flash* organised village-defence committees to alert peacekeepers to imminent attacks, reportedly through banging pots and blowing whistles.

The weaknesses of MONUC are also discussed. For instance, the authors argue that the EU mission *Operation Artemis,* which was launched in 2003 to shore up the UN mission, was an important turning point. EU personnel were better prepared than their UN counterparts to assume a protection role: their mission benefitted from appropriate capabilities including satellite equipment and a medical capacity; the presence of special forces; and an emphasis, assisted by the troops' knowledge of the French language, on bottom-up communication. It is also noted that MONUC has been criticised for employing excessively aggressive tactics – Médecins Sans Frontières, which claims to be treating large numbers of civilians injured in efforts to disarm militias, is particularly critical. There is further concern that MONUC is too closely associated with the Forces Armées de la République Démocratique de Congo (FARDC), which has absorbed several militias and preys on the civilian population. Thus, the title of *The Impossible Mandate?* refers to the difficulty of striking a balance between inadequate force (which fails to protect civilians as in Rwanda or Srebrenica or indeed the Congo) and excessive force, in which those who are supposed to be protected are killed, injured or forced to flee. Nevertheless, the authors conclude that coercive protection is possible provided states and international institutions make the necessary adjustments in capabilities, doctrines and training.

To some extent, this is already happening. Although the wars in Iraq and Afghanistan have discredited humanitarian intervention among the general public, they have caused a profound rethinking among militaries (especially the US military) and governments about how to protect civilians, how to link security and development and how to build legitimate states. The growing concern with coercive protection is evident, for example, in the new US *Counterinsurgency Field Manual* (published after Holt and Berkman's book went to press) prepared by General David Petraeus and General James Amos.[6] The manual puts the protection of civilians at the heart of US military doctrine. It argues for an 'appropriate level of force' and includes such protection-orientated observations as 'sometimes the more force you use the less effective it is'; 'some of the best weapons for Counter-insurgency do not shoot'; and 'sometimes the more you protect your force the less secure you will be'.[7]

Nevertheless, the overall document is still couched in the framework of national security, of war between the United States and its enemies. In Iraq, some of the new counter-insurgency techniques have been applied in the 'surge', and this has undoubtedly contributed to the reduction in violence and the improvement in security. But the Iraq mission suffers from two shortcomings. First, the continued emphasis on defeating enemies means that air-strikes – which involve 'collateral damage', or civilian casualties

– are still an important component of military tactics. Secondly, the surge has not been paralleled by political and economic efforts to increase the legitimacy of Iraqi authorities, which is necessary if improved security is to be sustained. In Afghanistan, NATO planners are similarly preoccupied with the need to adjust tactics to put more emphasis on protection and to somehow link security and development.

Human security or unending war?

The failings of the Iraq and Afghanistan missions underscore why I prefer the term 'human security' to either humanitarian intervention or the responsibility to protect. Human security is about the security of the individual and the community in which he or she lives; it thus involves the protection of individuals and communities. It also emphasises the inter-relationship between different types of security – freedom from fear as well as freedom from want. Perhaps most importantly, human security is what citizens experience in a law-governed society; hence intervention for human security is intrinsically linked to the legal framework and efforts to establish or restore the rule of law.

It is therefore useful to think about human security in terms of law enforcement. Law enforcement is different from either peacekeeping or war fighting – it is much more like policing. Treating humanitarian intervention as international law enforcement has several advantages. First, it highlights the fact that military personnel are not the only relevant actors – others include police, legal experts and development specialists. While Holt and Berkman do stress the need for civil–military coordination, the human-security approach goes beyond coordination in defining a shared mission and a new methodology or doctrine that applies to everyone. Second, 'spoilers' are treated as criminals rather than enemies; the aim is to arrest them and minimise their activities rather than to defeat them. Thirdly, it underlines the importance of establishing legitimate political authority, which affects the way that militaries are used. The aim is to create space for peaceful political processes rather than to impose a political solution through victory or defeat. Human security is thus radically different from counter-insurgency, which is what is practised by the Americans in Afghanistan and

Iraq, the Russians in Chechnya, and the Israelis in the West bank and Gaza. Civilian protection, development and state-building are being recognised as necessary in these regions, but as means to an end (defeating terrorists) rather than as ends in themselves.

This whole debate is profoundly challenged by Mark Duffield's original and stimulating book, *Development, Security and Unending War*. Duffield tends to assume that the international community knows how to implement humanitarian intervention, but he argues that such actions are not genuinely humanitarian – rather, they are part of a broader Western globalising agenda. In other words, they are effective but not universalist. Duffield points to the conclusions of the *Human Security Report*,[8] which shows that there has been a decline in wars and the number of people, including civilians, killed in them. He sees this as evidence of the success of the international community's pacification efforts. (Of course, pacification is not the same as protection, which Duffield himself points out; even where the international community has succeeded in sustaining ceasefires, there remain high levels of human-rights violations, organised crime, and violence against women.) But he sees this success not as a sign of a new universalism but rather as a new form of colonialism. He argues that human security is a technique of 'biopolitics' (as opposed to geopolitics), a Foucauldian term designating a 'form of politics that entails the administration of processes of life at the aggregate level of population' (p. 5). A human-security state is one in which 'the core economic and welfare functions of the population are designed and managed by international actors and agencies' (p. 28).

Duffield believes the global development project is a security project, a way of containing the excluded peoples of the underdeveloped world. According to Duffield, the underdeveloped world is irrelevant to the main economic blocs. 'Their only relevance is political, an excess freedom to move, flow and circulate, thus potentially destabilizing international society's finely balanced and interconnected way of life' (p. 187). For Duffield, the key difference between the populations of the developed and underdeveloped worlds is social insurance. Insurance companies, Duffield points out, estimated the cost of Hurricane Charlie in Florida, which killed 25 people in 2004, at $14 billion. The estimate for the Indian Ocean tsunami, which killed 200,000 people, was half that amount. Instead of insurance, the international community proposes self-reliant community-based development as a form of (inadequate) social protection for people in underdeveloped areas. Yet self-reliant development is necessarily subject to periodic crises, since people in underdeveloped states remain much more vulnerable to risk than people in the developed world. The consequence is a permanent emergency managed by humanitarian assistance. This permanent emergency is the unending war of the book's title. Notions like contingent sovereignty or fragile states are ways in which the new colonial paradigm of human security has been elaborated. Duffield compares development or human security to native administration in the colonial period. Like native administration, it is a more humane form of colonialism; the alternative, he argues, is extermination or eugenics.

Duffield's book turns the liberal vision of the world upside down. He causes us to question humanitarian impulses and treats well-meaning concern about the protection of civilians or the alleviation of poverty merely as methods of mitigating or condoning the fundamental inequity of contemporary capitalism. He discusses the way in which the NGO community has been co-opted by the international community in the post-Cold War world and has become the 'alter ego or conscience of capitalism', or 'the ambassadors of people-centred, community-level development that emphasize[s] self-reliance' (p. 62). He points to the implicit racism of terms such as 'good enough governance', espoused by the UK Department for International Development. But his is a counsel of despair. After all, concepts of humanitarian intervention, the responsibility to protect or human security are surely preferable to the 'war on terror' or to endless new wars, which might be the consequence of doing nothing. Duffield would probably agree, but he does not propose anything better. He talks somewhat vaguely about unlocking the emancipatory potential of development, but offers no guidance except to propose solidarity with the uninsured populations of the world.

Duffield's book could be regarded as a sort of deconstruction of books like those by Weiss, Holt and Berkman. It causes us to question whether we (the international community) can or should try to act as benevolent third parties in complex, difficult and dangerous crises in different parts of the world. Even if one profoundly disagrees with Duffield's cynicism about humanitarian efforts, the book does draw attention to two underlying truths of which all those engaged in humanitarian efforts should be aware. One is that crises are the 'dark side' of globalisation. What happens in the underdeveloped world cannot be isolated from what happens in the developed world. Problems of transnational crime – drug running, human trafficking or oil smuggling, for example – or of refugees and asylum-seekers are as much a responsibility for the states of the developed world as they are for what Duffield (actually rather optimistically) calls the human-security states of the underdeveloped world. The other is that much of what is undertaken in the name of humanitarianism or development is implicitly racist. In principle, humanitarianism, the responsibility to protect and human security presuppose the equality of all human beings. In practice, however, humanitarianism is often understood as something that is done abroad, where different standards of human rights and development apply. Human security ought to be about overcoming the division between the developed and underdeveloped parts of the world. It ought to be about providing insurance or protection for all. It ought to be about constructing a global rule of law, under which human rights override the military pursuit of geopolitical interest and everyone is treated as a citizen of the privileged parts of the world.

What *Humanitarian Intervention* and *The Impossible Mandate?* show us, of course, is that this is very difficult in practical terms – more difficult than Duffield allows. Weiss, Holt and Berkman have not convinced me that coercive protection is possible, but I do think that liberals have a responsibility to make the case and to investigate, as these authors do, the obstacles, problems and gaps that need to be solved if this is to happen, even if inadequately.

Notes

1 Adam Roberts has defined humanitarian intervention as 'coercive action by one or more states involving the use of force in another state *without the consent* of its authorities, and with the purpose of preventing widespread suffering or death among its inhabitants'. Quoted in Weiss, p. 5.

2 International Commission on Intervention and State Sovereignty, 'The Responsibility to Protect: The Report of the International Commission on Intervention and State Sovereignty', December 2001, http://www.iciss.ca/report2-en.asp.

3 Weiss, p. 23.

4 Kofi Annan, *A More Secure World: Our Shared Responsibility*, Report of the Secretary-General's High-level Panel on Threats, Challenges and Change, A/59/565 (New York: United Nations, 2004), http:/www.un.org/secureworld/report.pdf; Kofi Annan, 'In Larger Freedom; Towards Development, Security and Human Rights for All', Report of the Secretary-General, 21 March 2005, http://www.un.org/largerfreedom/.

5 This module was based on a draft prepared by the Office of the High Commissioner for Human Rights entitled 'Protection of Human Rights by Military Peace-keepers'. The draft offered different techniques for military protection.

6 Department of the Army and United States Marine Corps, *Counterinsurgency Field Manual No. 3-24*, Marine Corps Warfighting Publication No 3-33.5, Washington DC, December 2006.

7 *Ibid.* pp. 1–27.

8 Human Security Centre, University of British Columbia, *Human Security Report: War and Peace in the 21st Century* (Oxford: Oxford University Press, 2005).

Book Reviews

Middle East

Steven Simon

A Choice of Enemies: America Confronts the Middle East
Lawrence Freedman. New York: PublicAffairs, 2008.
£17.99/$29.95. 624 pp.

This magisterial book attempts to explain how and why successive US administrations have failed to get it right in the Middle East. Freedman is certainly the man for the job. Middle East experts focus on American cluelessness; right-wing pundits on Middle Eastern fecklessness; left-wing observers on Washington's hegemonic instincts; and self-proclaimed realists on the baleful role of the special relationship between Israel and the United States. Freedman sidesteps these clichés. He is decidedly level-headed, undogmatic, widely informed about things outside of his discipline, and alive to the ways in which governments actually work. The latter point is crucial and owes, among other things, to his access to senior policymakers and experience drafting the official history of the Falklands conflict. Freedman is a great archival historian in part because his grasp of the way decision-makers and bureaucracies interact with each other, their domestic political environment and the wider world enables him to read the fragmentary and self-serving sources more astutely than most scholars. He is also a writer who prefers to work in a jargon-free zone. *A Choice of Enemies* displays all these virtues.

Freedman's starting point is the 1979 Iranian revolution. Other junctures, such as the Suez Crisis of 1956, the year of revolutions in 1958, the Six-Day War of 1967, or even the Yom Kippur War of 1973, might have made good beginnings for his narrative. Yet it wasn't really until the 1980s that US involvement in the region began to deepen. Before then, no Washington policymaker could have conceived of, say, a US army of 150,000 situated in any Middle Eastern country, let alone Iraq. With Jimmy Carter's 1980 State of the Union speech, in which he said 'an attempt by any outside force to gain control of the Persian Gulf region will be regarded as an assault on the vital interests of the United States of America, and such an assault will be repelled by any means necessary, including military force', this eventuality acquired plausibility. The subsequent creation of the Rapid Deployment Joint Task Force – now the Central Command soon to be headed by General David Petraeus – provided the means to implement the Carter doctrine.

Freedman calls the 1979 revolution the 'second radical wave', which succeeded the prior generation's militant secular nationalism. He shows how bureaucratic warfare between the State Department and National Security Council staff, the absence of real expertise in Washington, and serious foreign-policy distractions, including Carter's own Camp David process, made it impossible to anticipate and prepare for regime change in Iran. This was to be the pattern in crises to come.

He also shows how and why it was so hard for Washington to grasp the implications of the radical wave launched by the Iranian revolution. The complex mixture of factors that had impeded Washington's ability to act effectively and constructively in the Middle East since 1979 was compounded during the Bush administration by the disorienting shock of the 11 September attacks and the ideological rigidity and incompetence of key officials. In consequence, the United States found itself at odds with everyone: Iran, Iraqi factions and al-Qaeda – true strategic failure. The lesson this holds for the next president is that 'choosing enemies is an art and not a science, and one that usually takes place in confusing and ambiguous circumstances'. Whoever wins the upcoming presidential election had better be able to see shades of grey.

Hamas in Politics: Democracy, Religion, Violence
Jeroen Gunning. London: C. Hurst & Co., 2008. £25.00/$34.50.
310 pp.

With Hamas's grip on Gaza tightening, it should no longer be possible to maintain the strange illusion that the group can somehow be strangled, as many believed following its electoral victory in 2006. Back then, when asked how he felt about the election results, a senior administration member was effusive, saying that the Bush administration now had Hamas 'where we want them'. The idea was that Hamas, in power, would have to deliver the quotidian goods to its various constituencies. But a US blockade would deprive the new government of the means to deliver. The ineluctable result, as presumably would be the case in any democracy, would be a new election in which angry voters would throw the bums out. Popular resentment against Hamas would be stoked by strongly preferential treatment for the secular Fatah faction that ruled the West Bank under tight Israeli supervision.

In the intervening two years, fantasy has had to concede to an awkward reality. The Hamas militia ejected Palestinian Authority (PA) forces from Gaza last year, essentially staging a coup that removed Fatah from the scene entirely. The organisation's control over its turf has gotten stronger, in part because of its confrontational posture toward Israel, and partly because it had a robust social-services infrastructure to build on. Israel inadvertently helped in this regard by targeting Fatah assets during the initial stages of the al-Aqsa intifada, thereby weakening the PA's capacity to provide crucial services and, in the process, stave off Hamas's challenge. In the meantime, the continuing flow of PA salaries to its employed but inactive personnel in Gaza has ensured that the crisis Hamas was expected to face has not materialised. Hamas has proceeded to professionalise its militia, with Iranian help, and allowed, or possibly abetted, the continued launch of *Qassam* rockets into Israel. There are signs that Hamas is triumphant, at least for now. It has won a truce from Israel, which was deterred from re-entering Gaza to suppress the missile launches, and manoeuvred Fatah leader Mahmoud Abbas into a process leading to a unity government that would accord equality to the two factions.

Gunning's book is a good introduction to what makes Hamas tick. It covers much the same ground as *The Palestinian Hamas: Vision, Violence and Coexistence* by two Israeli scholars, Shaul Mishal and Avraham Sela. That book was published in 2000, however, and reissued only in 2006 with a new introduction, but no substantive revisions. It is worth reading, but for those who want to be up-to-date and, moreover, have the benefit of interviews with key Hamas players, Gunning's book will prove quite useful. The implicit theme of this book is large: Can a movement like Hamas develop into a peaceful and pragmatic political party? Significantly, but unsurprisingly, Gunning has no answer. It is too early to tell. But one gets the impression that Hamas, if forced by diplomacy and politics to choose between its more moderate and more militant constituencies, will ultimately fracture, as did Fatah before it. This bodes ill for a final-status accord.

Bitter Friends, Bosom Enemies: Iran, the U.S., and the Twisted Path to Confrontation
Barbara Slavin. New York: St Martin's Press, 2007. $24.95.
272 pp.

This is not a specialist's book, in the sense that it is neither by nor for Iran experts. Indeed, rank-and-file Tehranologists will likely view some of the author's revelations as the embarrassingly unselfconscious disclosures of a naive American tourist. Slavin, however, is a respected reporter for *USA Today* and brings a journalist's eye to a complex and overheated subject. Writing for a general audience, she necessarily relies heavily on metaphor. Iran is Rodney Dangerfield, an American comedian whose signature line was 'I don't get no respect'. Together, the United States and Iran are like two teenagers, each waiting for the other's invitation to dance. But there is more to her book than homey analogies. It is actually two short books. The first is a readable introduction to the workings of the Iranian state. Her taxonomy, which includes 'reformers', the 'mullahs' and the 'opposition', will strike some as murky and unsystematic. The content, however, is valuable. The best of these chapters concerns Ahmadinejad, whom she places within the second generation of regime loyalists 'from humble backgrounds, [who] did not see the United States as a political or social model to be emulated'. For Slavin, Ahmadinejad represents an important new cohort, rather than the 'radical fringe'. The last chapter in this section describes 'the children of the revolution', born since the great upheaval, who have been marginalised by the insider elite that has dominated politics for nearly 30 years. Against this background, Ahmadinejad's ascendancy is both challenge to the old order and harbinger of a new dispensation.

The second book within *Bitter Friends, Bosom Enemies* traces the faultlines in the US–Iran relationship, particularly since the Clinton and Khatami administrations. She describes Madeleine Albright's apology for America's neo-colonial transgressions, Khatami's plea for a dialogue of civilisations and, of course, the rather close cooperation regarding Afghanistan in the wake of 11 September. These concededly limited attempts to establish a modus vivendi were derailed by, among other things, Washington's conviction that Iran was sheltering al-Qaeda fugitives who were still supervising, or at a minimum cheerleading, attacks against American allies. Catching Tehran covertly shipping a huge quantity of weapons and explosives to Yassir Arafat during the intifada reinforced US perceptions that Iran remained wedded to a radical agenda. Rapprochement at that point was probably not in the cards, but the White House's disregard for a mid 2003 'grand bargain' proposal and Bush's designation of Iran as a member of the 'axis of evil' no doubt precluded the possibility. And then there were the revelations about nuclear enrichment. Slavin's straightforward exposition of generational change in Iran and the extreme difficulty that even well-intentioned leaders on both sides face in trying to get the bilateral relationship on an even keel ought to prove useful to the 2008 presidential candidates' foreign-policy teams, but probably won't.

1948: A History of the First Arab–Israeli War
Benny Morris. New Haven, CT: Yale University Press, 2008.
£19.99/$32.50. 544 pp.

Morris is an academic turned journalist who was among the earliest crop of Israeli revisionists. His first book (*The Birth of the Palestinian Refugee Problem, 1947–1949*) was a systematic attempt to chart the origins of the Palestinian refugee crisis. Using newly available archives, Morris showed that there were instances in which Israeli actions deliberately precipitated the flight of Palestinians from their homes. In an Israeli context, this was a daring thing to do, since the refugee issue was so intimately bound up, as it is today, with the issue of Israel's legitimacy. Israelis fear that by taking responsibility for some, or all, of the refugee problem, they would tacitly validate the Arab claim that Zionism constituted a terrible injustice. The complexity of the issue – Jewish independence as original sin – coloured the debate in Israel over the recent celebration of its 60th anniversary.

Morris intended this new volume to be definitive. Journalistic style has been subordinated to balance, detail and documentation. The book is large, dense and dry. Given the contested nature of the territory, this is appropriate. He deals with the two phases of the 1948 war in sequence: the first, a savage civil war between Jewish and Arab Palestinians; the second, the invasion of Arab armies from outside Palestine, including Egyptian, Syrian, Jordanian, Lebanese, Saudi and Iraqi forces. He shows how the Yishuv, the pre-state Jewish government, prepared for the coming conflict, and how its military wing quickly moved to control the Palestinian road network, in part by seizing the land and villages essential to route security. On the basis of archival research, he refutes the notion that 'Plan D' aimed to cleanse Palestine of Arabs, as many believe. Indeed, if that had been Israel's intention, Arabs today would not constitute one-fifth of its population. On the other hand, he shows that Israelis were guilty of more atrocities than were Arabs. This, he argues, was a function of opportunity more than anything else. Israel was winning and taking more territory. Looking at instances of Arab abuses – at the Etzion Bloc, for example – it is hard to say that Arabs would have behaved better had they won the battle for Haifa or taken Tel Aviv. Civil wars are the worst, as the Lebanese and Iraqis know only too well.

Morris is also good at explaining the regional politics that led Arab regimes to commit forces to a fight they knew they would lose, and why Jewish units were more numerous and more operationally effective than their Arab counterparts. The one thing missing, of course, is insight from Arab archives. But this is unlikely to be forthcoming any time soon. Given the continuing hold of the two opposing narratives of 1948 – *ha-Tikva* ('the hope') and *an-Nakba* ('the catastrophe') – over Washington, regional capitals and the teeming slums of Gaza, Morris's book is essential reading.

Teaching Islam: Textbooks and Religion in the Middle East
Eleanor Abdella Doumato and Gregory Starrett, eds. Boulder, CO: Lynne Reinner Publishers, 2007. £37.50/$55.00. 267 pp.

Eleanor Doumato and Gregory Starrett have pulled together some solid essays about the state of curricular materials across the Arab world. This was a worthwhile exercise. The role of textbooks in Saudi Arabia and Palestine, in particular, in stoking students' animosities against 'the other' has attracted much attention. The predominant role of Saudis in the 11 September attacks and Israeli complaints about 'incitement' as a barrier to a lasting peace are cases in point. The Saudi *tawhid* curriculum stigmatises non-Muslims, including Shi'ites and, according to the editors, could be seen as endorsing violence against these 'outsiders'. Palestinian textbooks focus on the dispossession of Palestinian land rather than on recognising Israel's place in the region. There is some truth to this, but there is more to the story.

The bad-textbooks-make-bad-people argument took off after 11 September as part of the broader 'hearts and minds' discourse that characterised the response to the tragedy. Instances of intolerance and the centrality of religion that observers noted in textbooks used in several Arab countries were seen in the United States as obstacles to successful public diplomacy, the bureaucratic jargon for propaganda. To what avail were explanations of America's worthy goals if the target audience was raised from childhood on a diet of xenophobia? At the same time, Arab scholars enlisted by the United Nations Development Programme slammed the quality of education in the Arab world as grossly inadequate to the task of creating citizens capable of participation in the global economy.

Referring to textbooks as the 'home of official wish images', the authors collectively offer useful observations about regional pedagogy. First, with a couple of exceptions, references to war or jihad tend to justify violence only in self-defence. Offensive war is not valorised. Second, with the apparent exception of Saudi Arabia, curricular materials incorporate accounts of a generic Islam that downplays sectarian differences and links religious identity to support of the regime in power. To this end, the kind of Islam endorsed by textbooks runs counter to the sort of extremist versions that threaten local regimes. Third, what the editors call a 'master narrative' infuses religious-studies texts, 'portraying Islam and Muslims as eternal victims facing real and potential enemies'. Oddly, the book does not connect this conclusion explicitly to the positive characterisation of textbook justifications of violence only in a defensive context. One would think that the endorsement of defensive violence would mesh with a mindset of 'eternal' victimisation in dangerous ways. Fourth, like textbooks the world over, Arab curricula – again, with a couple of exceptions – stress ethical behaviour and civic virtues. Lastly, the country-by-country contributions show that curricular approaches vary considerably and that the Saudi model has not caught on. It would be interesting if the editors were to look outside the region to assess Saudi influence. This, too, is a controversial area that begs sober analysis.

Arms, Arms Control and Technology
Bruno Tertrais

The Seventh Decade: The New Shape of Nuclear Danger
Jonathan Schell. New York: Metropolitan Books, 2007. $24.00.
251 pp.

Why Nuclear Disarmament Matters
Hans Blix. Cambridge, MA: The MIT Press, 2008. £9.95/$14.95.
112 pp.

As the international community embarks on a new debate on nuclear disarmament, prompted by a flurry of national and private initiatives, two noted authors plead with nuclear-weapons states to take disarmament seriously.

Few people have written as eloquently and passionately about nuclear disarmament as Jonathan Schell. He devotes the first half of his new book to a discussion of three different historical rationales for the possession of nuclear weapons – the adherents of which he calls 'realists', 'romantics' and 'Wilsonians' – and emphasises the 'primacy of the psychological' in nuclear-weapons issues (p. 65). According to him, whereas the end of the Cold War should have led to disarmament, the turn of the century saw the coming to full maturity of nuclear thinking, bringing together all three strands:

> In the psychological field of action at the center of all nuclear strategy, the realist's fear, the romantic's ambition for greatness, and the Wilsonian's yearning for peace flowed together to provide a flexible, new, encompassing rationale for possessing nuclear arsenals. (p. 81)

Schell is right to underline the importance of sheer 'momentum' in nuclear policies, which often prevents fast or radical change. He is also right to remind us that when Western governments justify their arsenals by the existence of proliferation, it is no less than the fourth rationale they have offered: previously, the possession of nuclear weapons was justified by the German, then the Japanese, and then the Soviet threat.

The second part of the book, a critique of American nuclear policies, is much less original, and much less convincing. While Schell argues that 'President Bush arrived at the nuclear question … indirectly, through his reaction to September 11' (p. 100), he had in fact laid out a clear vision of his policies as early as May 2000. Schell claims that the Bush presidency has seen a 'grand return of nuclear war-fighting doctrines' (p. 127), but all the available evidence shows that US authorities, both civilian and military, continue to see nuclear weapons as a deterrent, not a war-fighting tool. Moreover, no administration has gone further than this one in marginalising the nuclear element in US defence policy, in favour of conventional forces and missile defence. Even Schell's contention that the use of force against Iraq was a clean break with past non-proliferation policies is open to question: Bush's two predecessors bombed Iraq's weapons installations in 1993 and 1998. The author has a point when he questions why some 2000 operationally available strategic weapons are needed if not for a large-scale war with Russia, but he fails to understand that 'Mutually Assured Destruction' has disappeared in US official thinking both as an organising principle and as a paradigm.

As he tackles nuclear disarmament (and expands on his previous work), Schell offers a well-crafted and coherent argument, according to which arms control could be the enemy of disarmament: 'Abolition … must be imported from the future to rescue the chaotic present' (p. 211). But he does not really answer several key questions: How would one foster a universal willingness to take abolition seriously? Why should one assume that a stronger commitment to disarmament will convince proliferators that they do not need nuclear weapons? And given that the existence of nuclear weapons seems to have discouraged the outbreak of a major war since 1945, would not the risk of such a war be significantly greater in a nuclear-free world? Schell's book offers penetrating insights on strategic issues, often summarised in pithy expressions (the suicide bomber as the 'nemesis of deterrence', p. 156), and for this reason is well worth reading. Unfortunately, his policy analyses and prescriptions are often too disconnected from reality to be truly useful.

Hans Blix, formerly the head of the International Atomic Energy Agency (IAEA) and the United Nations Monitoring, Verification and Inspection Commission (UNMOVIC), and now chairman of the Swedish government's Weapons of Mass Destruction (WMD) Commission, has published a much shorter book – more like a lengthy article. It is a worthy companion to the WMD

Commission report, issued in 2006, and benefits from the author's in-depth policy experience. Like Schell, Blix asserts that nuclear-weapons states do not take their obligations under Article 6 of the Non-Proliferation Treaty seriously enough. He criticises the Bush doctrine for justifying military action 'when the first milligrams of low-enriched uranium come out of a cascade of centrifuges' (p. 29), which even under the most lenient interpretation of self-defence is hardly consistent with the UN Charter. He emphasises that the UN Security Council is entitled to employ coercive measures when dealing with proliferation, and states that such actions should be reserved for the international community acting as a whole and employed only 'when there is an acute, not potential threat to peace' (p. 37). The trouble, of course, is that the Security Council would not necessarily be able to respond to an immediate threat.

Blix is right to emphasise the importance of security guarantees to limiting the risks of further proliferation. It is not certain, however, that these could solve the North Korean and Iranian crises: Pyongyang has been given assurances of non-aggression but has yet to give up its weapons-grade plutonium stockpile, and Tehran simply does not seem to be interested in such assurances (assuming it would believe them). Likewise, the reference to the 'Korean model of 1992' raises eyebrows given that 16 years later, North Korea has become almost a full-fledged nuclear-capable country. Where Hans Blix is on the mark is in suggesting significant but realistic proposals such as an enrichment- and reprocessing-free zone in the Middle East in exchange for fuel guarantees.

Doomsday Men: The Real Dr Strangelove and the Dream of the Superweapon
P.D. Smith. London: Allen Lane, 2008. £12.99. 553 pp.

Tools of Violence: Guns, Tanks and Dirty Bombs
Chris McNab and Hunter Keeter. Oxford: Osprey Publishing, 2008. £17.99/$24.95. 320 pp.

Doomsday Men by P.D. Smith tells the story of the twentieth-century search for the perfect weapon. It explores the fascinating, if uneasy and tortuous, relationship between scientists and war. The conflicts of the first part of the century hastened the advent of modern chemical and biological warfare, particularly through the efforts of Fritz Haber in Germany and Shiro Ishii in Japan. But this was just the beginning. As is well known, scientists went on to create weapons with a destructive capacity greater than anything previously imagined, based on the fission, and later the fusion, of atomic nuclei.

These developments led scientists to consider the possibility of creating a so-called 'doomsday weapon'. (As many *Survival* readers will be aware, this idea features prominently in Stanley Kubrick's film *Dr. Strangelove*. What they may not know is that Kubrick visited the Institute for Strategic Studies – as the IISS was then known – in 1961 for inspiration, and was reportedly met with a cold reception by Alastair Buchan.) Even though they were never the subject of serious research, doomsday devices remained a common theme in political debates and popular literature throughout the 1950s and 1960s. The Soviet Union came closest to actually building one: the *Tsar Bomba*, designed by Andrei Sakharov, could have attained a yield of 100 megatons. *Perimetr* was a semi-automated retaliation system designed to operate in case the country was destroyed by a nuclear attack. In the United States, Hungarian-born Leo Szilard, a key contributor to the Manhattan Project, developed the notion of a gigantic thermonuclear bomb 'salted' with cobalt, which would have the potential to end all life on Earth.

Doomsday Men points out that many weapons scientists – including Haber, Sakharov, Szilard and others – saw themselves not only as helping their countries, but also humanity as a whole, and believed, as did Alfred Nobel of his invention of dynamite, that their efforts would save mankind from war. (By contrast, their creations were often greeted with repulsion by military commanders.) Smith also illuminates, in his valuable account, the interaction between science and literature, with scientists and authors constantly inspiring one another throughout the century. For instance, *The World Set Free* by H.G. Wells (1914), the first novel about nuclear war, was a source of inspiration for many scientific pioneers, including Szilard.

Unlike doomsday devices, most weapons are not just objects of literary and scientific speculation, but are actually used to kill on a daily basis. These are the focus of *Tools of Violence*, an original work by Chris McNab and Hunter Keeter. The book is neither a technical catalogue of military equipment, nor an essay on contemporary violence. It has no particular thesis or agenda, but presents *in situ* the extensive array of instruments of armed violence that mankind is using today, from hand-held arms to chemical and biological munitions. Each category of weapon receives its own chapter: small arms, explosives, battlefield armour, artillery, military aviation, naval weapons systems, and chemical, biological, radiological and nuclear (CBRN) weapons. Densely written and packed with information, it aims to be comprehensive, but in fact focuses on traditional weapons and conventional tactics – nuclear weapons and missile defence, for instance, get a grand total of three pages, and perhaps should have been left out altogether. And it has a strong bias towards explaining American weapons and strategies – Russian, Chinese, Israeli or European technologies get a much less substantial treatment. But the book's US focus means it is strong on some contemporary defence issues with vital policy importance and political resonance that goes way beyond their tactical significance – for instance, the protection of armoured vehicles against improvised explosive devices (IEDs). The authors' extreme attention to detail is also commendable, particularly so as they avoid falling into the trap of 'data worship'. The presentation can be factual and sometimes dry, but most of the time the style is lively, and the use of case studies, anecdotes and quotations make the book easy to read. *Tools of Violence* could have formed the basis of a more ambitious essay, but it was intended as a reference work, which it succeeds in being.

On Nuclear Terrorism
Michael Levi. Cambridge, MA: Harvard University Press, 2007.
£16.95/$24.95. 210 pp.

The impact that a nuclear terrorist attack would have on our civilisation and way of life cannot be overestimated. If it happened in a major capital, the political, strategic and economic consequences would be truly devastating. However, seven years after the events of 11 September 2001, the likelihood of such an attack is still disputed. There are, broadly speaking, two schools of thought regarding the risk of nuclear terrorism. One says that it is only a matter of time before a nuclear attack takes place, unless we take drastic actions to reduce the risk. Another school insists on the enormous difficulties that any terrorist group would face if it decided to embark on such a plot.

Michael Levi clearly belongs to the second group. While shorter than other major studies on the same topic, his book is a careful, meticulous, balanced and dispassionate reflection on the subject. There is an abundance of technical detail, which testifies to the seriousness of the author and the rigorous approach he has taken, but the text is clearly written and easy to read – a valuable compromise. Simple diagrams illustrate some technical points that are often poorly understood. Levi starts with a realistic assumption: despite the extreme consequences of an act of nuclear terrorism, we will never be able to reduce the risk to zero. Therefore, 'we should seek to make nuclear terrorism as unlikely as possible, and we should also aim to minimize the consequences of any attack that might, despite our best efforts, occur' (p. 5). 'The right strategy', he says, 'can keep our gambling to a minimum, and tilt the odds in our favor' (p. 152). However, although a well-thought-out emergency response could save many lives, Levi rightly points out that more research has been devoted to preventing an attack than responding to one.

Levi also strongly emphasises the non-specific aspects of risk reduction: 'defense against nuclear terrorism is as much about bread-and-butter counterterrorism and homeland security as it is about nuclear-specific measures' (p.

143). He refuses to endorse the oft-quoted idea that 'terrorists have to be lucky only once, whereas we have to be able to succeed all the time'. Instead, he notes (correctly) that 'terrorists must succeed at every stage, but the defense needs to succeed only once' (p. 7). He stresses the technical, 'real world' difficulties that any group would face in actually building a reliable nuclear weapon with a significant yield. This is one of the strongest points of the book. Levi does not discuss at length the beliefs, mentalities and strategies of terrorist groups – in other words, the 'attractiveness' of nuclear terrorism. But this much we know: nuclear terrorism is *not* an option which is both technically easy *and* strategically attractive – otherwise, the proverbial mushroom cloud would already have appeared over one of our cities.

Nuclear Weapons: What You Need to Know
Jeremy Bernstein. Cambridge: Cambridge University Press, 2008. £16.99/$27.00. 312 pp.

Plutonium: A History of the World's Most Dangerous Element
Jeremy Bernstein. Washington DC: Joseph Henry Press, 2007. £14.99/$27.95. 194 pp.

A good understanding of nuclear policies, the risks of proliferation, or the economics of nuclear energy requires some knowledge of technical issues that are sometimes disregarded, even by the strategic community. Jeremy Bernstein, a professor of physics who is also a professional writer, has produced two short volumes on nuclear physics that are important additions to the growing body of scientific history aimed at a large public, but his books are nevertheless accurate and precise from a technical point of view. What makes them truly valuable is that they represent a rare combination of good historical research, impeccable science, a pleasant style and insightful personal anecdotes. Also, they illustrate the role of chance and coincidence in the world of scientific research – two factors that might very well have altered the course of the Second World War.

Nuclear Weapons: What You Need to Know is a well-documented history of the physics of nuclear weapons from Ernest Rutherford's discovery of the nucleus in the early twentieth century through the post-Cold War era. The book introduces the general public to critical but sometimes overlooked developments such as the Frisch-Peierls memorandum of 1940, which was the first paper to describe in detail the explosive properties of nuclear weapons; the famous lectures given at Los Alamos by Robert Serber, which became the material for the so-called 'Los Alamos Primer' (the first public document describing in detail the fabrication of nuclear weapons, declassified in 1965); or the Russian version of the Klaus Fuchs spy story, based on documents that became available after the fall of the Soviet Union. The book also contains strong explanations of the technology of implosion, boosted fission, and the effects of nuclear weapons.

Plutonium is a companion volume to *Nuclear Weapons*, but is more focused and also more scientifically oriented. In fact, one or two chapters are clearly not for those lacking an education in physics and chemistry. Why a book about plutonium? Simply because it is the most dangerous substance ever created, and may be the most bizarre element in Mendeleev's table: it has disappeared from the Earth's crust for natural reasons and its properties vary considerably from one form or 'phase' to another. Moreover, Bernstein's goal in recounting the history of plutonium, as revealed in the last pages of the book, is to show how mankind made a Faustian bargain in the twentieth century. (It is a fitting coincidence that, in keeping with the tradition of naming elements after planets, Plutonium was named after Pluto, itself named for a Roman god who was said to judge the souls of the dead.) We are now stuck with more than 150 tonnes of weapons-grade plutonium, and more than ten times as much civilian plutonium. The book does not address the critical economic and security issues that are raised today because of this inheritance. Will modern states choose to burn plutonium in electricity-producing reactors? Will some countries attempt to build a bomb by using 'civilian' plutonium? Bernstein provides no answers, but an understanding of the history and properties of this peculiar element is useful when dealing with the major challenges of energy security and nuclear proliferation.

Counter-terrorism

Jonathan Stevenson

Confronting Global Terrorism and American Neo-Conservatism: The Framework of a Liberal Grand Strategy
Tom Farer. Oxford: Oxford University Press, 2008.
£14.99/$29.95. 267 pp.

Worst-Case Scenarios
Cass R. Sunstein. Cambridge, MA: Harvard University Press, 2007. £16.95/$24.95. 340 pp.

As the title of his book suggests, Tom Farer, the erudite and articulate lawyer and legal scholar who serves as dean of the University of Denver's School of International Studies, considers the neo-conservative movement in the United States, as well as global terrorism, inimical to international security. He makes a strong case. In his view, the George W. Bush administration's illiberal policies in support of veritable torture, sloppy rhetoric of 'freedom' and 'democracy', reductionist lumping of all terrorists into a monolithic enemy, and militarisation of counter-terrorism constitute by turns hypocritical and simple-minded characteristics of an American grand strategy for containing and ultimately marginalising transnational Islamist terrorism that cannot succeed. The programmatic remedy, says Farer, is to re-establish the link between American constitutional values and international law.

While at first blush this may sound like just one more supercilious liberal bromide, he provides a considered array of five subsidiary objectives that make it appreciably more than that. They are, briefly, to signal respect for the bulk of Islamic beliefs and believers; to materially improve the lives and prospects of Muslim youth, especially in the Middle East; to empower mainstream Muslim thinkers in their confrontation with those who are irreconcilably hostile to non-Muslims; to encourage a more ecumenical understanding of the history and cultural interaction of religions; and to provide a viable educational model for Muslim countries (p. 246). Anticipating the 'fatuous' argument that the non-military public spending required to advance such an agenda would have little impact on the mainly middle- or upper-class Islamist terrorist ideological leaders, Farer points out that their ire derives substantially from their vicarious experience of the plight of their less fortunate brothers and sisters. 'Empathy can produce a Mother Teresa; it can also produce an Osama bin Laden' (p. 248).

While Farer wants to resurrect the technocratic liberal strategy that had brief currency in US policy circles after 11 September and before Iraq, University of Chicago law professor Cass Sunstein pointedly challenges the logic of any scheme that treats terrorism as a strategic threat while underplaying the greater devastation that, say, global climate change might bring. In his view, Americans since 11 September have focused on terrorism's 'worst case' for essentially cognitive reasons. The high public visibility and impact of the 11 September attacks provided Americans with a vivid example of what terrorists can do, establishing an 'availability bias' that obscured the relatively low probability of further comparable attacks and, when associated with a contemptible human face – bin Laden's – heightened the degree and durability of the emotional outrage associated with them. That is, the familiar is fallaciously equated with the probable, especially if its source is despised. The Bush administration has repeatedly exploited this cognitive reality, particularly to justify the invasion of Iraq and the application of abusive interrogation practices.

Although Sunstein maintains a cheerfully neutral pedagogical tone, he occasionally hints at his own political tilt. 'Fear is a powerful motivator', he says, 'and with respect to terrorism, drawing attention to worst-case scenarios is much in the self-interest of certain politicians' (p. 277). Insofar as Farer's re-orientation of US counter-terrorism policy would liberate intellectual and financial resources to deal with other problems more thoroughly and equitably, he and Sunstein appear to be in agreement.

Jihadi Terrorism and the Radicalisation Challenge in Europe
Rik Coolsaet, ed. Aldershot: Ashgate Publishing, 2008. £55.00/$99.95. 220 pp.

Leaderless Jihad: Terror Networks in the Twenty-First Century
Marc Sageman. Philadelphia, PA: University of Pennsylvania Press, 2008. £16.50/$24.95. 208 pp.

It is now well known that the US-led takedown of the Taliban and al-Qaeda in Afghanistan caused the latter's membership to disperse and its leadership to go underground, loosening its command and control over its followers and effectively devolving operational initiative to so-called 'self-starter' or 'homegrown' terrorist cells. As Rik Coolsaet's sensible and timely edited volume demonstrates, Europe is a focal point for the formation of such cells on account of the alienation of its growing Muslim population, the relatively high symbolic value of European targets, and Europe's ongoing utility as a platform for attacks against the United States.

Of particular interest are chapters contributed by Martha Crenshaw, Jocelyne Cesari and Glenn Audenaert. They show, respectively, that putative distinctions between 'new' and 'old' terrorism can be exaggerated and should not be construed so rigidly as to preclude constructive comparisons and continuities or elide analytic subtleties; that 'joining the jihad is a social process and not simply an individual decision' (p. 98), the remedy for which requires, among other things, clearer public-policy separation between international and domestic issues involving Islam; and that law-enforcement agencies need to establish institutional understandings of the radicalisation process and to integrate their core function of preserving security into a larger inter-agency strategy of de-radicalisation if that effort is to be effective.

In his chapter on European and global jihadis, Edwin Bakker frequently cites Marc Sageman, a forensic psychiatrist and former CIA case officer, whose highly influential book, *Understanding Terror Networks*, demonstrated the bottom-up evolution of terrorist networks and the centrality of social connections in that process. Sageman's new book – which has prompted a rancorous public feud with fellow American counter-terrorism expert Bruce Hoffman – takes this thesis a step further. In *Leaderless Jihad: Terror Networks in the Twenty-First Century*, Sageman essentially argues that 'the global Islamist terrorist social movement forms through the spontaneous self-organization of informal "bunches of guys," trusted friends, from the bottom up' (p. 69). Hoffman might have had considerable sympathy with this view a couple of years ago, but since then al-Qaeda has re-established a safe haven and physical base in the tribal areas of Pakistan, which suggests that it has regained some of the strategic and operational, if not tactical, command and control over affiliated groups that it had lost. Indeed, European analysts have observed enhanced operational links – including travel and communications – between al-Qaeda's core leadership in Pakistan and its franchise in North Africa, among others, and small training camps in North Waziristan appear to have re-materialised.

While these developments reinforce the characterisation of al-Qaeda as an organisationally flat, geographically spread-out network, they also tend to confirm that the group has partially rejuvenated a top-down recruitment and planning capability. This reality, in turn, supports challenges, like Hoffman's, to Sageman's position that the dynamics of global jihadist networks are predominantly bottom-up. For his part, Sageman acknowledges al-Qaeda's partial re-consolidation, but is explicitly 'skeptical of the claim of a resurgent al Qaeda Central' (p. 127), and sets forth a counter-argument. In any case, other aspects of his thesis – notably, the 'four prongs' of individual radicalisation, comprising a sense of moral outrage, perceptions of a 'war on Islam', alignment of that perception with everyday personal grievances, and mobilisation through social networks – remain analytically useful tools for meeting the radicalisation challenge.

War By Other Means: Building Complete and Balanced Capabilities for Counterinsurgency
David C. Gompert and John Gordon IV. Santa Monica. CA: RAND Corporation, 2008. $42.50. 516 pp.

Terrorism in Asymmetrical Conflict: Ideological and Structural Aspects
Ekaterina Stepanova. Oxford: Oxford University Press, 2008. £35.00/$70.00. 194 pp.

There is a firm consensus that the largely American invasion and occupation of Iraq has fuelled rather than quelled Islamist terrorism worldwide, and that flawed US counter-insurgency efforts, at best only partially and tenuously ameliorated by the 'surge', have intensified this perverse effect. The RAND

Corporation's capstone counter-insurgency study acknowledges as much. 'Lost in the fog of the GWOT [global war on terror]', it notes, 'is whether using armies to fight terrorists hidden among Muslim populations is spawning more hostility and resistance. The data suggest that it is' (p. 8). Yet the George W. Bush administration has appeared intent on using the military in general, and counter-insurgency in particular, as primary tools of counter-terrorism, and the new American administration will inherit ongoing insurgency challenges in Iraq and Afghanistan. Thus, the Office of the Secretary of Defense tasked RAND to do a comprehensive assessment of how to improve the United States' inadequate counter-insurgency capabilities.

RAND has done a characteristically thorough job, providing historical analyses, charts and graphs, policy prescriptions and resource-allocation recommendations. It has also tackled the assignment with admirable candour and bluntness. Recognising that 'large-scale conventional U.S. military power is, generally speaking, ineffective against a distributed, mobile, adaptable, uninhibited, and fearless enemy' and 'does not address the crux of the problem, which is the sentiment and direction of Muslim populations' (p. 350), RAND suggests that an excessively militarised approach to counter-insurgency has led to the overstretch of US ground forces and that enhancing counter-insurgency capabilities does not call for the expansion of those forces. Accordingly, the study sensibly concludes that better civil, informational, analytic, management and training – in a word, 'soft power' – capabilities are needed.

Ekaterina Stepanova, under the auspices of the Stockholm International Peace Research Institute (SIPRI), takes a conceptual look at the problem of asymmetrical conflict, and while much of her book merely recapitulates familiar distinctions between ethno-nationalist and expressive transnational religious terrorism, her efforts ultimately yield some interesting, even bold, results. In particular, she concludes that 'nationalism ... is the strongest force that can tie a militant organization to a certain location, territory, or national context and streamline and conventionalize its structure' (p. 125). No doubt the political success of Hizbullah within Lebanon, for example, has tamped down its out-of-area ambitions and extraterritorial terrorist operations, and Hamas's victory in the Palestinian Authority elections – at least before governing with Fatah became infeasible – rendered it less likely to make tactical alliances with al-Qaeda or its affiliates.

The corollary is that counter-terrorism strategies should include efforts to give radicalised Islamist groups a stake in the state so as to afford them something tangible to preserve, and thus render them easier to co-opt, influence and deter. Accomplishing this goal, says Stepanova, would entail 'nationalizing Islamist supranational and supra-state ideology' (p. 153) as opposed to 'using modern

Western-style democratic secularism' (p. 154) to tame Islamist terrorist groups. Even if such a policy does not result in a group's outright rejection of violence, 'it could stimulate it to abandon the most extreme violent tactics such as terrorism' (p. 163). The logic of this position is compelling and, as iconoclastic as it may seem, is not inherently inconsistent with the more comprehensive counterinsurgency model developed by RAND.

The Bin Ladens: An Arabian Family in the American Century
Steve Coll. New York: Penguin Press, 2008. £25.00/$35.00. 686 pp.

Steve Coll, a Pulitzer-winning journalist and now president of the New America Foundation, has written an expansive, probing book that gives rich social context to the phenomenon of transnational Islamic radicalism and terrorism. As such, *The Bin Ladens* complements seminal analyses such as Steven Simon and Daniel Benjamin's *The Age of Sacred Terror* and virtuoso investigative-reporting efforts such as Lawrence Wright's *The Looming Tower*. Coll's central thesis is that while post-1979 Islamic radicalism in the Gulf and the anti-Soviet jihad in Afghanistan were key formative influences on Osama bin Laden, his relationship to his family, and his family's embodiment of both transnational Arab cultural and commercial traditions and the invidious oil-based relationship between the United States and Saudi Arabia, 'bequeathed' to bin Laden 'not just wealth, but a transforming vision of ambition and religious faith in a borderless world' (p. 15).

In evocative prose, Coll tells how Mohamed bin Laden, father to Osama and 53 other children, came from the Hadhramawt region of Yemen to preside over a Saudi construction giant that built crucial industrial and military infrastructure for – and durable personal and business relationships with – the House of Saud. When a plane crash took Mohamed's life in 1967, he left an estate valued at about $150 million, of which only 2.27% went to Osama. But Osama evolved from being a marginal member of the bin Laden clan – like other bin Ladens, he was attracted to business and engineering and was fiercely self-reliant, but was atypically pious despite a fleeting adolescent affection for fast cars – to a respected manager in a moderately lucrative (he netted about $1m a year) international family business and, from his conversion in 1973, a religiously impressive and intimidating presence. The Soviet occupation of Afghanistan gave his radical side purchase and purpose, and his brothers supported his charitable activities on behalf of the Afghans.

The rest of Osama's story is better known (see Coll's *Ghost Wars*). His family, which largely embraced the US and the West, came to see him as a 'pest' (p. 282) and a potential political liability within Saudi Arabia, and encouraged his relocation to Pakistan in 1986 'to achieve his goals on the Afghan frontier' (p. 283). But however ambivalent towards Osama the rest of the family was, he could not have accomplished what he did as a militant, and ultimately a terrorist, without them. For example, his older brother Salem – an insouciant playboy and the most powerful member of the family's business empire – helped procure, with official Saudi assistance, surface-to-air missiles and AK-47 assault rifles for the Afghan mujahadeen at Osama's behest. Of course, in 1994 the bin Ladens publicly condemned Osama's anti-House of Saud diatribes premised on the Saudi royals' security dependence on the United States, and Riyadh stripped him of Saudi citizenship. Nevertheless, 'Osama would make three indispensable contributions to Al Qaeda, all derived from his experiences as a bin Laden: his emphasis on diversity and inclusion, his confidence about money and administration, and his attraction to the technologies of global integration' (p. 338). Yet none of the other bin Ladens remotely shared his revolutionary spirit or his hatred of the West. As Coll makes thoroughly clear, Osama bin Laden has always been, among other things, his own man.

The Mind of the Terrorist: The Psychology of Terrorism from the IRA to Al-Qaeda
Jerrold M. Post. New York and Basingstoke: Palgrave Macmillan, 2007. £16.00/$27.95. 318 pp.

Counter-terrorism professionals and academics most commonly handle the psychology of the terrorist interstitially, as part of a broader analysis of terrorists' political, ideological and religious motivations. A good example is Mark Juergensmeyer's *Terror in the Mind of God*. If the tendency to subordinate the subject of terrorist psychology signals a need for a more direct and comprehensive treatment, Jerrold Post – founder of the CIA's Center for the Analysis of Personality and Political Behavior and now a professor at George Washington University – purports to fill it. His book does bring together well-tested typologies of terrorism (ethno-nationalist, leftist-ideological, religious extremist), and explores, across a broad spectrum of terrorist organisations, the inspirational effects of martyrdom, charismatic (and narcissistic) leadership, identity politics, jailhouse or refugee-camp indoctrination, and imperatives of asymmetric warfare. The bulk of *The Mind of the Terrorist*, however, merely rehashes the histories and grievances of terrorist groups without integrating any considered assessment of their particular psychologies into largely standard accounts.

The final three chapters of the book are more focused, and contain a number of useful insights, but in some respects remain problematic as current guidance.

For instance, Post states that 'part of al-Qaeda's leadership genius under bin Laden and Zawahiri is not to focus on differences, but to coopt and embrace potential rivals' (p. 222). The primary example cited is Abu Musab al-Zarqawi, the head of al-Qaeda in Mesopotamia who was killed by an American air-strike in June 2006. While it is true that al-Qaeda's core leadership did acquire more control over Zarqawi by reinforcing his self-proclaimed allegiance, Post admits that Zarqawi did not completely change his tactics – which involved indiscriminate and gruesome killing of civilians in general and Shi'ites in particular – despite Zawahiri's celebrated protests, lodged in an intercepted letter. Thus, the example raises doubts about how effective the core leadership's flexibility has been in establishing cohesion. Recent challenges to the maximalist logic of al-Qaeda's jihadism by respected figures within the larger movement – including Sayyid Imam al-Sharif ('Dr Fadl'), Sheikh Salman al-Oudah and Noman Benotman – only intensify those doubts.

Likewise, the book's discussion of mass-casualty terrorism – especially the blithely simplistic claim that 'religious fundamentalist terrorist groups, who follow the dictates of charismatic religious leaders, are not constrained by their audience on earth, as their acts of violence are given sacred significance' (p. 240) – seems inconsistent with the disputes that are arising in global jihadist discourse. That is not to say that calmer voices are clearly prevailing, or will prevail: the extremist counter-arguments are comparably defensible in theological terms; militant radicalism remains highly appealing; the United States is still a supremely antagonistic target; provocative 'apostate' Muslim regimes persist; and the reconstitution of al-Qaeda's physical base of operations in Pakistan's tribal areas is proceeding. Post sketches some sound prescriptions for 'an integrated strategic information operations program' (p. 246), including efforts to reduce the public's psychological susceptibility to terrorist threats. But the aforementioned complicating factors do not catch sufficient light in *The Mind of the Terrorist*, which diminishes the book's applicability to present-day challenges.

Brief Notices

Middle East

American Policy Toward Israel: The Power and Limits of Belief

Michael Thomas. Abingdon: Routledge, 2007. £75.00/$150.00. 253 pp.

Thomas looks at the domestic, social, religious and political factors that have shaped US policy towards Israel, arguing that 'policy debates have been struggles to embed and enforce beliefs about Israel and Arabs'. He argues that the 'nearly unconditional American support of Israel' was institutionalised during the Reagan and first Bush administrations, and applies the lessons learned.

Beyond the Façade: Political Reform in the Arab World

Marina S. Ottaway and Julia Choucair-Vizoso, eds. Washington DC: Carnegie Endowment for International Peace, 2008. £13.99/$22.95. 304 pp.

Essays on ten Middle Eastern countries explore the dilemmas of political reform in that region. The authors seek to highlight the diversity of problems, actors and solutions in the region and to draw lessons for making the promotion of democracy more effective. The limitations of external actors hoping to bring about reform are discussed.

Bad Days in Basra: My Turbulent Time as Britain's Man in Southern Iraq

Hilary Synnott. London: I.B. Tauris, 2008. £17.00/$26.95. 287 pp.

Once the UK's most senior representative in Southern Iraq, Synnott provides a first-person account of the chaotic way in which occupied Iraq was governed. His memoir records the corruption, apathy and dishonesty of Iraqi and Coalition leaders.

The Epicenter of Crisis: The New Middle East

Alexander T.J. Lennon, ed. Cambridge, MA: The MIT Press, 2008. £16.95/$25.00. 363 pp.

The essays in this collection (first published in *The Washington Quarterly* between 2005 and 2007) paint a portrait of the nations at the centre of what some call 'an arc of crisis': Saudi Arabia, Syria, Iraq, Iran, Afghanistan and Pakistan. The authors address the changing role of Islam, the danger posed by failed states and the evolving terrorist threat, touching on such topics as the relationship between the Saudi royal family and al-Qaeda, and Afghanistan's opium industry.

The Politics of Chaos in the Middle East

Olivier Roy. London: C. Hurst 7 Co., 2008. £12.99/$24.95. 167 pp.

Roy argues that a narrative of 'us and them' prevents the West from understanding the complex political dynamics of the Middle East and the discontent that has led to them. He suggests that dialogue with influential political actors such as Hamas and the Muslim Brotherhood is the only way to reduce tensions.

Globalization and Geopolitics in the Middle East: Old Games, New Rules
Anoushiravan Ehteshami. Abingdon: Routledge, 2007. £75.00/$150.00. 258 pp.

Ehteshami discusses how patterns of globalisation in the Middle East and North Africa differ from other regions, such as East Asia. Whereas globalisation is usually associated with greater economic, societal and cultural openness, the Middle East has seen poor state formation, minimal interregional trade and investment, and a reassertion of traditional identities.

Identity and Religion in Palestine: The Struggle Between Islamism and Secularism in the Occupied Territories
Loren D. Lybarger. Princeton, NJ: Princeton University Press, 2007. £23.95/$39.50. 296 pp.

Based on more than 80 interviews and his own experience living in the region, Lybarger discusses the ways in which the identities of ordinary Palestinians have changed under the competing influence of the Islamist movement and secular-nationalist factions. He paints a complex picture of divided loyalties and internal struggles in a society coping with ongoing processes of occupation, peace negotiations and fragmentation.

Inside Hamas: The Untold Story of the Militant Islamic Movement
Zaki Chehab. New York: Nation Books, 2007. £17.99/$29.95. 256 pp.

Palestinian journalist Zaki Chehab provides a window into the high-profile but still mysterious radical movement Hamas, showing how, with the implicit encouragement of the Israelis, Hamas built a strong social base through the provision of welfare programmes. The group's more violent activities are also examined, as Chehab reveals a group 'driven above all else by a desire for power'.

International Assistance to the Palestinians after Oslo: Political Guilt, Wasted Money
Anne Le More. Abingdon: Routledge, 2008. £70.00/$130.00. 239 pp.

Le More examines flows of foreign aid to the Palestinians between the creation of the Palestinian Authority and the death of President Arafat, concluding that funds from the international community were intended to substitute for substantive diplomatic engagement. She discusses the effects this money has had on the Palestinian population, Israeli policy and the conflict itself.

Iran's Foreign Policy from Khatami to Ahmadinejad
Anoushiravan Ehteshami and Mahjoob Zweiri, eds. Reading: Ithaca Press, 2008. £35.00/$54.50. 149 pp.

This collection covers Iranian foreign policy from the time of President Khatami to the present. It discusses the four main policy priorities during this period: resisting all forms of foreign domination; preserving Iran's independence and territorial integrity; defending the rights of Muslims; and maintaining peaceful relations with non-belligerent states.

Iran in World Politics: The Question of the Islamic Republic
Arshin Adib-Moghaddam. London: C. Hurst & Co., 2007. £18.99/$32.50. 272 pp.

Adib-Moghaddam seeks to move past the limitations of mainstream representations of post-revolutionary Iran to achieve a deeper understanding of such complex issues as the nuclear question, tension with the United States and Iranian–Arab relations. He advocates a new methodological and theoretical approach to 'critical Iranian studies'.

The Iran Threat: President Ahmadinejad and the Coming Nuclear Crisis
Alireza Jafarzadeh. Basingstoke: Palgrave Macmillan, 2008. £15.99/$14.95. 284 pp.

Jafarzadeh, who claims to have access to dissident groups inside Iran, provides a detailed account of Ahmadinejad's rise to power and the state of Iran's nuclear programme, including such trends as the military's growing control of the programme and efforts to bury facilities in tunnels. He also discusses the country's involvement in Iraq and its broader goals for the Middle East.

An Iraq of Its Regions: Cornerstones of a Federal Democracy?
Reidar Visser and Gareth Stansfield, eds. London: C. Hurst & Co., 2007. £19.99/$27.50. 350 pp.

This volume looks at the influence of regionalism on contemporary Iraqi politics. The authors note that geographic divisions exist alongside ethno-religious ones and that the former could provide the 'building blocks of the new Iraq', assuming the Iraqi constitution is upheld.

Israel's National Security: Issues and Challenges since the Yom Kippur War
Efraim Inbar. Abingdon: Routledge, 2008. £70.00/$140.00. 304 pp.

Inbar offers an overview of Israel's security challenges since 1973. He explores both Israel's and the international community's responses to events including the Cold War, the intifada, the peace process, the recent war with Lebanon and Iranian nuclearisation. The ways in which current trends might influence future Israeli actions are also discussed.

Making Islam Democratic: Social Movements and the Post-Islamist Turn
Asef Bayat. Palo Alto, CA: Stanford University Press, 2007. £14.95/$21.95. 320 pp.

Bayat argues that there is nothing in the essence of Islam that renders it incompatible with democracy: what matters is how it is practiced. He shows how various social movements across the Middle East have used religion to unleash social and political change, either in support of authoritarian rule or to build 'an inclusive faith that embraces a democratic polity'.

The Nuclear Sphinx of Tehran: Mahmoud Ahmadinejad and the State of Iran
Yossi Melman & Meir Javedanfar. New York: Carroll & Graf Publishers, 2007. £9.99/$16.95. 336 pp.

Two Middle East specialists offer insights into the rise of the Iranian president, from his modest roots to the present. They explore the leader's 'vituperative populism', 'apocalyptic theology', nuclear ambitions and links with terrorists in other Middle Eastern states.

Muslim Communities of Grace: The Sufi Brotherhoods in Islamic Religious Life
Jamil M. Abun-Nasr. London: C. Hurst & Co., 2007. £16.95/$27.50. 256 pp.

Abun-Nasr seeks to explain the emergence, appeal and teachings of Sufi brotherhoods across the Muslim world, noting that these religious communities have become players in the struggle between secular modernising nationalists and Islamists in many Muslim nations.

No End in Sight: Iraq's Descent into Chaos
Charles H. Ferguson. New York: Public Affairs, 2008. $17.95/£9.99. 352 pp.

Based on interviews conducted for the 2007 film of the same name, this book documents the aftermath of the fall of Baghdad in 2003. Authorities such as Deputy Secretary of State Richard Armitage, analysts George Packer and Christopher Hitchens, and other US and Iraqi witnesses to the Iraq War discuss early tactical mistakes, the insurgency and prospects for the future.

Pen and Swords: How the American Mainstream Media Report the Israeli–Palestinian Conflict
Marda Dunsky. New York: Columbia University Press, 2008. £16.50/$27.50. 444 pp.

Dunsky examines US media coverage of the Israeli-Palestinian conflict from the failed Camp David summit of 2000 through the second Palestinian uprising of 2004, concluding that the media routinely fail to acknowledge the significant impact of US policy in the region and the international legal and political consensus that exists on the key issues of Israeli settlements and Palestinian refugees.

The Road to Democracy in Iran
Akbar Ganji. Cambridge, MA: The MIT Press, 2008. £9.95/$14.95. 113 pp.

Ganji's advocacy of secular democracy and human rights in Iran earned him a six-year prison sentence. Writing in English for the first time, he calls for nonviolent, domestically driven democratic change in the Muslim world, and for Islamic recognition of human rights, including womens' rights.

The Umma and the Dawla: The Nation State and the Arab Middle East
Tamim Al-Barghouti. London: Pluto Press, 2008. £17.99/$35.00. 240 pp.

Arguing that the colonially created states of the Middle East represent a failed compromise between Islamic notions of identity and modern nationalism, Al-Barghouti analyses the Muslim concepts of 'umma' (roughly, 'nation') and 'dawla' (state) and explains how these differ from comparable Western ideas.

The United States and Iran: Sanctions, Wars and the Policy of Dual Containment
Sasan Fayazmanesh. London: Routledge, 2008. £70.00/$140.00. 264 pp.

Fayazmanesh draws on primary sources to provide a detailed analysis of US policy towards Iran, staring with the role played by the Carter and Reagan administrations in the Iran–Iraq War. He discusses the sanctions regime imposed in 1979, the role of lobby groups and 'so-called neoconservatives' in shaping policy, and the nuclear issue.

The Quest for Democracy in Iran: A Century of Struggle Against Authoritarian Rule
Fakhreddin Azimi. Cambridge, MA: Harvard University Press, 2008. £22.95/$35.00. 492 pp.

Azimi traces the evolution of Iranian government, society, civic culture, ideology, foreign relations and economy over the last century. He argues that Iran has taken steps towards democracy in the past, only to have these attempts thwarted by repressive rulers (particularly Reza Shah and his son) and imperialist interventions led by the British and Americans.

U.S. Foreign Policy and Islamist Politics
Ahmad S. Moussalli. Gainesville, FL: University Press of Florida, 2008. £39.50/$59.95. 224 pp.

Moussalli defends the ability of Islamic movements to promote pluralism, democracy and human rights in the Middle East, provided the United States ends its damaging policies in the region. The Iraq War and the unresolved Arab–Israeli conflict present obstacles to the forces of globalisation in Muslim societies.

Treacherous Alliance: The Secret Dealings of Israel, Iran and the U.S.
Trita Parsi. New Haven, CT, and London: Yale University Press, 2007. £18.99/$28.00. 384 pp.

Parsi draws on a decade of foreign-policy experience to analyse the evolution of the relationships between Israel, Iran and the United States since 1948. Revelations include the Iranian prime minister's request that Israel assassinate Khomeini; Israel's attempt to engage Saddam Hussein after the Gulf War; and American interference in Iranian plans to withdraw support from Hamas and Hizbullah.

Unity in Diversity: Interfaith Dialogue in the Middle East

Mohammed Abu-Nimer, Amali I. Khoury and Emily Welty. Washington DC: United States Institute of Peace Press, 2007. $19.95. 336 pp.

As they explore the dilemmas, difficulties and prospects for interfaith dialogue in Israel–Palestine, Lebanon, Egypt and Jordan, the authors present the views and experiences of numerous 'frontline' workers, including laypeople, who seek to the bridge the religious divides in these societies.

The New Iranian Leadership: Ahmadinejad, Terrorism, Nuclear Ambition, and the Middle East

Yonah Alexander and Milton Hoenig. London and Westport, CT: Praeger Security International, 2007. £27.95/$49.95. 344 pp.

This book offers an overview of the Iranian state, the country's nuclear ambitions, and its support of terrorist groups, particularly Hizbullah and Hamas.

Arms, Arms Control and Technology

The International Politics of Space

Michael Sheehan. London: Routledge, 2007. £21.99/$41.95. 238 pp.

Fifty years after the launch of Sputnik, space technology continues to shape military affairs around the world. Sheehan analyses the space programmes of the United States, Russia, China, India and the European Space Agency and explains how our ideas of space will shape its use – for peace or for war – in the future.

The Nuclear Jihadist

Douglas Frantz and Catherine Collins. New York: Twelve Books, 2007. £10.99/$25.00. 413 pp.

Journalists Frantz and Collins provide a detailed account of the A.Q. Khan nuclear-weapons network, following the story around the world. They note that intelligence authorities were aware of Khan's activities for years and might have stopped him but for their passive 'watch-and-wait' approach.

Terrorism and Weapons of Mass Destruction: Responding to the Challenge

Ian Bellany, ed. London: Routledge, 2007. £70.00/$140.00. 256 pp.

The fear that nuclear, chemical or biological weapons will be used by non-state actors against civilians, as in the case of the Tokyo subway attacks, is now widespread. Specialists in each category of weapon ask whether existing arms-control treaties can be expanded or strengthened to combat this threat.

Nuclear Insecurity: Understanding the Threat from Rogue Nations and Terrorists

Jack Caravelli. London and Westport, CT: Praeger Security International, 2007. £27.95/$49.95. 192 pp.

Caravelli critiques US efforts to prevent the spread of nuclear weapons and materials. He makes recommendations to address the many problems his analysis identifies.

Counter-terrorism

Beyond al-Qaeda Part 1: The Global Jihadist Movement

Angel Rabasa et al. Santa Monica, CA: RAND Corporation, 2007. £18.50/$30.00. 226 pp.

In addition to examining the evolution of al-Qaeda since 11 September 2001, the authors outline the threat posed by al-Qaeda affiliates and other groups that share its worldview and operational goals. They conclude with a four-pronged strategy to defeat terrorist groups.

Beyond al-Qaeda Part 2: The Outer Rings of the Terrorist Universe
Angel Rabasa et al. Santa Monica, CA: RAND Corporation, 2007. £15.50/$25.00. 210 pp.

Arguing that terrorist groups without strong links to al-Qaeda can still threaten the United States and its allies, the authors profile major 'independent' terrorist organisations – both Islamist and non-Islamist – around the world, and offer strategies that could be used to prevent their destructive activities.

Blood & Rage: A Cultural History of Terrorism
Michael Burleigh. London: HarperPress, 2008. £25.00. 545 pp.

Burleigh plots the evolution of contemporary terrorism from the first violent acts of the Irish Republican Brotherhood to the deadly attacks of present-day jihadists. He argues that the West's past experiences with terrorism show that it can be contained, and that terrorist organisations almost always have weaknesses that can be exploited.

Chronologies of Modern Terrorism
Barry Rubin and Judith Colp Rubin. Armonk, New York: M.E. Sharpe, 2008. £65.50/$99.95. 405 pp.

This reference work provides details on the history of terrorism from the French Revolution to the present. Each chapter centres on a specific region or theme and consists of an analytical introduction followed by a chronological account of the development and activities of terrorist (and counter-terrorist) groups.

Terrorism Today (2nd ed.)
Christopher C. Harmon. London: Routledge, 2007. £20.99/$39.95. 248 pp.

Harmon draws on the statements and writings of terrorists themselves to provide a complete overview of global terrorism. His wide-ranging analysis touches on terrorist financing and strategies; he also discusses counter-terrorism techniques and how terrorist groups end.

The Confrontation: Winning the War Against Jihad
Walid Phares. Basingstoke: Palgrave Macmillan, 2008, £13.99/$24.95. 296 pp.

The author of *Future Jihad* and *The War of Ideas* forecasts the 'global clashes to come' and provides strategies for pre-empting them. He discusses how the forces of terror can be defused in war-torn Iraq and Afghanistan, Hizbullah-dominated Lebanon, defiant Iran and even in the West, where terrorist movements threaten to grow.

Al Qaeda in its Own Words
Gilles Kepel and Jean-Pierre Milelli, eds. Pascale Ghazaleh, trans. Cambridge, MA and London: Belknap Press, 2008. £18.95/$27.95. 363 pp.

The editors have collected and annotated key texts by leading al-Qaeda figures, including Osama bin Laden, Abu Musab al-Zarqawi and Ayman al-Zawahiri. These texts, along with the accompanying introductions and critical commentary, provide insights into the historical, intellectual and doctrinal development of a movement that is synonymous with Islamic terrorism.

Global Security and the War on Terror: Elite Power and the Illusion of Control
Paul Rogers. London: Routledge, 2007. £21.99/$41.95. 240 pp.

In this collection of essays, Rogers argues that the current international security paradigm is misguided and unsustainable because it requires that power and control be concentrated in the hands of (mainly Western) transnational elites without addressing the underlying issues that lead to insecurity. He calls for a new paradigm 'rooted in justice and emancipation'.

Radical Islam and International Security: Challenges and Responses
Hillel Frisch and Efraim Inbar, eds. London: Routledge, 2007. £70.00/$140.00. 227 pp.

Researchers from around the world lend their expertise to a study of the political challenges posed by the rise of radical Islam. Part one looks at the phenomenon in comparative and historic terms, part two provides regional case studies, and part three suggests responses to the Islamic challenge.

Unmasking Terror vol. 3: A Global Review of Terrorist Activities
Jonathan D. Hutzley, ed. Washington DC: The Jamestown Foundation, 2006. £17.99. 500 pp.

Jamestown Foundation analysts from all over the world provide detailed analysis of terrorist organisations and activities, based on indigenous source material. The authors aim to provide information that is not readily available elsewhere.

Sharing the Dragon's Teeth: Terrorist Groups and the Exchange of New Technologies
Kim Cragin et al. Santa Monica, CA: RAND Corporation, 2007. £12.50/$20.00. 136 pp.

Noting that terrorist groups have increased their effectiveness through exchanges with other groups, the authors provide suggestions for disrupting these channels of communication and preventing the uptake of new technologies and strategies by some of the world's most dangerous organisations.

From the Archives

Survival 1978–1987

Editor's note

Between now and the end of the year, each issue of *Survival* will include brief archival selections as part of the 50th anniversary of the journal and the International Institute for Strategic Studies. In this issue we present excerpts from the third decade of our publication. The selections here cannot be fully representative but are intended to give a flavour of the events, concerns and personalities of the period. Material in italics is editorial comment reproduced verbatim from the archival issues.

Helmut Schmidt, 'The 1977 Alastair Buchan Memorial Lecture'

Survival, vol. 20, no. 1, January–February 1978, pp. 2–10.

The Alastair Buchan Memorial Lectures have been established as a tribute to the Institute's first Director. The 1977 Lecture was delivered by Helmut Schmidt, Chancellor of the Federal Republic of Germany, on 28 October 1977.

> Most of us will agree that political and military balance is the prerequisite of our security, and I would warn against the illusion that there may be grounds for neglecting that balance. Indeed, it is not only the prerequisite for our security but also for fruitful progress in East–West detente.
>
> In the first place we should recognize that – paradoxical as it may sound – there is a closer proximity between a hazardous arms race, on the one hand, and a successful control of arms, on the other, than ever before. There is only a narrow divide between the hope for peace and the danger of war.
>
> Second, changed strategic conditions confront us with new problems. SALT codifies the nuclear strategic balance between the Soviet Union and the United States. To put it another way: SALT neutralizes their strategic nuclear capabilities. In Europe this magnifies the significance of the disparities between East and West in nuclear tactical and conventional weapons.
>
> We are all faced with the dilemma of having to meet the moral and political demand for arms limitation while at the same time maintaining a

 DOI 10.1080/00396330802329121

fully effective deterrent to war. We are not unaware that both the United States and the Soviet Union must be anxious to remove threatening strategic developments from their relationship. But strategic arms limitations confined to the United States and the Soviet Union will inevitably impair the security of the West European members of the Alliance *vis-à-vis* Soviet military superiority in Europe if we do not succeed in removing the disparities of military power in Europe parallel to the SALT negotiations. So long as this is not the case we must maintain the balance of the full range of deterrence strategy. The Alliance must, therefore, be ready to make available the means to support its present strategy, which is still the right one, and to prevent any developments that could undermine the basis of this strategy.

* * *

Valerie Yorke, 'Retaliation and International Peace-keeping in Lebanon'

Survival, vol. 20, no. 5, September–October 1978, pp. 194–202.

On 11 March 1978, Al Fatah's commando raid against a bus on the Tel Aviv road killed 37 Israelis. In reply, on 15 March, Israel intervened against Lebanon in her largest military operation in peacetime: up to 20,000 troops backed by artillery, naval and air power occupied a six-mile-wide security belt and two days later extended that occupation to the Litani River. An estimated 1,000, most of whom were civilians, were killed. Israel's massive incursion reflected two aspects of her security policy: the requirement for 'defensible borders' and the doctrine of retaliation – a combination that produced uncertainty among the main parties concerned about Israel's overall intentions.

…

For thirty years, Israel's answer to threats to her security by infiltration and terrorism has been retaliation (an integral part of her policy of self-reliance). As Palestinian commando tactics changed from infiltration and sabotage to border raids and shelling, so the form of retaliation evolved. The border policing and punitive raids of the 1950s were replaced by a policy of graduated response in the mid-1960s: if her villages were shelled, Israel's artillery shelled Jordanian army positions; against rocket-fire on her towns, Israel used long-range guns against neighbouring Arab towns; and if Jordanian or Syrian artillery supported the commandos, Israel carried out air-strikes against their positions. The three-fold objective of this graduated 'price-list' has been to seek out and destroy guerrilla training-camps; to compel neighbouring Arab states to refrain from equipping and financing infiltrators and to restrain *fedayeen* based on their territory; and to induce the greater cooperation of Arab states in peace-settlement negotiations.

...

In the Israeli view, retaliation is a reaction, not an act of aggression. Although based on the offensive principle of carrying war onto enemy territory, it aims to deter and prevent, but also to punish. However, with her regular forces operating against foreign states, Israel's policy of self-help falls uncomfortably between armed aggression and self-defence. Nevertheless, Israel perceives retaliation as a necessary response to guerrilla attack in order to channel conflict into fixed and recognized boundaries; otherwise, it is argued, Arab operations could evolve into large-scale and continuous warfare, thus compelling Israel to use large forces in a frustrating and costly war of attrition.

* * *

Raymond Aron, 'The 1978 Alastair Buchan Memorial Lecture'

Survival, vol. 21, no. 1, January–February 1979, pp. 2–7.

It is a well-known but striking fact that over the last thirty years the political map of the world has changed with startling rapidity, with one exception: the map of Europe. Elsewhere, some hundred new States have arisen. Who would have thought that the lines of demarcation traced by the ambassadors at London, ratified by the Three at Yalta, would remain unchanged, frontiers between two worlds, separating two parts of a city – Berlin – like two parts of a continent? Yet despite the division of a continent, of a nation, of a city, political, commercial and human relations have multiplied. An agreement on the status of West Berlin has been concluded among the Four. The Communist zone is in debt to the West to a figure of almost $50 billion. The Olympic Games will take place in Moscow in two years. In this sense, detente today constitutes a probably irreversible fact. The same politico–military situation which fed the fears of Europe in 1950 is now experienced as if it were normal, almost stable. Soviet troops are still there, but nobody, outside certain political circles, fears the massive push of Soviet tanks towards the Atlantic.

This sense of security appears as paradoxical as was the great fear felt at the end of the 1940s and beginning of the 1950s. The Fondation pour les Etudes de Défense organized an opinion poll a few years ago on the subject of threat. Automobile accidents headed the list. The average

Frenchman fears his neighbour behind the wheel more than a Soviet tank driver.

The Soviet Union has lost her prestige in Europe as the first Socialist country or the centre of Marxism–Leninism. Even the Parisian intelligentsia – which, after World War II, had taken over the reinterpretation of Marxism from the Germans – rejects not only the Soviet model but Marxist philosophy itself, which Sartre called until recently 'insurpassable'. If the cold war was fought for men's minds, it is the West which has gained the victory in Europe.

The Soviet Union owes her super-power status to her military strength. Neither the functioning of her economy nor her standard of living are particularly impressive. Authoritarian centralized planning is scarcely an attractive prospect. Even the Eastern European States try to lessen the system's defects and to 'make the best of it'.

* * *

Edward N. Luttwak, 'The American Style of Warfare and the Military Balance'

Survival, vol. 21, no. 2, March–April 1979, pp. 57–60.

National styles differ in war, as they do in the pursuits of peace. Embodied in the tactical orientation of military forces and revealed by their structures, these national styles reflect not only the material and human attributes of societies but also their collective self-image. That is why the attempt to transplant a national style of warfare into the armed forces of another nation, with a different pattern of strengths, weaknesses and social relations, usually fails. One recalls vividly the failure of Egypt to practice Soviet-style armoured warfare in 1967, and equally her success with her own tactics, at least during the first days of the 1973 war.

To each his own, therefore. But even so a fatal dissonance can arise: national styles of warfare, embedded as they are in culture and society, may retain their domestic authority even while being overtaken by changes in the external military environment. Particularly dangerous are those changes which are subtle and cumulative rather than overt and dramatic. The latter may awaken attention and stimulate a re-thinking of military methods and structures which may yet save the situation. But when change is slow and not manifest, routines are apt to go on as before, until the sudden and catastrophic discovery of inferiority in war itself.

* * *

Shahram Chubin, 'Repercussions of the Crisis in Iran'
Survival, vol. 21, no. 3, May–June 1979, pp. 98–106.

The revolution in Iran removing the Shah after a thirty-seven-year rule will have a profound effect both on the political balance in the Middle East and the East–West strategic balance. Whatever the new regime, its policies will be less favourable to Western interests than before: it will be politically non-aligned, militarily and diplomatically passive, militant on oil prices and conservationist in production policy. The upheaval in Iran is also important as a model of an authentically and markedly anti-Western populist national revolt. Furthermore, throughout the months of turmoil, Western, especially American, policy has been ineffective either in anticipating events or in limiting their damaging consequences for other interests in the region. Certainly this was due in part to the policy inherited by the Carter Administration and to the intractability of Iran's domestic problems to external influence, but it was equally due to Washington's inconsistency, incoherence and equivocation.

* * *

Gregory F. Treverton, 'Issues and Non-Issues',
Survival, vol. 21, no. 5, September–October 1979, pp. 194–7.

It is self-evident that SALT II alone will not solve the strategic problems of the United States; to expect that is to expect too much of SALT. Yet the treaty does embody a number of advances on SALT I; SALT II, unlike SALT I, provides for equal numbers on both sides, as was mandated by the American Senate at the time of SALT I (which allowed the Soviet Union quantitative advantages for presumed American qualitative ones). For the first time the Soviet Union will be required to reduce her strategic forces, by some 250 launchers. Certainly, the launchers dismantled by the Soviet Union will be older ones, but the fact of reduction remains important.

SALT will not solve, however, the principal problem confronting American strategic forces – the growing vulnerability of the *Minuteman* land-based intercontinental ballistic missile (ICBM) force. This fact has been plain enough, however, since the Vladivostok summit between President Ford and Mr Brezhnev, in 1974. At the same time it seems clear that SALT II will not preclude necessary American responses to the problem, such as mobile basing of ICBM. At least SALT II does set an upper limit on the Soviet counter-force capability. Since Soviet sea-based forces are not yet accurate enough to threaten missile silos, the SALT ceiling of 820 on land-based ICBMS armed with multiple independently-targetable re-entry vehicles (MIRV), in combination with a limit of ten warheads per missile, means, in practice, that the Soviet Union will be unable to field more than 9,000 warheads in a counter-force first strike against American ICBMS. This is at least a worst-case limit against which to plan.

* * *

Lawrence Freedman, 'Time for a Reappraisal'

Survival, vol. 21, no. 5, September–October 1979, pp. 198–201.

For committed arms controllers, SALT has now become a melancholy affair. Satisfaction at the achievement of an agreement between the superpowers that is comprehensive in its scope and thorough in its detail, is tempered with the slight relevance of its provisions to the force structure of either side and the disruptive consequences of the acrimonious debate which will accompany its passage through the Senate. Whereas once the arms controllers might have hoped for severe restraints on the development and production of new weapons, they must now watch ruefully as the Administration insists to its hawkish critics that favoured weapons programmes can be protected from SALT. Whereas once there might have been hopes that the SALT process would result in an improvement in East–West relations, these have steadily deteriorated despite, and possibly because of, SALT. The Treaty has to be sold on negative grounds – it does not do any actual harm and non-ratification could seriously damage detente, NATO cohesion and the general authority of the President in his dealings with the outside world. It is doubtful whether the positive accomplishments of the Treaty (agreed ceilings which require cuts in Soviet force levels, a start on controlling qualitative improvements and co-operation in intrusive verification measures) are sufficiently appealing in themselves to result in ratification. Even if all goes well and the Treaty passes through the Senate in a form acceptable to the USSR, the next stage in SALT, which will begin immediately, is full of issues that appear even more controversial and intractable.

* * *

Zalmay Khalilzad, 'Pakistan and the Bomb'

Survival, vol. 21, no. 6, November–December 1979, pp. 244–50.

Pakistan's attempt to construct a centrifuge uranium enrichment plant, with possible Libyan financial assistance, has brought about a dramatic upsurge of US and European interest in the implications of her nuclear programme.

Reportedly, the Carter Administration regards Pakistan as the next candidate for the nuclear club. Because of the establishment of an Islamic Republic in Iran and the reported 'return of Islam' throughout the Middle East, Pakistan's nuclear efforts are increasingly being described as part of an aggressive Islamic revival. Therefore, reference is often made to an 'Islamic bomb' or a 'nuclear jihad'.

To have an effective non-proliferation policy, it is essential to analyse the motivations of other states in wishing to acquire nuclear weapons capabilities and to have a clear picture of the consequences of such an acquisition. Only then can the proper measures be taken to dissuade countries such as Pakistan from pursuing their programmes. Recent commentaries on Pakistan's nuclear efforts, however, do not reflect such analysis; rather, they suggest an atavistic fear of the 'Muslim threat' retained from the age of the Crusaders. In order to realistically assess the proliferation and diplomatic aspects of Pakistan's nuclear programme, I believe it is important to bear in mind that Pakistan's desire to acquire nuclear weapons arises largely from a perception of a nuclear threat from India dating back several years and not from an impulsive militancy within the context of an Islamic religious revival.

* * *

Alton Frye, 'Nuclear Weapons in Europe: No Exit from Ambivalence'

Survival, vol. 22, no. 3, May–June 1980, pp. 98–106.

One of modern man's greatest achievements lies in the fact that his studies of nuclear war consist entirely of speculations. Nevertheless, it is obvious that the technological, military and political features of nuclear conflict today would differ greatly from those of a war fought a decade or two ago. The possible scale of devastation has increased, and the instruments and methods by which such destruction would be wrought have changed enormously, as have the political circumstances in which it might occur. So, too, have the possibilities and requirements of deterring or limiting the resort to nuclear weapons. This is true both for central war between the Soviet Union and the United States, in which the emergence of threats to land-based strategic missiles is now the dominant worry, and for theatre war in Europe, in which drastic shifts in the regional nuclear balance have reinforced the Warsaw Pact's perceived advantages in conventional forces – heightening anxiety at a time when the broad political trends had been working to reduce tensions between East and West. That anxiety triggered NATO's December 1979 decision to deploy new long-range theatre nuclear systems (ground-launched cruise missiles and *Pershing* II ballistic missiles), as it had previously spurred commitments to strengthen the Alliance's conventional capabilities during the next few years.

* * *

William E. Griffith, 'Super-power Relations after Afghanistan'

Survival, vol. 22, no. 4, July–August 1980, pp. 146–51.

The Soviet invasion of Afghanistan is important for two major reasons. First, it marked the first time since 1945 that Soviet troops have invaded a country which is not a member of the Warsaw Pact. Second and more important, because of Afghanistan's strategic location, the invasion improves the Soviet strategic position in the direction of the Indian Ocean and the oil of the Persian Gulf.

In comparison, the question of whether or not the immediate, minimal Soviet purposes in invading Afghanistan were primarily defensive, to prevent the loss of what Moscow had gained there, is a secondary one. The indefinite presence of massive Soviet air and land forces in Afghanistan – which is what we must anticipate, since otherwise the regime in Kabul would fall – is bound to have major geopolitical results, regionally and globally favourable to the Soviet Union.

Whether, and how much, the response to the Soviet invasion, particularly by the United States and the Islamic countries, will outweigh these Soviet strategic gains is the most important question for the making of American foreign policy today.

* * *

Edward Heath, 'The 1980 Alastair Buchan Memorial Lecture'

Survival, vol. 22, no. 5, September–October 1980, pp. 199–202.

This is why it is so urgent for the Western countries to develop a clearer idea of which are the greatest threats to their security and to which of these threats military power can be credibly and responsibly committed. In no case is this more important than in the region of the Persian Gulf, for which the United States has now proclaimed a security doctrine. Many would agree that given the existence of an effective quick-strike force and a substantial military presence in the Indian Ocean, American military power could be credibly committed to deterring a frontal assault by the Soviet Union on any of the countries in the region. Yet this is not the only possible threat to the region, nor even the most likely. What of the other potential threats to its security? What, for example, do we do if the Soviet Army pursues the Afghan freedom fighters to their sanctuaries inside Pakistan? What do we do if war breaks out between Iraq and Iran which threatens the Iraqi oil fields? What do we do if a leader emerges in Baluchistan who proclaims Baluchi independence and invites the Soviet Army to ensure that it is secured? What, indeed, should we do, and could we do, if an internal uprising in an oil-rich country of the Gulf were to threaten its production of oil for any prolonged period? These are not abstract questions. They are serious and pressing. Responsible answers will not be found in demagogic certitudes, tempting though it may be to resort to them.

* * *

Jiri Valenta, 'Soviet Options in Poland'

Survival, vol. 23, no. 2, March–April 1981, pp. 50–9.

As 1981 began the continuing instability in Poland presented a serious threat to Soviet interests in that country. The Stanislaw Kania government has so far been unable to stop the growth or curtail the activities of the free, independent trade union called *Solidarnosc* (Solidarity). Solidarity claims that more than seven million workers (out of thirteen million in the socialized sector) have decided to shift their membership from the party-supervised trade unions to the new organization. Two million of these are also members of the Communist Party of Poland, which has a total membership of 33 million. The Polish government has made many concessions to the workers, and by November the free trade unions, led by Lech Walesa, had won several battles with Mr Kania's administration, including the struggle over the legal registration and statutes of Solidarity. Moreover, they won the right to publish their own weekly union newspaper, and to express their views each week during an hour-long programme on the state-run radio network. In the face of new strikes, the Polish authorities were made to release a printer and a government employee arrested on charges of stealing a secret police plan for a crackdown on dissidents.

* * *

Raymond L. Garthoff, 'The Soviet SS-20 Decision'

Survival, vol. 25, no. 3, May–June 1983, pp. 110–19.

Most official, and many unofficial, Western discussions have tended to disparage Soviet 'claims' of 'modernization' as a justification for the Soviet SS-20 deployment decision. Public discussion has been regrettably ill-informed. It seems highly likely that, in the Soviet place, US and NATO military and political leaders would have done exactly the same thing, and would have considered such a modernization programme as fully justified. It would probably have been seen as a step depriving the *other* side of TNF superiority and thus enhancing deterrence of any initial use by the other side. We cannot confirm that this was the Soviet view, but it would logically have fitted her frame of reference and perspective.

Did the Soviet Union also see an opportunity to gain political–military advantage and leverage *vis-à-vis* Western Europe by the SS-20 deployment? This, as we have seen, has been the Western assumption, and this assumption, as much as the fact of deployment, stimulated both Western concern and counteraction with the NATO LRTNF decision in 1979. Certainly the Soviet Union would prefer a 'margin of safety' or advantage in the theatre balance, and would welcome any inhibitions this might place on NATO self-confidence. But there is no evidence to support the idea that the Soviet leaders saw a political 'option' flowing from their SS-20 military deployment decision, or that such a political purpose even entered into their consideration in making the decision. And there is considerable indirect evidence that it did not.

* * *

Lord Carrington, 'The 1983 Alastair Buchan Memorial Lecture'

Survival, vol. 25, no. 4, July–August 1983, pp. 146–53.

Confidence should not of course shade into complacency. But it is perhaps a good moment to reflect coolly on the strength of the West as well as on our weaknesses, and to compare them with those of the Russians. Taking stock in this way can be a heartening exercise. True, the West has serious economic and social problems. But our economic malaise is more cyclical than caused by our system, and our social troubles are, I believe, soluble. We do not think in terms of emerging into sunny uplands – a style of thinking more appropriate to Soviet propaganda – but simply of moving into a new phase of the cycle in which the West will need all its powers of adaptation.

The Russians, by contrast, are subsiding into a slow crisis because of their system. The economy and the ideology of Communism are moribund. What we are witnessing in Poland, and imperceptibly in the corpulent body politic of the Soviet Union itself, is the onset of rigor mortis in a whole system – limb by limb.

* * *

Harold Brown and Lynn E. Davis, 'Nuclear Arms Control: Where Do We Stand?'
Survival, vol. 26, no. 4, July–August 1984, pp. 146–55.

Advocates of the freeze oppose all modernization, arguing that new weapons increase the risk of nuclear war. Opponents suggest that modernization is required to reduce the vulnerability of US nuclear forces and to ensure comparable counterforce capabilities with the Soviet Union. Underlying the arguments of both groups is a concern for stability. Stability is in fact primarily a matter of how each side manages its overall political relations. But to the extent that the strategic nuclear force postures play a role, their survivability is most critical.

Arms-control agreements should, therefore, be designed to improve the overall survivability of the nuclear forces of *both* sides. This can best be done through a combination of steps: by reducing the overall number of nuclear weapons and particularly of ballistic missile warheads; by permitting certain kinds of modernization (e.g., mobile missiles); by allowing the rebasing of ICBM by regulating the introduction of new missiles; and by phasing out or preferentially reducing certain kinds of older systems (e.g., MIRV missiles).

* * *

Prime Minister H.E. Yasuhiro Nakasone, 'The 1984 Alastair Buchan Memorial Lecture'
Survival, vol. 26, no. 5, September–October 1984, pp. 194–99.

Out of the ashes and ruins of World War II, and with deep remorse for the past, the Japanese people dedicated themselves to international peace, and resolved never again to go to war. They set, as their goal, to make Japan a 'nation of peace and prosperity'.

Left with the ruins of war and lacking its own natural resources, Japan needed peace if we were to rebuild our economy and feed our hundred million people. Japan also needed to achieve domestic stability by forming the broadest possible popular consensus. For these reasons, our objective of 'peace and prosperity' was chosen carefully and wisely.

Japan has been especially careful in its handling of security questions. The Japanese people sincerely believed that their nation should never again fall prey to militarism or become a military power. And this belief was consistent with the wishes of Japan's neighbours.

* * *

Harold Brown, 'The Strategic Defense Initiative: Defensive Systems and the Strategic Debate'
Survival, vol. 27, no. 2, March–April 1985, pp. 55–64.

From my own experience, the fact of American vulnerability to utter destruction by nuclear attack erodes the confidence that political leaders have in US nuclear policy. It affects all of US national security policies and limits American military and diplomatic behaviour. I have seen this in the five presidents I have served, and in my own actions as Secretary of Defense. I have also seen the frustration that this vulnerability has created in senior US military leaders, as well as their frustration with public and Congressional criticism of efforts to modernize strategic offensive systems. Their advocacy of defensive systems, and even a defensive strategy, can thus be explained even though they may have doubts about its efficacy. I sympathize with this desire to find an alternative. But political and military leaders also have a responsibility not to deceive themselves or to mislead, however unintentionally, the American people. And their advisers have a responsibility, as difficult as that can sometimes be, to give realistic evaluations to those leaders.

If technology promised the certainty of a successful defence of the American population against strategic nuclear weapons, or even a high probability of overall success, it is likely that policy-makers and defence analysts would agree that the United States should seek that objective. There would then no doubt be a different debate, dealing with the appropriate means of moving through the transition to this new nuclear strategy, of avoiding potential problems of instability, and of managing relations with US allies and with the Soviet Union. But technology does not offer even a reasonable prospect of a successful population defence.

* * *

Ambassador Paul H. Nitze, 'The 1985 Alastair Buchan Memorial Lecture: The Objectives of Arms Control'
Survival, vol. 27, no. 3, May–June 1985, pp. 98–107.

New defensive systems must also be cost-effective at the margin, that is, it must be cheaper to add additional defensive capability than it is for the other side to add the offensive capability necessary to overcome the defence. If this criterion is not met, the defensive systems could encourage a proliferation of counter-measures and additional offensive weapons to overcome deployed defences, instead of a re-direction of effort from offence to defence.

As I have said, these criteria are demanding. But they are necessary if we are to move towards a more stable balance at lower levels of arms. While our SDI research programme will seek technical answers to technical questions, we are simultaneously examining the broader strategic implications of moving towards a more defence-reliant balance

If the new technologies cannot meet the standards we have set, and thus not contribute to enhancing stability, we would not deploy them. In that event, we would have to continue to base deterrence largely on the ultimate threat of nuclear retaliation, though hopefully at lower levels of arms.

* * *

Joseph S. Nye, Jr, 'Nuclear Winter and Policy Choices'

Survival, vol. 28, no. 2, March–April 1986, pp. 119–27.

Would a major nuclear war mean the end of the human species? The answer is uncertain. For the past two years, scientists and policy-makers have been studying the theory of 'nuclear winter' – the proposition that the smoke created by a major nuclear attack would block the influx of sunlight, thus causing a drop in temperatures that might eventually destroy human life on this planet.

...

Although the uncertainties about nuclear winter are great, its prospect cannot be ruled out. Recent reports by the National Academy and by the Pentagon both admit that it is possible. And in terms of policy implications, its political effects are already here, well before the scientific evidence is adequate.

* * *

Gregory F. Treverton, 'US Strategy in Central America'

Survival, vol. 28, no. 2, March–April 1986, pp. 128–39.

Whatever else may be said about the debate over American policy in Central America, there is not much strategic thinking apparent in it. Neither the Reagan Administration nor its critics have articulated an approach that meets the basic requisites of strategy – that links a clear statement of national interests with a sober sense of national capabilities. A few years ago Michael Howard redirected the attention of strategists to what he called the 'social' or 'societal' dimension of strategy. Any strategy must be supported by the people it is intended to serve; they must be prepared to pay the price requested of them to meet the strategy's objectives.

It is in linking national purposes to what the American people are prepared to support that the debate is weakest. That fact is most obvious in the debate over US policy towards Nicaragua. For its part, the Reagan Administration, despite occasional disclaimers, seems to mean what much of its rhetoric suggests: that it is not prepared to live with a Sandinista regime in Nicaragua under any conditions. In February the President spoke of his desire to 'remove' the 'present structure' in Nicaragua and make the Sandinistas 'say uncle'.

* * *

Elizabeth Pond, 'The Security Debate in West Germany'

Survival, vol. 28, no. 4, July–August 1986, pp. 322–36.

The security debate has gone underground in West Germany since that surprisingly uneventful day at the end of 1983 when the first *Pershing* IIs went operational at Mutlangen. But it's only dormant, waiting to be revived. Depending on how the super-powers now manoeuvre, the American Strategic Defense Initiative (SDI) and arms control could well become much more divisive issues between the US and West Germany than Euromissile deployment.

Briefly, if progress is seen to be made in Soviet–American arms control, then German–American security issues will probably revert in West Germany to the *status quo ante* of the mid-1970s, when they were the arcane preserve of specialized bureaucracies. If, however, the arms-control talks begun in 1985 bog down as did their predecessors from 1973 onwards and lead to no ratified agreements – and if Washington is perceived as the obstacle – then a West German public which has been sensitized to security choices by the Euromissile debate is likely to re-engage in the issue. At its worst, what would then amount to an unprecedented common front between the West German government and public in resisting American defence policy could lead to an unprecedented common front between the West German Left and American Right in pressing to get US troops out of West Germany.

* * *

Brian Urquhart, '1986 Alastair Buchan Memorial Lecture: The Role of the United Nations in Maintaining and Improving International Security'

Survival, vol. 28, no. 5, September–October 1986, pp. 387–98.

Due largely to the limitations imposed by the relationships of the permanent members of the Security Council, current methods of conflict control are a pale shadow of what was envisaged in the Charter. Although much time is now spent on Chapter VI procedures for the Pacific Settlement of Disputes, we rarely hear much about Chapter VII – Action with Respect to Threats to the Peace, Breaches of the Peace, and Acts of Aggression – the once famous 'teeth' of the United Nations of which everyone was so proud at the Organization's birth. It seems as if the international body politic is now too weary, too distracted, too divided, too lacking in common purpose ever to decide to use its teeth.

It is tempting, for instance, to wonder what would have happened in the Iran–Iraq War if the Security Council had from the start acted upon the precepts of the Charter. After all, neither Iran or Iraq were exactly the favourite countries of any of the permanent members, and the initial and massive violation of the Charter was clear. The situation was, and is now more than ever, an evident threat to international peace and security. In those first weeks in 1980, however, the Council, in spite of the efforts of the then Secretary-General, showed an amazing and myopic capacity *not* to act or even to consider action. And later, when the war dragged horribly on in a strategically sensitive area of the world, it showed no disposition to consider measures under Chapter VII. One can only imagine the effect on the capacity of both countries to wage continuous war if economic relations had been cut and arms embargoes imposed by the international community as a whole.

* * *

Charles Tripp, 'Iraq – Ambitions Checked'

Survival, vol. 28, no. 6, November–December 1986, pp. 495–509.

The Iraqi decision to embark on a war with Iran was based on an ultimately disastrous misperception of the significance of the Iranian revolution for the region, and of the part Iraq had to play in countering the challenge it posed. Iraq could not fail to recognize the danger of the revolution both to the security of the Ba'athist government – and, thus, to the survival of the Iraqi state – as well as to the growing influence of Iraq in the affairs of the Gulf. However, in deciding to confront that threat through invasion and war, Iraq was still playing by the old rules of the region, appropriate to the days when the Shah ruled in Tehran.

The Iranian revolution had not simply transformed the nature of the Iranian threat, but had radically altered the terms under which state to state relations could be conducted in the region. Pre-emptive and limited though Iraq's initial war aims might have been, it failed to recognize how irrelevant such aims were now that it was dealing with a regime which saw war neither as limited nor as an extension of diplomacy. Consequently, when the Iraqi army crossed the border in force, it was in effect attacking not the state but the revolution. As a result, the Iraqi armed forces brought down on themselves and on Iraq the fury of a revolution which senses itself under threat.

* * *

Gail Warshofsky Lapidus, 'KAL 007 and Chernobyl: The Soviet Management of Crises'

Survival, vol. 29, no. 3, May–June 1987, pp. 215–23.

Both the shooting down of Korean Air Lines (KAL) flight number KE 007 on 1 September 1983 and the disaster at the Chernobyl nuclear power station in May 1986 engaged the post-Brezhnev Soviet leadership in unforeseen and politically-damaging crises with serious international as well as domestic repercussions. Although there were significant dissimilarities between the two episodes – above all, in the fact that the downing of KAL 007 had no direct consequences for the Soviet population – nonetheless, a comparison of the way in which the two events were handled offers a revealing window into persistent features of Soviet organizational behaviour, as well as evidence of interesting departures from earlier practices. Moreover, as the first real test of the new Gorbachev leadership, the handling of the Chernobyl disaster offers some insights into the scope and limits of General Secretary Gorbachev's commitment to increased *Glasnost'* (openness or candour) in Soviet political life.

* * *

Professor Raymond Barre, '1987 Alastair Buchan Memorial Lecture: Foundations for European Security and Co-operation'

Survival, vol. 29, no. 4, July–August 1987, pp. 291–300.

Everything that tends towards a loosening of the isolated nature of the USSR and brings it into closer relations with Western Europe is to be encouraged. Mr Gorbachev has broken sharply with his predecessors on several major issues: a younger generation of political leaders, better social discipline, the drive for improved economic efficiency, the many steps taken to reduce intolerance and promote greater freedom of speech, and the start made in the release of political prisoners. We must welcome these changes and not belittle them, while suspending judgment as to whether they will ultimately turn out to be marginal or fundamental.

However, this does not mean that their extent should be over-estimated. Brezhnev's social and economic legacy is not being challenged in order to undermine a system, the merits of which the new Soviet generation believes in. Rather it is to guarantee its more efficient working. It is by no means certain whether the measures now being taken to increase productivity and introduce new technologies are intended to raise the standard of living, or to satisfy the ambitions of the military. Moreover, in his speech to the 28th Congress, Mr Gorbachev stressed that his proposed internal changes were justified, in particular, by concern for maintaining his country's international image and standing.

...

First, we observe a pernicious tendency to re-open the debate on the validity of nuclear deterrence. Initially confined to Soviet propaganda, it rapidly permeated Western societies through the action of pacifist movements, and has now come to dominate the official discourse of our main ally, the United States. Since it launched the Strategic Defense Initiative four years ago, the American government has claimed that its objective is to abolish nuclear weapons all over the world; incidentally, this ratifies one of the major objectives of 1950s Soviet diplomacy.

Of course, nuclear weapons are abhorrent weapons which we might wish the scientists had never let out of their Pandora's box. But it is precisely because the damage they can do is so atrocious that the use of force is necessarily kept out of the political calculations of governments. Let us not mistake the objective: we want to avoid war, and this is exactly why nuclear arms remain, and will doubtless remain for a long time, indispensable to the security of Europe. Conversely, the 'denuclearization' of Europe would signify the end of deterrence by freeing the USSR of the risk of escalation which would threaten its territory and could lead to unacceptable destruction. It would simultaneously maximize the vulnerability of Western Europe because of its inferiority in essential conventional weapons, and terminate the Atlantic Alliance through the departure, sooner or later, of American forces, for the men follow the arms.

The latest version of the anti-nuclear campaign in Europe is the zero option, i.e., the elimination of all intermediate-range nuclear missiles in Europe: the SS-20s on the one hand, *Pershing* II and cruise missiles on the other. Much could be said about the wisdom of the 'twin-track decision' taken by the NATO countries in 1979, which made the Soviet Union, through the arms-control negotiations, the arbiter of their decisions on what arms are needed for their defence. After many episodes, Mr Gorbachev, who shares the same opinion on this matter as Mr Sakharov, has now proposed to focus on INF arms control as a matter of priority, independent of other issues, probably in the hope that the President of the United States, pressed by his domestic difficulties, will yield to the temptation of a foreign-policy success. I am told that all the Western countries in which these missiles are deployed are sympathetic to the zero option and that, in any case, considering that they have maintained this stance since 1981, the public would not understand if they were to change their position now.

As an independent observer who has always argued that the deployment of the *Pershing* missiles was necessary to strengthen the Alliance while remaining aware that France was not a party to this NATO decision, allow me to make three observations regarding the famous zero option:

First: implementation of the zero option could weaken – in particular via negotiations on the shorter-range missiles – NATO's ability through the presence of tactical nuclear weapons to offset the conventional and chemical superiority of the Warsaw Pact. This consequence should be avoided.

Second: also to be avoided is the probability that the zero option, by removing an intermediate stage of escalation, could weaken NATO's capacity for Flexible Response, thereby bringing about the dilemma, if not 'all or nothing', at least 'all or too little'. The *Pershing* II missiles are not solely a response to the SS-20's, as was claimed some years ago. They are an indispensable link in the chain of deterrence that should continue to bind Europe and the United States, since they can reach Soviet territory directly from Western Europe.

Third: since Europe is within range of both the USSR's tactical and strategic arms the countervailing power can only come, in the present situation, from the United States. But just as the credibility of extended deterrence by the United States implies the physical presence of American forces, those forces can only stay in Europe so long as they remain protected by extended US deterrence.

For these reasons, I have never considered the formula 'neither SS-20, nor *Pershing*' as a desirable objective. Those who proposed the zero option in order to make the deployment of the *Pershing* missiles palatable, believing that the USSR would never agree to withdraw the SS-20s, have been caught in their own trap.'

* * *

IISS ADELPHI PAPERS

ADELPHI PAPER 395

Selective Security: War and the United Nations Security Council since 1945

Adam Roberts and Dominik Zaum

ISBN 978-0-415-47472-6

In contrast to the common perception that the United Nations is, or should become, a system of collective security, this paper advances the proposition that the UN Security Council embodies a necessarily selective approach. Analysis of its record since 1945 suggests that the Council cannot address all security threats effectively. The reasons for this include not only the veto power of the five permanent members, but also the selectivity of all UN member states: their unwillingness to provide forces for peacekeeping or other purposes except on a case-by-case basis, and their reluctance to involve the Council in certain conflicts to which they are parties, or which they perceive as distant, complex and resistant to outside involvement.

The Council's selectivity is generally seen as a problem, even a threat to its legitimacy. Yet selectivity, which is rooted in prudence and in the UN Charter itself, has some virtues. Acknowledging the necessary limitations within which the Security Council operates, this paper evaluates the Council's achievements in tackling the problem of war since 1945. In doing so, it sheds light on the division of labour among the Council, regional security bodies and states, and offers a pioneering contribution to public and governmental understanding of the UN's past, present and future roles.

ADELPHI PAPER 394

Ending Terrorism: Lessons for defeating al-Qaeda

Audrey Kurth Cronin

ISBN 978-0-415-45062-1

Like all other terrorist movements, al-Qaeda will end. While it has traits that exploit and reflect the current international context, it is not utterly without precedent: some aspects of al-Qaeda are unusual, but many are not. Terrorist groups end according to recognisable patterns that have persisted for centuries, and they reflect, among other factors, the counter-terrorist policies taken against them. It makes sense to formulate those policies with a specific image of an end in mind.

Understanding how terrorism ends is the best way to avoid being manipulated by the tactic. There is vast historical experience with the decline and ending of terrorist campaigns, yet few policymakers are familiar with it. This paper first explains five typical strategies of terrorism and why Western thinkers fail to grasp them. It then describes historical patterns in ending terrorism to suggest how insights from that history can lay a foundation for more effective counter-strategies. Finally, it extracts policy prescriptions specifically relevant to ending the campaign of al-Qaeda and its associates, moving towards a post al-Qaeda world.

Closing Argument

Are We At War?

Michael Howard

I

This year we are celebrating the 50th anniversary of the foundation of the IISS. I shall not bore you with a blast on our own trumpet, except to remark how astonishing and gratifying it is to see how the acorn that Alastair Buchan then planted should have grown into such a flourishing tree and continued to bear such nourishing fruit. But I would stress the point that the founders of the Institute never had the audacity to claim to tell people *what* to think about strategic affairs, much less what to *do* about them. Our hope was simply to persuade people at least to *think* about them – not only the military and political experts whose job it was, but everyone with a vote – and to provide them with accurate information so that they could think intelligently; possibly also to provide some guide to priorities, as to what was important and what less so.

At that time there could be no doubt as to what was most important: it was the acquisition by the major powers of the world, at a time when they were bitterly divided by incompatible ideologies, of nuclear weapons capable of destroying mankind several times over. The destruction of Hiroshima and Nagasaki seemed to open a new and grimmer era in the history of mankind, and we were only beginning to learn how to come to terms with it. So, unsurprisingly, the work of the Institute focused for several years on questions of nuclear deterrence, disarmament and arms

---

Michael Howard is President Emeritus of the International Institute for Strategic Studies. This essay was presented as the 2008 Alastair Buchan Memorial Lecture at the IISS, London, on 6 April 2008.

 DOI 10.1080/00396330802329147

control before broadening out to consider less existential, if more immediate, questions. Now I would just say that those questions of nuclear war have not gone away: the proliferation and control of nuclear weapons remains one of the ineluctable problems of our time. The nuclear dragon may be sleeping, but it is certainly not dead, and the IISS continues to keep a wary eye on it.

Then seven years ago another event occurred that was in some ways even more epoch-making than the development of nuclear weapons: '9-11', the destruction of the World Trade Center in New York by a dozen or so terrorists, with the massacre of some 3,000 people who were peacefully working there. The perpetrators had themselves been virtually unarmed, with none of the resources of a major state behind them. The implications were terrifying. How many more of them were out there? What if they had access to nuclear weapons? We had to come to terms with the fact the most powerful state in the world could now be seriously harmed, not by another state equally powerful, but by small private groups owing allegiance to no state at all. For the past 300 years wars had been waged, but also peace had been kept, by States, one of whose defining characteristics was that they enjoyed a monopoly of violence. That monopoly had now been seriously breached by elements apparently beyond state control. Fifty years ago the challenge to world order had come from the transformation of weapons systems. Now it appears threatened by the transformation, if not disintegration, of the entire states-system that has provided the framework for international relations for 300-odd years.

The American government reacted to 9-11, understandably enough, as if the attack had come from an enemy state. It declared war, and from that day to this many, if not most, Americans still believe that they are 'at war', although the precise definition of the adversary has varied over the years. But many, if not most, of America's friends and allies believed this reaction to be mistaken. For what it is worth, I was one of them. We have now had seven years to think about it and I still believe that America was wrong, and dangerously wrong. The United States and her allies are certainly engaged in armed conflicts in many parts of the world, but that is a different matter from being 'at war'; and the difference matters. I hope that you will forgive me if I take this opportunity to share with you some further thoughts on the question. I need hardly add that they are my own thoughts, and they certainly don't carry any imprimatur from the IISS as such.

II

When I use the term 'epoch-making' to describe 9-11, I choose the words carefully. What we are witnessing is the close of an epoch that opened some 350 years ago; an epoch generally known as 'Westphalian' after the Peace of Westphalia, concluded in 1648, that remoulded the decaying feudal order of Europe into discrete sovereign states with distinct frontiers, whose rulers went to war to protect or extend their national interests very much as they thought fit. National loyalties might be complicated by transnational affiliations: in the seventeenth century by loyalty to the Catholic Church; a century later by the appeal of revolutionary France; in our own day by that of international communism. But on the whole the state could rely on the overwhelming support of its citizens – never more so than during the First World War, when the loyalties of armies fighting for their countries was unadulterated by considerations of transnational ideologies. The object of war was simple – victory; and victory was attained by the overthrow of the enemy, the destruction of his will and capacity to resist. Once victory was achieved a peace was made that enhanced the power and interests of the victors, but the framework of the system, not least the sovereignty of its members, normally remained unaffected.

But there was one belligerent to whom this simple Westphalian pattern did not apply – the United States; or rather, the president of the United States, Woodrow Wilson. When Wilson brought his country into the European war in April 1917 it was not as an ally of either side, nor did he endorse the war aims of his co-belligerents. For him the war was a crusade, one, as he himself put it, 'for a universal domination of right by such a concert of free peoples as shall bring peace and safety to all nations and make the world itself free'. It was a war, in fact, to change the world.

This was not a path down which Wilson's own people were yet prepared to follow him, let alone those of his European allies. The Europeans were still thorough Westphalians. They had made war to protect their national interests and those interests determined the peace that they eventually made. Nevertheless, Wilson's vision, of Westphalian wars being replaced by what we might term 'Enlightenment Wars', crusades for the establishment of 'a Universal Domination of Right', was to remain the declared objective of the United States throughout the twentieth century. Her wars were fought not simply to defeat her adversaries but to convert them so as to make further war inconceivable.

So unlike Westphalian wars, Enlightenment wars were fought not for purely national interests but on behalf of mankind. The object was to create a *community* of nations which, if they went to war at all, would do so not to prosecute quarrels with one another, but to enforce a commonly accepted law against a transgressor. To bring such a community into existence it might certainly be necessary to use force against a member who did not share its values. This was the case both with Imperial Germany and its Nazi successor, both of which had to be converted to democracy before they could be admitted to the comity of nations. But after the defeat of the Axis powers in 1945 the United States was able to put its principles into practice, with 'democratic values' and the principle of 'collective security' being accepted, if only notionally, by all members of the United Nations.

As we know, this happy state did not last for long. The Cold War quickly brought it to an end as the leading powers divided into two blocs, each identifying itself with a different concept of 'democracy' and a different vision of 'world order'. But stability of a curious kind did result, if only from the fact that, in the nuclear age, neither side dared go to war. New states were thus able to emerge peacefully onto the world stage, largely because, with a few exceptions, their former imperial masters had neither the will nor the capacity to prevent it. Some of them flirted with the Soviet Union so long as its ideology and power gave them some leverage on the world scene, but most joined the world of the market economy, even though this made them dependent on the West. Ultimately, the failure of the communist dream forced both the Soviet Union and People's Republic of China to do the same. It was the stability provided by the Cold War that by the end of the twentieth century enabled a new global order to come into being that was gradually to render the Westphalian system of states obsolescent, if not yet obsolete.

This order was of a different kind from that visualised by Wilson and implemented in some measure by Franklin Roosevelt. It was not international, but transnational. It did not result from agreement between governments; indeed it had often come into being in spite of them. It had been created by the silent operation of a market economy that had originated in Europe and the Atlantic region in the early nineteenth century and developed ever faster as sail gave way to steam, steam gave way to oil, electricity gave birth to electronics, telegraph was replaced by radio and television, which in turn led to the Internet that has now made instant communication possible not only between every nation, but every man, woman, and, not least, child, on the planet. It is a process that has swept away social structures, political hierarchies and religious beliefs, opening up unimaginable opportunities for mankind but leaving in its wake a trail of confusion, bitterness and anomie. No state, even the most powerful, can remain immune from its effects: the communist world struggled in vain to insulate itself, and eventually gave up in despair.

In this post-Westphalian world the function of the state is no longer simply to create and preserve an acceptable order for its citizens and defend them against their rivals. It is also to enable its citizens to participate fully in this new transnational global order while protecting them so far as possible from its ravages; to cooperate with other like-minded states in so doing; and to assist in the evolution of such states where they do not yet exist and to restore them when they are threatened.

The Westphalian system is far from extinct and traces of it will be with us for many years yet. States may no longer enjoy a monopoly of violence but wars between them are still possible, especially between small new states with ill-defined frontiers. It is also still conceivable between great powers – China, the United States, Russia, India, and as some would have it, the European Union – and all arm to face that possibility. But today the major threats to world order do not come from rivalry between great powers, but from the inability of weak states to exert control either over their own citizens or over highly volatile regions where no effective writ runs; and this weakness creates threats of disorder with which traditional military power has shown itself ill-adapted to deal. The world is in fact increasingly divided, not between freedom and tyranny, nor between democracy and dictatorship, but between states that are successfully adjusting themselves to membership of global civil society and those that are not.

This 'new world order' has three primary characteristics. It is *global*, embracing the entire planet. Disorder anywhere in the world may have universal implications. It is *dynamic*: today there is no region that is not experiencing increasingly rapid and socially disruptive change. The effectiveness – indeed the *legitimacy* – of governments depends on their capacity to manage that change, a capacity itself dependent on social consensus, uncorrupt administration and the rule of law.

Above all, this global society is highly *vulnerable.* I shall say nothing here about climate change, which is perhaps the greatest threat of all, but in addition to that, increasing urbanisation is making an ever larger proportion of the world's populations dependent on exogenous supplies of vital fuel, and creating huge conglomerations – hardly deserving the name of 'cities' – whose critical infrastructure can easily be disrupted by a few malevolent individuals who can cause at best widespread inconvenience, at worst destruction on a scale far transcending that of 9-11.

There is no lack of people ready to so disrupt it. Although the transformation of our societies increases the wealth, the health, the life expectancy and the opportunities open to mankind to a degree inconceivable even a century ago, it also creates losers: uprooted peoples whose livelihood and lifestyles have been destroyed, whose traditional political structures have been demolished, and whose core beliefs – beliefs that held their societies together for centuries – have been dissolved. Their grievances may be regionally and politically specific as were those of the Irish or the Jews a generation ago, or those of the Palestinians today. They may be based on a more general resentment at the injustice and oppressions inherent in a global economy that may put the prosperity of entire societies at the mercy of decisions taken in boardrooms at the other end of the world. They may be provoked simply by visceral reaction against the hedonistic secular materialism that has destroyed faiths that sustained their ancestors for millennia. Whatever the cause, there will be no lack of angry young men and women in a generation whose numbers are swollen by increased life expectancy beyond their capacity to find employment, and who will not hesitate to use violence to redress or revenge their grievances. They may revert to atavistic tribalism. They may be recruited to messianic creeds, religious or secular, that promise a new and glorious future. Sometimes their protests may be channelled into political parties that gain control of a state, as happened so disastrously in the case of Germany after 1918. But initially they are all likely to turn to 'terror': first *demonstrative*, 'the propaganda of the deed', to give expression to their resentment, advertise their existence and recruit supporters; then *intimidatory*, to cow their opponents into submission; finally *provocative*, to tempt the government into overreaction and so delegitimise its authority.

There is nothing new about these techniques: in Europe they have a pedigree dating back nearly two centuries. But in our own day they have been rendered far more lethal: first by the vulnerability of urban societies to which I referred; and secondly by a readiness for self-sacrifice that was perhaps more common in our own societies a couple of generations ago – when young men were positively encouraged 'to lay down their lives for their country' – than it is today. For whatever our political leaders may say about the atrocities perpetrated by suicide bombers, these are not 'mindless'. They are often carefully calculated and regrettably effective. And they are certainly not 'cowardly': people who are prepared to die for a cause in which they believe may be misled, but they are not cowards. If we do not accept that we are often dealing with people who are both intelligent and courageous we would be very stupid indeed.

III

The threat of terrorist protest thus accompanies the development of our global society like an inescapable shadow, and is likely to remain a major social problem as far forward as we can foresee. In our own day it has been made especially lethal by the coincidence of the problem of Palestine, affecting as it does the entire Muslim world, with a profound crisis of modernisation within Islam that has produced a school of extremists whose influence extends beyond the Middle East into the Muslim diaspora in Western cities – a diaspora that has its own problems of cultural assimilation. It is a combination that presents a formidable challenge to the stability of the entire world order. But there is no point in 'declaring war' on it, let alone adopting the apocalyptic language of religious extremists who stigmatise their opponents as the embodiment of evil.

This is not a mere matter of semantics. There is no harm in speaking of wars against poverty, or crime, or disease. These are mere metaphors: they do not give a license to kill. But in the world of international politics 'war' has a specific meaning. It means quite specifically the abandonment of civil restraints and the legitimisation of the use of whatever force is necessary to achieve one's objectives. Restraints inherent in the culture of the belligerent societies may be observed in the conduct of war – restraints recently described by one American attorney general as 'quaint' – but they will be very quickly abandoned under duress. The leaders of nations at war have always considered themselves entitled, if all else fails, to use any means to defeat their adversary and avoid defeat themselves, whether it be the torture of individuals or the destruction of entire cities, and they will usually enjoy massive popular support when they do so. Let us be clear about it. To 'declare war' is formally to espouse a set of values and to legitimise activities normally outlawed in civil society.

But in dealing with terrorists our object should be not to abandon those values. It is to enforce them. '9-11' and similar atrocities should be seen, not as acts of war, but as 'breaches of the peace' – not just the peace created by international treaties, but the peaceful order that makes possible the functioning of a global civil society on which the well-being of the entire planet depends. Our approach in dealing with them should not be that of 'warriors' but of *police*, whose function is the preservation of civil order, and for whom the use of force is the last and least desirable resort. The object of terrorism is to destroy the legitimacy of the incumbent authority. The object of government must be to preserve and exert it, and to avoid being dragged into a conflict on the same level as its adversary. That is possible only so long as it retains the confidence of the community on whose behalf it claims to act.

This should not be too difficult in dealing with domestic terrorism, unless the extremists have a cause – as they did in Northern Ireland – that can command substantial public support. But intervention to deal with terrorist activity in foreign countries is a very different matter. It is true that the global civil society whose peace we are trying to keep has yet to develop its own transnational structure of government, so its agents have often to be the armed forces of old-fashioned Westphalian states whose very presence, however well-intentioned, is likely to arouse a very natural xenophobia; especially if they carry a great deal of their own tribal culture with them. However well they may behave, however many sweets they give children, foreign soldiers can never be very popular, certainly not for very long, and certainly not if they believe that they are 'at war' and are therefore immune from normal civil restraints. It then becomes all too easy for their opponents to depict them as the agents, not of a global civil society, but of an alien hegemony, and condemn those who support them as traitors.

For all these reasons we should not become involved in the affairs even of the most incompetent and failing states unless our intervention is a matter of vital importance to global stability and has clear international legitimacy. I would argue that our intervention in Afghanistan meets these criteria, while that in Iraq did not. And if we do become involved, our object must be neither to subdue nor to convert – not even convert to Western-style democracy. It is to assist where necessary in destroying hard cores of nihilistic extremists and to aid the construction, or reconstruction, of a civil society whose government can fulfil its basic obligations: to maintain a socially acceptable order; to connect its citizens with the benefits of transnational civil society while protecting them from its hazards; and to act as a dependable member of the community of states. If there is no immediate prospect of doing any of this, we would be ill advised to try.

I am afraid that all this is now pretty platitudinous, but it would not have been seen as such in Washington – or even, I am afraid, Downing Street – five years ago. Experience in Iraq and Afghanistan has now made us sadder and I hope wiser people. After a similar if rather less traumatic experience suffered by the British in South Africa at the beginning of the last century, the poet Rudyard Kipling – whose observations on war in Afghanistan still have a poignant relevance – remarked:

> Let us admit it fairly, as a business people should
> We have had no end of a lesson; it will do us no end of good.

At least, I hope it will.

Re-launching in 2008 with a brand new look!

Survival

GLOBAL POLITICS AND STRATEGY

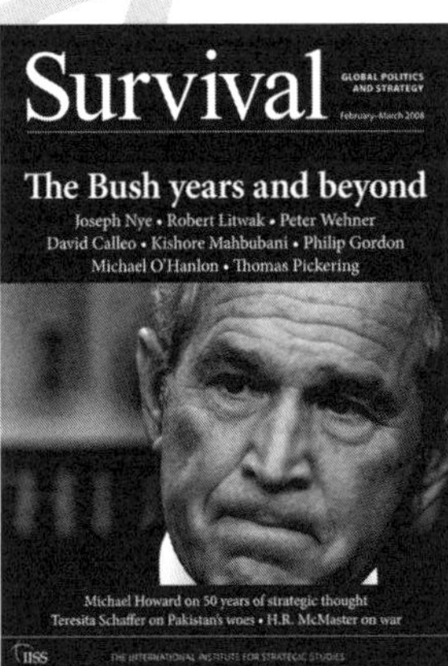

- Increasing from 4 to 6 issues per year
- Expanded Reviews and Brief Notices from a team of Contributing Editors
- Informative and thought-provoking statistics, maps and reports, and quotations from IISS events and the wider strategic and policy community
- Regular commentary and debate

Published by The International Institute for Strategic Studies

Subscription Rates

Institutional (Print & Online)	☐ £279.00	☐ US$488.00 (US only)	☐ $513 (ROW)	☐ €410.00
Institutional (Online Only)	☐ £265.00	☐ US$464.00 (US only)	☐ $487 (ROW)	☐ €390.00
Personal	☐ £85.00	☐ US$145.00		☐ €116.00

Please send my Journals to:

Name ____________________

Address ____________________

____

Methods of Payment

☐ Payment enclosed. Cheques should be made payable to **Informa UK Limited** and be drawn on a UK or US bank.

Please charge ☐ Visa ☐ MasterCard ☐ Eurocard ☐ American Express (AMEX – US$ / £ only)

Card Number Expiry Date

Security Code (Last 3 digits found on reverse of card)

Signature Date / /

Payment has been made by bank transfer to one of the following accounts (please indicate):

☐ **UK** - National Westminster Bank Plc, 25 High Street, Colchester, Essex, CO1 1DG, UK • Account Name: Informa UK Ltd.
£ Account No: 01825550 • Sort Code: 60-06-06 • Swift Code: NWBKGB2L • IBAN:GB25NWBK60060601825550

☐ **USA** - Bank of America, 100 33rd Street West, New York, 10001 NY, USA • Account Name: Informa UK Ltd.
Account No: 2753109322 • ABA No for Wires: 026009593 • ABA No for ACH: 021000322 • Swift Code: BOFAUS3N

☐ **Europe** - National Westminster Bank Plc, 25 High Street, Colchester, Essex, CO1 1DG, UK • Account Name: Informa UK Ltd.
Account No: 06880185 • Sort Code: 60-72-11 • Swift Code: NWBKGB2L • IBAN: GB08NWBK60721106880185

Please fill in your bank details, or alternatively send a cheque, in an envelope, to the address below:

Louise Armstrong, Marketing Executive, Politics, Geography and Area Studies
Routledge, Taylor & Francis Group, 4 Park Square, Milton Park, Abingdon, Oxfordshire OX14 4RN, UK

Promo code: YE06001L

Subscription Rates

Institutional (Print & Online)	☐ £279.00	☐ US$488.00 (US only)	☐ $513 (ROW)	☐ €410.00
Institutional (Online Only)	☐ £265.00	☐ US$464.00 (US only)	☐ $487 (ROW)	☐ €390.00
Personal	☐ £85.00	☐ US$145.00		☐ €116.00

Please send my Journals to:

Name ____________________

Address ____________________

____

Methods of Payment

☐ Payment enclosed. Cheques should be made payable to **Informa UK Limited** and be drawn on a UK or US bank.

Please charge ☐ Visa ☐ MasterCard ☐ Eurocard ☐ American Express (AMEX – US$ / £ only)

Card Number Expiry Date

Security Code (Last 3 digits found on reverse of card)

Signature Date / /

Payment has been made by bank transfer to one of the following accounts (please indicate):

☐ **UK** - National Westminster Bank Plc, 25 High Street, Colchester, Essex, CO1 1DG, UK • Account Name: Informa UK Ltd.
£ Account No: 01825550 • Sort Code: 60-06-06 • Swift Code: NWBKGB2L • IBAN:GB25NWBK60060601825550

☐ **USA** - Bank of America, 100 33rd Street West, New York, 10001 NY, USA • Account Name: Informa UK Ltd.
Account No: 2753109322 • ABA No for Wires: 026009593 • ABA No for ACH: 021000322 • Swift Code: BOFAUS3N

☐ **Europe** - National Westminster Bank Plc, 25 High Street, Colchester, Essex, CO1 1DG, UK • Account Name: Informa UK Ltd.
Account No: 06880185 • Sort Code: 60-72-11 • Swift Code: NWBKGB2L • IBAN: GB08NWBK60721106880185

Please fill in your bank details, or alternatively send a cheque, in an envelope, to the address below:

Louise Armstrong, Marketing Executive, Politics, Geography and Area Studies
Routledge, Taylor & Francis Group, 4 Park Square, Milton Park, Abingdon, Oxfordshire OX14 4RN, UK

Promo code: YE06001L